Racism in Indian Country

PETER LANG
New York • Washington, D.C./Baltimore • Bern
Frankfurt am Main • Berlin • Brussels • Vienna • Oxford

Dean Chavers

Racism in Indian Country

PETER LANG
New York • Washington, D.C./Baltimore • Bern
Frankfurt am Main • Berlin • Brussels • Vienna • Oxford

Library of Congress Cataloging-in-Publication Data

Chavers, Dean.
Racism in Indian country / Dean Chavers.
p. cm.
Includes bibliographical references and index.
1. Indians of North America—Ethnic identity. 2. Indians of North America—Public opinion. 3. Indians in popular culture. 4. Racism—United States. 5. Public opinion—United States. 6. United States—Race relations. I. Title.
E98.E85C53 305.897—dc22 2008025238
ISBN 978-1-4331-0393-3

Bibliographic information published by **Die Deutsche Bibliothek**.
Die Deutsche Bibliothek lists this publication in the "Deutsche Nationalbibliografie"; detailed bibliographic data is available on the Internet at http://dnb.ddb.de/.

Cover design by Joni Holst

The paper in this book meets the guidelines for permanence and durability of the Committee on Production Guidelines for Book Longevity of the Council of Library Resources.

29 Broadway, 18th floor, New York, NY 10006
www.peterlang.com

Printed in the United States of America

To my beautiful wife Antonia Navarro Chavers. She has suffered the sting of discrimination as I have.

She remembers vividly growing up in south Texas. She remembers how she and her brothers and sisters would have to eat their ice cream sitting on the sidewalk. The restaurant would sell them ice cream out the side door, but they could not go inside to eat it.

She still remembers vividly the landlady who tried to evict her from her first apartment when she finished nursing school. Thank goodness for her roommate Diane who threatened the landlady with a lawsuit. The landlady backed down.

She remembers as recently as 1985 how she was discriminated against in Tulsa. She would select her purchases at the store. But when she would go to pay for them, the clerks would always wait on the white ladies first. If she did nothing she was wrong. If she protested she was wrong and uppity. We soon left Oklahoma.

Thank you, Toni, for hanging in there.

CONTENTS

INTRODUCTION

This has been the hardest book I have ever written. It is my 24th book. (Almost all of the others have been about education, grant seeking, and proposal writing.) It is the only negative one I have written, and probably the last negative one I will ever write. Even so, I feel it is necessary.

Writing it was emotionally hard. At times I got depressed and had to stop for a few days. Normally when I am writing I work every day from the time I start until it is done. I wrote my last book, *Modern American Indian Leaders*, in ten months. It is 792 pages long.

For a long time, many practices of discrimination against Indians have not been reported and have gone untouched. For years I have heard reports about Indian people being discriminated against. I knew what happened to me when I was growing up, but like most people, did not think to put my personal experiences into a larger framework. I think about education every day, not discrimination. (I run a scholarship program for Native college students called Catching the Dream.)

Indian people do not think in terms of violation of their civil rights. At least we do not appear to think in terms similar to those of Black or Hispanic people. The National Association for the Advancement of Colored People (NAACP), the Southern Christian Leadership Conference (SCLC), the Southern Poverty Law Center (SPLC), and the Mexican-American Legal Defense and Education Fund (MALDEF) have fought many battles in the courts over civil rights for Blacks and Hispanics. They have been aided and abetted by the American Civil Liberties Union (ACLU) and the legal aid societies.

They have brought court actions, legislation, petitions, and numerous other techniques to the forefront of national consciousness. Protests, sit-ins, marches, and other more radical approaches are now almost accepted as a way of life in the United States, at least by some people.

Indian Country, though, has never had a civil rights organization. The closest thing to it has been the American Indian Movement (AIM), which in terms of philosophy has been more like the Student Nonviolent Coordinating Committee and the Black Power movement than they have to any of the other ethnic minority civil rights organizations.

Indian people have tended to use other types of tactics. There have been occupations of land, a few marches, and some armed confrontations in Indian Country in the past 40 years. Generally Indian people tend to get very emotional and involved in questions of land, and in questions of tribal sovereignty. I have wondered for years if there were some basic rights that are being denied to Indians, and which no one is investigating or attempting to rectify.

Reports have circulated all over Indian Country about Indian people being sick and being denied hospital care. Are there Indian people being denied the right to live in housing of their choice because of their race? I would think so. Even so, I hear little about this type of gripe in Indian Country.

I have heard about gerrymandering, voter registration funny business, and at-large voting being used to deny Indians representation on school boards, on county commissions, on city councils, and in state legislatures. The only investigation that I knew about was done by the National Indian Youth Council (NIYC) and the American Civil Liberties Union (ACLU). These organizations have done research on voting in Indian Country and have brought lawsuits to break up at-large voting schemes that are designed to deny Indians the vote.

Racism is an irrational belief that some "races" of people are superior to other "races." We put the word race in quotation marks because the concept itself has largely been discredited over the past 50 years. In 1850, most of the white people in the United States believed that Indians, Blacks, and other minorities were clearly inferior to them. In 2000, only the die-hard stoners still believe this. So we have made progress as a nation. However, as in other areas, progress for Indians has come last and takes longer to achieve.

The diehards are a clearly defined bunch of people—Ku Klux Klan members, Aryan nations members, skinheads, and ideological Southerners. However, there are other groups who are not as ideologically conservative or backward as the diehards. For protection of their privilege, for desiring to take Indian lands and minerals, and other reasons, they still act as racist people.

Racism leads to violence, prejudice, oppression, stereotyping, social isolation, bigotry, institutionalizing of beliefs, values and actions, and the passing of laws to maintain the separation of the races. Everyday racism—the treatment of a person of another race as different—is different from institutional racism, which is the intentional subordination of special racial groups through organizational norms. Institutional racism is much more powerful than the relations between two individuals. It carries norms, and at the extremes carries the force of law.

Marriage between a white person and a Black person and between an Indian person and a white person was illegal in all states of the South as of 1900. The miscegenation laws were wiped off the books by court order as late as 1967 in the Supreme Court case of *Loving v. Virginia.* The decision also applied to the 16 states that still had miscegenation laws on the books. *Loving v. Virginia* involved the 1958 marriage of Mrs. Loving, an African American, who died in May 2008, and Mr. Loving, who was white. Mr. Loving was killed in a car accident in 1975.

When my friend in the Air Force, who was a weather man and a Chinese American, wanted to marry his Anglo girlfriend in Mississippi in 1966, they could not get a marriage license in the state. They had to go to New Orleans to get married.

Similar laws and norms keep cities segregated. Los Angeles and Greensboro are as segregated today as they were in 1955. It is norms and rules now that keep Blacks, Indians, and Hispanics from being allowed to move into white areas, or have white jobs, or marry whites. Racism keeps them from being able to get loans to buy houses and cars.

This is a book that is long overdue. Racism against American Indians has been present from the first days of English, Spanish, French, Portuguese, and Russian colonization. The attitude of the European conquerors of the "New World" has been that Indians were only savages, heathens, simple children who did not know right from wrong.

White people assumed, and many still do, that Indians had no religion, no culture, and no language. In the modern age, many of the unenlightened still believe these things. They, of course, have never lived in Indian Country, have never known an Indian person, and have never had contact with an anthropologist or linguist who has studied Indian cultures or Native languages.

It is not surprising that a Nixon appointee to the U.S. Supreme Court would greatly limit the power of tribal governments over non-Indians. In *Oliphant v. Suquamish Indian Tribe,* written by Justice William Rehnquist in 1978, the Court made a very broad ruling saying that Indian tribes cannot prosecute non-Indians on tribal lands.

Even the most enlightened white people, including Justice William O. Douglas and Justice Ruth Bader Ginsburg of the U.S. Supreme Court, have used racist, demeaning, stereotypical, and misleading terms to describe Indians. The notions of Indians as savages, as ignorant, as heathens, as primitives, are strongly engrained in the U.S. psyche. Many people talk about the "Indian language," revealing their ignorance of the fact that more than 1,000 Native languages were spoken in the U.S. as of 1492, and that 300 still survive today. Non-Indian people still say Indians were heathen savages, when in fact Indians are some of the most religious people in the world. Indian people still pray every morning when they arise, in contrast to people who only pray once a week, in church.

Racism has long been ignored, suffered through, and dealt with by Indian people. In addition, there are still Indian people who object to bringing up the subject. I am not one of them. I think hatred, racism, and discrimination should be exposed and dealt with, even though people who hate Indians are some of the most ignorant and violent people in the nation.

A survey in 2007 by Dr. Dennis Combs in Tulsa, Oklahoma, found that white students are more likely to regard Indians with prejudice rather than other ethnic groups. In what may be the first survey of its kind, the white students, all of whom had been in college for more than a year, found that they regarded Indians less favorably than they did Black people. Some of the students resent what they perceive as free services, such as health care, that go to Indians and not to others. Most prejudice, Combs found, is subtle instead of being blatant. The students thought that Indians have a poor work ethic, are different culturally, and are freeloaders.

Indian people are starting to react, and some of them are the Indian leaders who can make a difference. When "shock jock" radio DJ Tom Barnard made a racist remark on KQRS Radio in Minneapolis in September 2007, the leader of the Red Lake Chippewa Tribe, Floyd Jourdain, the leader of the Shakopee Mdwekanton Sioux Tribe, Stanley Crooks, and Clyde Bellecourt of the American Indian Movement (AIM) led a protest meeting with the station management.

Barnard and his co-host Terri Traen had made light of the high suicide rate in Beltrami County, next to Red Lake reservation in northern Minnesota. "Maybe it's genetic," Barnard said. "Isn't there a lot of incest up there?"

The tribal leaders demanded in the meeting that the two radio personalities be fired. The station made no promise to fire them. The Indian leaders also demanded that the station issue a written public apology to the two tribes.

(I thought about my mentor, the late Roger Jourdain, and what he said. "The people in Bemidji just call us savages," he told me one time when I was visiting at Red Lake. "They stop our people just for driving with our tribal license plates on their car.")

Many people still think it is fine to kill Indians. They reflect the thinking of George Custer, who was killed along with all his men at the Battle of the Greasy Grass, which white people call the Battle of the Little Big Horn. Custer wrote his senior honors thesis at West Point on the need to kill all the Indians in the nation, so there would be no more Indian problem. He also finished last in his class at West Point.

There were somewhere over 10 million Indians living in the United States and Canada Before Chris (BC), in 1492. By 1900 the total in the United States was down to under 400,000, which is a death rate of over 96%. People in California, Utah, Nevada, and Oregon were still hunting Indians for Sunday sport as late as the 1890s. None of them was ever charged or prosecuted for shooting down innocent Indian women and children. Those facts perhaps say more about the attitude toward Indians in the United States than any others. The only good Indian is a dead Indian.

We no longer espouse this extreme attitude as a nation. However, we have a long way to go to come around to the belief that Indians are full human beings, as capable in their pursuits as other people. Indians can love, work hard, get an education, raise families, write books, build businesses, and do all the other things other people can do; however, barriers are built to prevent Indians from doing almost all these things. That is what this book is all about.

The United States, Australia, New Zealand, Canada, and a few other countries have become very adept at victim blame. They have created institutions to keep their minorities poor, weak, undereducated, malnourished, and dependent. However, then when the institutions work, they blame the victims for their conditions instead of blaming the government that carried out the work or the public that supported the policies. What a fine mess you have gotten us into!

The government confined Indians to reservations, took over most of even the poor reservation lands, and rented them out to white farmers and ranchers. It forced Indian kids into boarding schools where they were humiliated, beaten, punished for speaking their Native languages, and forced to work at hard labor. These kids returned home to no jobs, no prospects, and no future. The white population and the government then proceeded to blame the Indians for not working, for being on the dole, and for having too many people addicted to alcohol.

The government put together a series of second-rate vocational schools, forced Indians to leave home and stay at them for four to eight years, and shaved off all their sacred hair the first day they were there. This made Indians hate the BIA boarding schools. Then the BIA and the public blamed Indians for not having a good education.

So it goes, from housing to health care to family welfare to jobs to businesses on reservations (or the lack of them). The government designed a rotten system, forced Indians to live with it, and then blamed Indians when the system only made Indians worse off financially, educationally, and socially.

A handful of Indian organizations have been founded in the past decade to work toward lessening the effects of blatant racism, subtle racism, and institutional racism. The oldest such group was Honor Our Neighbors Origins and Rights (HONOR). It was started in 1988 as the result of protests about Ojibwa treaty rights in Wisconsin. It disbanded in 2006 with a positive bank balance and a good record of accomplishments.

Students and Teachers Against Racism (STAR) started in the 1990s as a protest against the ingrained racism in South Dakota schools. It expanded its interests to include hate crimes, barriers to Indian voting, alcohol abuse, racial profiling, and related issues. STAR is still going strong and has much to work against the racism in Indian schools in South Dakota and elsewhere.

Institutionalized racism is a powerful thing, and something that most of us don't think about very often. We simply accept things as they are, without question, because it takes too much effort to challenge the system. Rules are rules, whether they are right or wrong, and most of us follow the rules. Society could not function otherwise.

James Riding In (Pawnee), a professor of American Indian Studies at Arizona State University, decries the invasion of the Tohono O'odham Nation on the Mexican border by the Border Patrol. The Tribe shares over 100 miles of border with Mexico and is a prime area through which illegal immigrants from Mexico, Guatemala, Costa Rico, and other Central American countries enter the United States.

"The color line has always and continues to impact Indians in harmful ways," he told *Indian Country Today* in July 2006. "Many of the new immigrants are Indians from south of the border. They suffer deprivation and death for the promise of a better life."

"Canada is not under the same scrutiny," he said. "Most people coming across the Canadian border are light-skinned people. Most of the people coming across the southern border are brown-skinned people, Mayans and others."

"These immigrants, who largely have brown skin, are being targeted in the name of national security. There are millions of white Canadians in this country illegally. Why aren't they subjected to the same level of scrutiny and oppression as are those from south of the border?"

There have been three main bad guys in the Indian racism drama—the federal government, the anti-Indian people, and developers. However, all are much bigger than might be supposed. The Bureau of Indian Affairs

(BIA) has 15,000 employees. Ryser counted some 50 different anti-Indian groups. Many teachers of Indian students in their heart of hearts are also anti-Indian people, or people who want to "save" Indians by destroying their language and culture. Developers include commercial real estate people, miners, ranchers, farmers, loggers, manufacturers, and others who lust after Indian land and resources. There are many more of all of them than needed to make life miserable for Indian people.

We need to look at the ways in which Indian people are mistreated, brutalized, raped, murdered, cheated, and denied jobs, housing and even transportation. Then maybe we can start to do something to end it.

This book is about people who are racist. Most U.S. citizens are decent people and have no hate in their heart for Indian people. This book is not about that majority. It is about the minority that engages in racist treatment of Indian people—the majority of the whites with whom Indians come into contact in their daily lives. This book is about the hateful actions of these folk.

ONE

The Infernal BIA

The government's deliberate destruction of Indians started when the Bureau of Indian Affairs was created. Prior to 1848 Indian Affairs had been part of the War Department. It was responsible for such things as delivering blankets infected with malaria and other diseases to Indians to kill them.

When the Department of the Interior was created in 1848, Congress moved the BIA there. It was no longer responsible for helping to kill Indians. Instead, it was there to take care of them, along with taking care of the minerals, the waters, the trees, the national parks, and later the dams and national forests, which the rest of the Department of the Interior is supposed to manage.

Interior is composed of the Bureau of Indian Affairs (BIA), the Bureau of Reclamation, the National Park Service, the U.S. Geological Survey, the Bureau of Land Management, the Minerals Management Service, the U.S. Fish and Wildlife Service, and the Office of Surface Mining. BIA is the only bureau responsible for people. All the others are responsible for trees, water, coal, oil, minerals, parks, dams, rivers, and other nonhuman things.

The BIA had responsibility for both the social service functions and the health functions of Indian reservations until the Indian Health Service was split away in 1955. It went to the Department of Health and Welfare (HEW), which was renamed the Department of Health and Human Services when Education got its own Department under President Jimmy Carter.

BIA had the initial responsibility to take care of Indians through treaties, to make treaties with them to take to the President for his approval and to distribute rations to keep Indians from starving. Treaty making was its main responsibility from 1848 until a half a decade after the end of the Civil War. The last Indian treaty was made in 1871; that year Congress put a rider on a bill saying it would make no more treaties.

In the meantime, BIA started in 1878 to educate Indians. It took its cue from a military man, and has kept at it until today. Captain Richard Henry Pratt, fresh from taking Apache prisoners in Arizona, got sent with them in 1876 to St. Augustine, Florida. He was in charge of guarding Indians as prisoners of war while they cooled off. However, while he had them there, he decided to see if he could teach them some English.

They were surprisingly good students. After a year of this, he asked the War Department if he could use the old Carlisle Army Barracks in Pennsylvania as a school for Indians. It was sitting empty. The Army gave its approval, and Carlisle Indian School was born. It set the example for a series of abandoned Army bases being turned into Indian schools. They included Fort Wingate (still in use today as an Indian school), Fort Stewart, Fort Chilocco, and eventually over 200 others. (There are still 184 of these schools in operation today.)

The next year, Pratt sent recruiters to the tribes of the southwestern and the north central states. They tried to recruit as many children of the headmen and chiefs as possible. He put the children in Carlisle Indian School, with no visits from parents allowed. The message was clear—we have your kids a long way away, in Pennsylvania. Any acting up on the part of the parents could put their children in harm. For decades, the parents were not allowed to leave the reservations anyway.

And the system worked. Within less than a decade the so-called "Indian wars" of the Great Plains were over. By now, the Indian school in Carlisle, Pennsylvania, has reverted to military use and is now the home of the War College. A small poorly maintained cemetery adjacent to a thoroughfare road is the last resting place for some of the Indian children who died at the boarding school.

"Captive education" became the order of the day. The main function of the schools was to "kill the Indian and save the man," as Pratt put it so ineloquently, but his philosophy held. The BIA was to be the agent of social change in one of the largest social change experiments in world history. Its purpose was to obliterate any traces of Indian language, culture, and history and replace it with English customs. The Indian problem would be gone; there would no more Indians to worry about.

The school cut the hair of the Indian students on their first day. Their pride in their long hair was gone. For many tribes long hair was and still is sacred. The matrons at the schools subjected them to de-lousing, looking at all parts of their bodies, and shaming them. They were forbidden to speak their Native languages, and got whipped if they were caught.

Pratt wrote a book *Battlefield and Classroom* about his four decades trying to forcibly turn Indians into white people. He told how the students had to march to class like military cadets. They had to milk cows, put up hay, run huge washing machines, clean their rooms, and do all sorts of manual labor.

If they spoke their Native language to each other and got caught, they would either get beaten or have their mouths washed out with soap. The ill treatment they received for five to seven generations has led directly to the many social problems facing Indian Country today. High suicide rates, huge unemployment rates of 45%, sexual abuse, physical abuse, drug abuse, and other social problems can be laid largely at the foot of the BIA and its failed social experiment.

The main curriculum for boys was agriculture. The main curriculum for the girls was home economics. The boys were supposed to become farmers on their reservations when they got home, and the girls were supposed to become wives and homemakers. This type of curriculum stuck. The 184 BIA schools now are largely vocational schools. When a couple of them tried to change to a college-prep curriculum, the change held for a couple of years and then went away.

The master plan for the development of Indian boarding schools came in "Grant's Peace Policy" of 1867. The leading churches, not wanting to see genocide happen to Indian people, met in Philadelphia that year to develop a plan for Indians. The thing to do with them, it said, was to create reservations for them, in out of the way places, and confine them to the reservations until they could learn English and learn how to be farmers. Then they would no longer be problems. They would just be brown white people.

Pratt got to implement a huge piece of it with his school experiment. Educators in the classroom took the place of cavalrymen raiding Indian villages. Indian schools ignore the reality of modern life, which is that three-quarters of high school graduates in the U.S. are now going to college. Only 17% of Indian students are going on to college, and 80% of them flunk out without ever earning a college degree. Many of these college dropouts are successful anyway. The jobs on reservations are often filled with the most qualified person available, which may be an Indian with two or three years of college.

The BIA schools were about to undergo some changes when I did my dissertation at four of them. In fact, in the decade before 1975 they had changed from being in business to serve students from rural isolated areas that had no other schools to attend. They became holding pens for problem children and slow learners. In 1966 the last two categories accounted for 30% of the students; by 1976 they accounted for 80%.

One student at Stewart Indian School when I surveyed teachers there in 1975 for my dissertation had beaten a man to death with a motorcycle chain. The judge gave him three options—Indian school, the Army, or reform school. He chose the Indian school.

When I worked at the Southwestern Indian Polytechnic Institute (SIPI) in Albuquerque from 1985 to 1986, the administration was constantly being frustrated by the BIA agents in the field. They wanted college-level students, while the BIA people wanted to send the problem kids from the reservations there to get rid of them. That battle is still going on.

The BIA, though, went much further than education in achieving its goals. It controlled Indian lands, Indian housing, Indian health, Indian transportation, Indian records, Indian minerals—everything Indian, in fact. If that were not enough, it tried to dispossess Indians of as much as possible.

The BIA was complicit in the largest theft of land in U.S. history, the theft and giving away of 100 million acres of Indian reservation lands. The Dawes Act of 1888 put Congress on record as wanting to give as much Indian land as possible to homesteaders, ranchers, and miners. Almost all Indian reservations now are "checkerboarded," with Indian trust land next to white-owned land, next to Forest Service land, next to land owned by the state, and next to land owned by Indians in fee simple title. In short, it is a mess. In fact, the BIA wanted it that way.

Furthermore, the BIA is still trying, in its simple-minded way, to divide up the income from a piece of land with 160 or 80 acres on it among 20 or 120 people. Some of that land is being rented for twenty-five cents an acre, so that a plot of 80 acres may only bring in a few dollars. In some cases, that pittance of money never gets to the rightful owners, who in many cases are living in poverty.

The BIA recorded the names of babies when they were born. It recorded the deaths of people when they died. It recorded the deeds to private lands when they were deeded to individual Indians. It handled the rations the government intermittently provided to the starving Indians so they would not starve to death. It assigned houses to people if they were available. As Indian people have said, it was the BIA from cradle to grave.

It has always been beyond my understanding why white people, including the BIA, after defeating Indians in the eighteenth and nineteenth centuries, still feel they have to take out their hatred on us. Was it not enough to take everything we owned and confine us in barren isolated lands? Why do they still have to punish Indians?

I can almost understand why they would want to punish the Lakotas at Pine Ridge and Rosebud. They are the ones who defeated and killed George Custer and part of the Seventh Cavalry. There are many white people in the Dakotas and Montana who feel a special hatred for the Lakota and Cheyenne for this defeat. To them the Seventh Cavalry are national heroes. Even the massacre of the starving Indians at Wounded Knee in 1890 is not enough for them to make up for Custer's loss.

Indeed, their campaign has worked. I can still remember my first trip to Pine Ridge and Rosebud 40 years ago. To me it was like being back in Viet Nam. People were walking around with a look of defeat on their faces. I had not seen that look since Nam. It was so frustrating to me to see that. I felt so helpless at not being able to do anything to help them.

(My uncle, Tom Godwin, who lives in Denver, has been dealing with this on a personal level for two decades. He and his wife, Ruth, adopted a son from Pine Ridge when he was a baby. Tom has been raising money and buying house trailers for Pine Ridge for years. When they have enough money for one, they hook it up to a truck and haul it up there and set it up. There is a special place in heaven for people like that, I think.)

The big thing the BIA has been pushing in Indian Country for 150 years is assimilation. They believe the solution to the Indian "problem" is to have no more Indians. They are the ones who have pushed for obliterating Indian languages, forbidding the practice of Indian religions, and wiping out Indian culture, and they have been very effective at it. After all, they hold the purse strings to most of Indian Country.

Scandals, misspending of money, under-the-table dealings, and other shady tactics have been the hallmark of the BIA. In the early reservation days, Indian agents often got rich or partly rich by taking part of the beef, commodities, and other food that was supposed to go to Indians. They often almost starved Indians to death by withholding rations (see Di Silvestro).

At the same time, they determined that the way to maintain peace on reservations was to take the children of the chiefs and headmen as hostages. When Pratt got permission to start the first BIA boarding school in Pennsylvania, the BIA agents were all for it. They scoured the northern plains, the southern plains, and the southwest to find these children and send them to Carlisle. Then they told the chiefs they had better stay in line, stay on the reservation, and keep the peace. They did not have to tell the chiefs they were holding their children hostage. The chiefs already knew that.

In short, the BIA has been one of the leaders in racist practices and discrimination against Indians. This method, of course, contravenes what it is supposed to do—protect the trust resources of Indians against theft from outsiders and protect Indian people from harm by others. It has been hard for the BIA to provide protection for Indians when it has been one of the leading agents doing the opposite.

In January 2008, Gwen Francis of Farmington, New Mexico, filed a lawsuit against the Bureau of Indian Education (BIE), the part of the BIA that is now semi-autonomous and handles the schools and scholarships.

She claims she was fired illegally for calling attention to a student at Tiis Nasbas Community School who was not getting proper services.

The student, a Navajo, was placed into Special Education, but the school did not provide Special Education services for him. Consequently, he was afraid to come to school, but he had no other choice. Within a few months his fear of school required him to be admitted into a hospital. When Ms. Francis pointed this out, she was fired on October 19, 2007. She claims her firing was motivated by this case. She also claims the local BIE official who oversees the school harassed her sexually and created a hostile work environment.

Susanna Turose of Mancos, Colorado, also filed a lawsuit the same month, claiming misspending of Special Education funds at Red Rock Day School in Arizona. The school is on the Navajo Reservation. She claims that when she complained, she was downgraded from principal to Special Education teacher and moved from Red Rock to Tiis Nasbas Community School. The BIE official, Joel Longie, lowered her pay by $6 an hour, she claims. At the end of the school year, she was fired after a 16-year career in education.

Newton Lamar, the President of the Wichita Tribe, accidentally found a document in the files of the BIA Anadarko Area Office in the 1960s. It showed that significant amounts of money from the Individual Indian Monies (IIM) and Indian Monies from the Proceeds of Labor (IMPL) accounts were going into a slush fund.

His reward for exposing this theft was that BIA removed him from office, without giving a reason. Newton went to court and won a lawsuit against the BIA. The court ordered BIA to restore him to his tribal office, which he then held for another 20 years, until his death.

James Milam was elected Chief of the Seminole Nation in 1983, and the BIA promptly threw him out of office. Jim was outspoken about his opposition to the high-handed way the BIA acted. As a former Marine who had retired, he was not used to being stepped on.

The BIA promptly threw him and his Vice Chief, my Alcatraz friend Al Miller, out of office. They went to court and won their lawsuit, and were restored to office. Out of spite, the BIA then "retroceded" or took away all the tribe's budget for the year, leaving Jim and Al with offices in name only.

The last "Seminole War" followed this piece of chicanery. The opposite sides were actually shooting at each other across the road in front of the tribal office building. The leader of the opposition, who had been anointed tribal leader by the BIA, was Edwin Tanyan. He won the next election with support from the BIA and ended the Milam/Miller government. The BIA then promptly reversed the retrocession of the tribe's contracts and continued to support Tanyan with an adequate tribal budget.

The BIA is like good soldiers, one of my friends told me 20 years ago. He was a top level BIA manager, but one who had to report to a GS-15 (top-level manager) in Washington. "If the top political people in Washington say to save the Indians, they ask where the Bible is. If the top people say to kill the Indians, they ask where the gun is."

In fact, this way of doing things has been the major fault of the BIA from the beginning. It is especially vulnerable to the whims or the anticipated whims of the White House. During Nixon's time, ironically, when we took over Alcatraz, the BIA was in the business of saving Indians. Nixon doubled the budgets of both the BIA and the Indian Health Service. He was under pressure from the Alcatraz occupation. He also adopted the most progressive Indian policy statement of the past half century. The main writer was Browning Pipestem (Otoe), who was our main Alcatraz attorney.

Under Jimmy Carter, who never adopted or developed an Indian policy, the BIA sat on its hands. Under Ronald Reagan, who had a love-hate relationship with Indians, the BIA tried its best to cut tribal budgets, reduce work forces, and otherwise carry out what it thought were the mandates of the Reagan administration. Interestingly, Reagan had the most Indian-hating Interior Secretary of all time, James Watt.

Question: How much energy does it take to power all the electrical plants in the U.S.? Answer: One Watt.

James Watt tried to drive a hard bargain as much as possible with Indians, gaining all the advantages he could for his oil company friends. Indians were getting 2% on royalties for oil and gas when they should have been getting 20%. It took lawsuits, investigations, and whistleblowers to expose the corruption under Reagan and Watt.

Similarly, when the government announced in the early 1950s that it was going to "relocate" Indians off reservations and into the cities, the BIA went to great lengths to get every Indian it could to relocate. Russell Means, who used to be one of the top AIM people, went on relocation three or four times.

The BIA grabbed people up and stuck them on buses bound for Los Angeles, Seattle, San Francisco, Dallas, Denver, Chicago, Phoenix, and Minneapolis. There, people either learned how to live in a big city or they failed. Studies showed that about 65% of Indians who were relocated actually returned home to the reservation, many of them worse off and damaged by the experience.

When the government announced in 1953 that it planned to terminate all Indian treaties, promotion within the BIA became tied to the success of terminating tribes. The man who forced termination on the tribes of New York later got the top job of Area Director of the huge Sacramento Area Office. By 1969 some 152 tribes had been terminated. The Alcatraz occupation caused Richard Nixon to reverse the termination resolution, HCR 108, which the Congress had passed in 1953. His policy of not terminating Indian treaties is still the official law of the land. It was passed as official Indian policy in the Indian Self-Determination Act. Nixon had stated the end of termination as part of his Indian policy, announced in July 1970.

The last word about the BIA is its incompetence. Many of the folk in the BIA could not get hired by an employer who demanded excellent work. This attitude showed through in a speech made by a top BIA person in Sacramento in the 1970s.

"We go to work every day," he said, "and we get things done. It may be right or it may be wrong, but every day we get something done."

You could literally hear the groans in the audience of 200 tribal leaders that Saturday morning. Many of them were hearing this type of stupidity for the first time, apparently. They normally were given the mushroom treatment—kept in the dark and covered with feces.

I personally know BIA people who got "gimme" degrees. They did not earn the degrees; someone else did the work, or they played basketball as the way they got through college. Incompetence is the word of the day in the BIA.

The BIA needs reform in the worst way. The following are the minimums that Congress needs to do to reform the BIA.

- Authorize a major study of BIA administration from top to bottom, similar to the Merriam Report of 1928. The Merriam Report is the last comprehensive study of the BIA, and it is a shame that there has not been another study in so long. The BIA needs to have light shined on it more than any other federal agency. After all, it is the only Interior agency that deals in people.
- Congress needs to authorize a review of the myriad of Indian laws to make sense of them. The Congress has reportedly passed over 5,000 Indian laws, acts, bills, and other pieces of legislation. Many of them are outdated, racist, and in need of either updating or throwing out. For instance, it is still within the purview of the BIA to accept or not accept any attorney an Indian person or tribe tries to hire. This is how the famous attorney Melvin Belli was thrown out of court in Ukiah, California. He had been hired to represent the Indians of California in a land

claim for 98% of the state. The BIA lawyer cited the law, stated they had not approved Mr. Belli's hiring, and the judge threw him out of court. Belli never got to say a word in his defense or in defense of his clients. Other attorneys eventually settled the lawsuits for 47 cents an acre, the biggest act of thievery ever permitted against Indians.

- Develop and enforce a code of ethics for BIA employees. They often act now as if they are gods, and no one can make them do the right things. They are often right about that. However, ethics and fair treatment should be part of their daily routines.
- Establish an office of Ombudsman for the BIA, reporting directly to the Secretary of the Interior, and outside the normal chain of command of the BIA.

TWO

Stereotypes of Indians

The movie producer John Ford is alleged to have killed more Indians than the Seventh Cavalry. He shot several movies at the famous Monument Valley on the border of Arizona and Utah, which is on the Navajo reservation. His most famous one was *Stagecoach* in 1938, which starred John Wayne.

Wayne was also a famous Indian killer who was alleged to have killed 10,000 Indians in movies, using only a rusty switchblade knife. In his personal life he apparently also thought Indians were a breed to be disdained, and he regretted that all Indians hadn't been killed in the 1800s.

Television was almost as good as John Wayne at portraying Indians in a bad light. Ward Bond and his long running series *Wagon Train* killed a few hundred Indians. *Bonanza* and its crew of a father and three sons killed quite a few. The number of TV series where Indians were killed numbers in the dozens, including the longest running series ever, *Gunsmoke.*

In my California days (1968–1978) I got asked many times to talk to a class of students at a school about Indians. My mentor Joseph Nettles at the University of Richmond (I was there 1960–1962) had actually had me to do this a few times around Richmond, but I didn't like doing it. However, in California after Alcatraz I got a few requests and honored all of them.

One of the most frequent was to talk to the cadets at the police training academy in Oakland, which I did for a few years. I had a soft spot in my heart for policemen, and still do. The selflessness of putting yourself in harm's way to help others is one of the noblest acts of humankind.

The instructors would have me come in to talk to the recruits for two hours on Indians in the Bay Area—where they came from, what they did, what problems they got into, what their culture was like, and so on.

I used to ask them, "What do you do with a teenager from the Oakland hills when you catch him drinking and driving? Do you take him to jail or do you call his parents?" They knew the answer: you call his parents. A cop could be in a lot of trouble if he put a rich white kid in jail.

Then I would ask, "What do you do with an Indian kid from East Fourteenth Street when you catch him drinking and driving?" They knew the answer to that one, too. Throw him in jail. Indians have no clout to cause a cop trouble. Some of the more sensitive recruits became upset when I asked these questions. However, I hope that at least some of them took a different attitude toward Indians when they hit the streets.

The number of stereotypes about Indians found in history books, movies, comic books, radio shows, television shows, stage plays, and dime novels is staggering. The effects they have on Indians are still in debate, but to me the debate is over. I think they are all harmful and lead to bad effects.

These two white men were talking one day in Muskogee, Oklahoma. One said, "You know, I can't believe the number of Indians in this town. Everywhere I look all I see is Indians, Indians."

The other man said, "It's that same way in Tahlequah. I was over there the other day, and I must have seen a hundred. Everywhere I looked all I saw was Indians."

This old Indian man overheard them and said, "Well, why don't you go to hell, then. You won't find any Indians there!"

Indians are savage uncivilized heathens: The "noble savage" stereotype is the worst cruelty ever pulled on Indians. For the life of me I can't figure this one out. Someone is noble, that is, worthy of honor or praise, and is at the same time a savage animal?

Cowboys and Indians: When we Indian kids were little we went to the Gene Autry and Roy Rogers movies on Saturday afternoons when we had a dime. Later we played cowboys and Indians ourselves. All the boys wanted to be the cowboys; the losers got to play the Indians.

Later, though, when we boys realized we were Indians, the roles changed. The winners got to play the Indians, who in our games won, while the losers had to play the cowboys. I have often wondered if Indian kids from other tribes did the same thing. However, in the world of non-Indian kids, the Indian is always the loser, and the cowboy is always the winner. That's the way the movies always portrayed it, so that's the way it has to be.

Indians live in squalor. Unfortunately this one is true. Anyone who has been to an Indian reservation knows that poverty is widespread, but this poverty is on purpose. The government has tried its damnedest to make beggars out of Indians. They put us on the poorest lands available and then proceeded to rent these lands out on long-term leases to farmers, ranchers, and potato growers. However, this stereotype is about the only one that is true.

Indians live in teepees. Sebastian "Bronco" LeBeau (Lakota) from Cheyenne River said on the Blue Comics Web site that "In my short lifetime—I'm only 42 years old—I have experienced on occasions too numerous to count encounters with non-Indians who have asked me, 'What was it like to grow up living in a teepee?' And it never fails that once I have responded to the teepee question I always get the follow up, 'But I thought all Indians lived in teepees.'"

Teepees were part of the Plains Indian culture. My tribe lived in log houses, as did the Creeks, the Cherokees, the Choctaws, and many other eastern tribes. In fact, the log cabin of the frontiers was a direct adaptation of Indian housing. The Northwest tribes lived in plank houses, and the Southwest people lived in permanent pueblos constructed of stone and mortar. Indians lived in a wide variety of types of dwellings, of which teepees are just one example.

Indian dancing: An Indian mother reported that "Last year I remember my 5-year-old daughter coming home very excited and saying she learned how to be 'Indian' in school. At first I was shocked and upset because she's Navajo; I then decided to find out what she was talking about. I asked her, 'What is it to be Indian?'" She replied, "We put paint on our faces, wore feathers in our hair and did Indian dances." I asked, "Who showed you the Indian dance?" She answered, "My teacher." I said, "Show me the dance." She started prancing around in circles—it was cute."

Attacking wagon trains: When I used to give talks to elementary schools, the most obnoxious question the ten-year-olds would ask me was, "Why do you Indians always attack the wagon trains?" Another question was, "Why do you Indians always kill the women and children?" At a young age the white kids have some horrible stereotypes in their mind about Indians.

Shaving: Indians don't have facial hair: For a long time, when people would ask me my ethnicity and I would tell them Indian, sometimes the men would say, "You can't be Indian. I can see where you shaved this morning." In their minds, Indians don't have beards and don't shave. I just wish that were true. I hate shaving. But most folk think real Indians don't have to shave. The truth is that facial hair varied widely in Indian America, from people with little or no hair to people with heavy beards.

Indians are invisible: This ranges from believing Indians can walk silently through the woods and sneak up on you to believing that Indians are seen no more because they are confined to reservations and hardly anyone ever sees them. I still have people asking me if it is all right if they drive to a reservation. Can they be admitted to the reservation? Some of them don't believe me when I tell them there are no guards, no gates, and no passes needed to drive onto a reservation.

Indians are sneaky: Supposedly an Indian could sneak up on you in the woods, without making a sound or breaking a twig, and hit you in the head with his tomahawk. This is bunk. We boys used to try to walk silently in the woods, which is impossible.

The **"rain dance"** has been so overplayed that it is not only a stereotype—it is a cliché. In watching the Ellen DeGeneres show a little while ago, the announcer, after watching her dance, said he thought it might rain. In fact the rain dance is a very serious dance engaged in by the Hopi people. Living on the high mesas of northeastern Arizona, rain is a very serious subject. So when they do a rain dance, it is a prayer asking God to bring them rain. So it is a prayer, and not a heathen fun time. (Outsiders are not allowed into either the Rain Dance or the Snake Dance.) Ellen DeGeneres's announcer denigrated Indian people with his uncaring remark, apparently without thinking about it.

Indians don't pay taxes. I wish we didn't have to. However, the fact is that Indians living on reservations have to pay state income taxes, federal income taxes, and other kinds of taxes. They are not subject to state property taxes, which still irks local county, city, and state officials, who want to tax everybody everywhere. The local officials want to tax tribal casinos (which they cannot), tribal tobacco shops (which they cannot), and Indian businesses (which they cannot). By the same token, non-Indians living on reservations don't pay taxes to the tribes, who are the rightful government providing services to them. Tit for tat, I reckon. The kicker is that the BIA and land developers made sure Indians were assigned to the poorest land available.

Indians can't vote. In fact, Indians have been citizens since 1924. To me there is a supreme irony in finally making Indians citizens of the land where we have lived for ten or twenty thousand years. The fact, though, is that Indians were not legally citizens before. The fact is that Indians don't vote very well. They will vote pretty well for an election to the tribal council, but they will only turn out at a rate of 15% or 20% in an election for the local sheriff or the local congressman. That's one reason we have so many unfriendly politicians representing Indian Country.

Indians get everything for free. This is a biggie, setting white people's teeth on edge across the nation. Nonetheless, Indians do pay for housing, even though it may be provided by HUD, a federal agency. Indians do not pay for dental care, health care, and education in the sense that non-Indians pay property taxes. Recognizing that Indian kids need to be educated, and that states could not tax tribal trust property, Congress passed a law in 1950 (the Impact Aid Act) that has the U.S. paying money to local public school districts for Indians living on reservations, students living on military bases and attending public schools, for students living on Forest Service lands, and for students living on National Park Service lands.

Heather Gonzales, a senior at Gallup High School, stunned and mortified the Indian students at a leadership forum in February 2007. She said Indians get everything for free, while others had to work for it.

"I don't understand why they're always getting mad when they get free stuff," she said to a reporter, Natasha Kaye Johnson. "We have to get jobs to pay for our shoes and jackets."

As a teenager, she was somewhat naïve. Gonzales had not obviously internalized what any adult in Gallup could have told her. We believe these things, they could have said, but we never say them out loud except to each other. After all, Indians spend hundreds of millions of dollars a year in Gallup. They buy food, clothes, cars, trucks, shoes, fertilizer, toothpaste, and a thousand other items. Indians alone keep Gallup afloat.

Shundiin Holyan, a Navajo senior at Tohatchi High School, said about Gonzales, "She's supposed to be a leader. I think she just spoke out of being ignorant and naïve. She doesn't understand why we get what we get. She doesn't understand how our people suffered."

In response, Gonzales, rubbing salt into an open wound, said, "The land was exchanged a long time ago. By now, the (federal) government has paid it off. African Americans were our slaves, but we didn't give them anything for what we did to them."

What upset the Indian students the most was that Gonzales's peers from Gallup were giving her high fives and commending her after she finished. Senator Jeff Bingaman from New Mexico, who sponsored the forum, changed the topic quickly.

Bloodthirsty savages is a term pasted on Indians by the first explorers, Columbus and Amerigo Vespucci (who by a fluke got the continents named after him). After capturing some Indians as prisoners and taking them back with him to Spain on his first voyage, Columbus proceeded to give Indians a bad name. Vespucci, a converted whoremaster, claimed that Indians were cannibals and murderers—this was his way of showing his gratitude for being saved by Indians in South America.

War paint is responsible for white children crying. It is symbolic, intended to disguise people, to ward off evil spirits. To most non-Indians, however, it is scary. I have seen little white kids start crying and screaming at powwows if their parents haven't told them in advance what to expect.

Racist stereotypical words are things you will never hear an Indian say, except when he is making fun of white people. They include ugh, many moons ago, me go, savages, and the like. The worst is squaw (which refers to the female sexual organ) and buck, which equates Indian men with wild boar or deer.

Stereotypes are useful in some ways, but they are worthless in dealing with Indians. The farcical nature of the great majority of them is clear. Indians are alcoholics, they are mean, they are dirty, they are lazy, they are dishonest, they are raiders, and they scalp people.

Indians drink "firewater" and cannot handle their alcohol. A white lady from UC San Francisco came to our campus at Cal State Hayward when I was teaching there. She wanted to hire some of the Indian students for a test. She wanted them to drink a six pack of beer each, and sit in a room for a few hours. Every so often she would take a sample of blood from them to see how well their bodies were getting rid of the alcohol. Her "theory" was that Indians metabolized alcohol at a slower rate than whites. I told the students not to do it, and they all refused. This was totally racist, it seemed to me, and the worst stereotype.

Indians are mean people. Indians are not mean. The kindest people I have ever met are Indians. I have been stabbed in the back by the best—faculty members, consulting firms, company presidents, and journalists. However, the best friends I have ever had were in Indian Country. Indians are the gentlest people in the world, but it is nigh impossible to convince non-Indians who don't know any Indians of the truth of this statement.

Indians are dirty. Indians are not dirty. In the old days, before there were reservations, Indians traditionally took a bath every day, usually in a stream or river. It was only after Indians were reduced to poverty and water became scarce and polluted that the problem of dirty bodies came about. I have smelled some awful smelling people in my life, but they were mostly not Indians. Non-Indians talk about Indians as being dirty, when in fact Indians are some of the cleanest people in the world, often bathing twice a day on a regular basis. At the time of English colonization, the typical Englishman only bathed a few times a year. The typical Indian at that time bathed at least once a day. Who is the unwashed here?

Indians are lazy. Indians are not lazy. If you have ever had to herd cattle or sheep for 12 hours a day, or put up fence all day, or do any of the many other kinds of things that Indians have to do, you would believe Indians are hard workers. My mother put me in charge of the family farm when I was 11 years old, and I did all the man's work the next six years. Daddy was in the hospital most of that time. If you have ever cut wood all day, dug ditches all day, harvested tobacco and broken tobacco suckers all day, plowed cotton all day, and so on, you would know that I was not lazy.

Neither were the great majority of the other Indians in our community. The lazy Indian is that way because white folk won't hire him.

Indians are all thieves. I lock my car all the time when I am at home in Albuquerque. However, when I go to work at schools on the reservations, I never bother. I leave it unlocked on purpose; I want to feel at home. And in 35 years of doing that, nothing has ever been taken out of my car when it was on an Indian reservation.

Indians are raiders. This is patently a lie, made up in colonial times to justify having wars with Indians, burning down their houses and villages, making slaves out of them, exporting them as slaves, taking their women as servants and prostitutes, and worse. The raiders have been the settlers, the colonists, the militia, the Army, and the local law enforcement people.

Indians scalp people. Scalping originated with the Europeans. The colonists started in the sixteenth century to offer rewards for every Indian scalp brought in to the port of Charleston and other places. Indian scalping continued through the raping and pillaging of California after the Gold Rush. One old white settler allegedly had a blanket made up of Indian scalps; he slept under it every night. American Indians did not invent scalping. Herodotus, the Greek historian, wrote in 440 BC: "The Scythian soldier scrapes the scalp clean of flesh and softening it by rubbing between the hands, uses it henceforth as a napkin. The Scyth is proud of these scalps and hangs them from his bridle rein; the greater the number of such napkins that a man can show, the more highly is he esteemed among them. Many make themselves cloaks by sewing a quantity of these scalps together."

Indians wear feathers and beads. The typical non-Indian associates Indians with feathers, war paint, buffalos, bows and arrows, teepees, beads, and animal skins. While all these things were important in the culture of some tribes, each one was restricted to only a portion of the 1,000 tribes in pre-Columbian America. Feathers were part of the Plains Indian dress, especially war bonnets. However, the Woodlands, Pueblos, and practically all other Indians did not use feathers. When you see a Southwest Indian wearing feathers, he is doing it for the tourists. Beads originally were a trade item. Animal skins were part of the clothing of many tribes, and some used them as ornaments, such as otter hair braids, moccasins made of buffalo or deer hide, and so on.

Indians hunt buffalo. Buffalo were also restricted to the Plains tribes—Lakota, Osage, Ponca, Umon Hon, and so on. The buffalo were so important to the Plains tribes that the government deliberately urged Buffalo Bill and the other buffalo hunters to kill them off to starve Indians to death. In the

15 years after the end of the Civil War, the commercial hunters almost completely wiped out over 50 million buffalo. They often took only the tongue, salted it, and shipped it to expensive restaurants in eastern cities. Most of the meat from the buffalos was allowed to rot. People were still picking up buffalo bones from the plains for decades afterward.

Indians hunt with bows and arrows. Indians were happy to give up bows and arrows when rifles came along, although as boys we loved to make our own bows and arrows.

Indians are at the end of the trail or Indians are all dead. This was almost true. From a population of perhaps 10 million in the United States, by 1900 there were fewer than 400,000 Indians left in the United States. That means that about 96% of Indians were killed by gunpowder, infected blankets deliberately given out by the Army, wars, pillaging, Sunday hunts in California and Oregon that went on for 50 years (1850–1900), and diseases. However, the small population of 1900 has now grown to over 2.5 million, and is the fastest-growing population in the United States except for perhaps "illegal" immigrants. (Since we didn't give permission for any people from Europe to come here, just who is illegal?)

Indians had no religion, were pagans, worshipped trees, or some such nonsense. None of this is true, but it is one of the most enduring myths about Indians. Indians are some of the most religious people in the world. The traditional Indians of today still arise early each morning and immediately say a prayer. If you have ever been to an Indian religious meeting, you will know how hard Indians pray. In a white church, a long prayer would be five minutes. In an Indian church, a long prayer would be twenty minutes. It goes a long time. My non-Indian friends do not understand why I won't kill a spider. But there is no reason to kill one. The spider clears your house of insects you don't want there anyway. A spider is part of nature.

Indians were a hunting culture. Again this was true of the Plains Indians, but 90% of the Indians in the United States relied mainly on agriculture for their livelihood. Indian people all over the United States relied on such animals as deer, elk, antelope, moose, buffalo, turkeys, grouse, and other animals for part of their food. However, it was the corn, beans, squash, cantaloupes, watermelons, peas, hominy, grapes, berries, potatoes, figs, and other plants that provided the bulk of Indian foods.

Indians sneaked up on settlers and burned down their houses, killed the men, raped the women, and killed the women and children. Non-Indian kids have been known to start crying when they heard an Indian was coming to their school. Indians are supposed to be the embodiment of evil.

Indians surrounded the wagon trains. This is pure bunk, made up by people in Hollywood and passed on through about 10,000 Indian and western movies. The number of Indian attacks on wagon trains, which undoubtedly happened, was very small. After all, Indians knew the settlers had rifles and some of them had repeating rifles. Their bows and arrows were no match for these rifles.

Talking Indian is a whole level of ignorance. Other terms ignorant people use are the Indian dialect, the Indian language, the Indian tongue, and so on. The fact is that there are hundreds of Indian languages, not one. Having a Lakota talk to a Navajo is like having a Frenchman talk to a Chinese person. They won't understand each other. Some Indian languages are related, in the sense that French and Italian are related; both came from Latin. Apache and Navajo are so close that my Apache friends tell me if they hang around Navajos for a couple of weeks they will pick up a few of the words. However, the "Indian tongue" myth is one of the hardest things to get people to understand.

Indians can commune with nature. I doubt Indians can commune with nature any better than an Episcopalian or a hippie can. Andy Rooney, the *60 Minutes* funny man, said when asked about the racist sports names like the Atlanta Braves and the Washington Redskins, "American Indians have more important problems than to worry about sports teams calling themselves by Indian nicknames."

"Their genius," he said, "was for living in a wild state … without damaging the ozone layer."

He really laid on the stereotypes and racial misconceptions. They "shot flaming arrows into the stagecoach carrying the new schoolmarm …," he said. Also, "they surrounded the wagon trains …"

"There are no great Indian novels, no poetry."

"There's no memorable Indian music."

He decried "an Indian belief, involving ritualistic dances with strong sexual overtones, is demeaning to Indian women and degrading to Indian children."

Terri Jean of the Red Roots Educational Project responded by calling Rooney's remarks stereotypes. A stereotype, she said, is made up by people who believe they are superior to another people. It is misconstrued, exaggerated, generalized, and negative. It is based on assumptions about another race, "when one group refuses to find the truth and relies on false information, forming their own opinions."

Mayor Pro Tem Michael Berry of Houston had no idea he was letting a genie out the bottle on March 27, 2007. The temporary mayor, who is really a three-term member of the city council, also hosts a talk radio show on KPRC. He intends to provoke listeners.

"We need to stop wasting all this time and energy apologizing to the American Indians, which we continue to do," he said. "We do it with incredible resources from our Treasury. Our entire Department of the Interior, practically, is the Department of Indian Affairs."

"We continue to give land, you know. At the Grand Canyon this group that got a private developer to come in and put this $30 million glass skywalk out over the Grand Canyon, which I will go and see, I admit it, as tacky as it is. Why are we still giving Indians exclusive rights to gamble, exclusive rights to print money, which is also known as a casino?"

"First of all, the treaty involved land and sovereignty. It did not require that we continue to pay for education. It did not require welfare programs. It did not necessarily mean we had to grant them casino licenses."

Berry, who was obviously trying to increase the size of his audience by stirring up controversy, got an answer from the Hopi Tribal Chairman, Ivan Sidney. "First," he said, "The Hopi people did not fight a war with America. Second, the Hopi people do not have a treaty with the United States. Third, the Hopi people do not have casinos. Fourth, the Hopi people do not ask for handouts. Fifth, we are a proud nation of people as are all American Indians."

Berry was clearly wrong. Of the 388 treaties that tribes "signed" with the United States, fully 114 of them promise education, health, and other things in return for the Indians giving up land. In fact, this promise was given for as long as the rivers flow and the grass grows, or maybe it meant until people didn't really mean it any more. The United States gives Indians land? How wrong could you be? All land in the United States is Indian land.

On April 1, 2008, the show "Bob and the Show Gram" on WDGC/GL105 radio in Raleigh, North Carolina, had a field day insulting American Indians. The station is owned by Clear Channel Communications Corporation. The three on-air people were Bob Dumas, Mike Morse, and Kentucky Kristin, a woman.

They included Asians, Latinos, and Blacks as well. They specifically included the Lumbee Tribe and the Eastern Band of Cherokees. They questioned the work ethic of all Indians. They also said "All Indians are lazy."

They referred to the housewarming party of an Indian and a white as a teepee warming party. In referring to Pocahontas and Sacagawea, they called them "Poca-Ho-tas" and "Saca-cooter."

The references stimulated the NC Commission of Indian Affairs to call a press conference to condemn the station's racist comments. The Commission also asked the Federal Communications Commission to levy heavy fines against the station and fire the disk jockeys that made the comments. Just to make things interesting, the show got its female co-host to admit that she cannot back up a car, and neither can most women.

- Students in grammar schools, high schools, and colleges need to be exposed to Indian art, history, music, literature, and philosophy as part of their regular curriculum. Only education and learning will diminish the strong impact that negative stereotypes now place on Indian children.
- We need an Indian television series, something like George Lopez's show, to let people see the human side of Indian people. And they need to see Indian humor, which is fantastic.

THREE

Racial Name-Calling

Perhaps nothing hurts worse than being called a racist name. Children do it without seeming to think about how much it hurts. I got called "Big Lips" and "Nigger Lips" so often when I was a kid that I was surprised when I grew up and realized that my lips are only slightly larger than normal.

Lee Brightman, one of the founders of the Bay Area organization United Native Americans (which was a model for the later American Indian Movement), used to tell me how he was always called "Chief" in college at Oklahoma State University. Lee was a starting lineman on the football team, so few people gave him a lot of grief. However, when he arrived in San Francisco and was working as a doorman at nightclubs on North Beach, he got called "Chief" numerous times. At first he kind of liked it, but soon got tired of it and would tell people not to call him that.

Indians get called all kinds of names. In South Dakota Indians are called prairie niggers. In North Carolina, where I grew up, and in Florida, they are called swamp niggers. In Wisconsin, they are called timber niggers. In Washington State they are called salmon niggers. In Arizona they are sand niggers or desert niggers. Most of these names are used behind the back of the Indians being so called.

Some of the other names Indians are called are **Squaws, Bucks, Warriors, Lazy Indians, Welfare cheats, Dumb Indians, Thieving Indians, Welfare warriors,** and **Spear Chuckers.** That's right—Black people aren't the only ones who are called spear chuckers.

My favorite phrase to hate is **"You people,"** which lots of teachers of Indians students use constantly. It instantly sets the teacher, an Anglo, and the student, an Indian, apart. Any white man who marries an Indian woman becomes **Squaw man.**

In the Flagstaff area, according to Jo Tallchief, editor of the *Red Lake News,* the name for Indians is "Trog," as in the Latin word troglodyte, meaning caveman. The acronym is also translated into "Total Reliance on Government."

When I first visited South Dakota in the middle of the 1960s, there were still signs up in bars, restaurants, and stores saying **"No dogs or Indians allowed."** If a white woman saw an Indian woman try on a dress or a pair of shoes, that was a sure sign that she would not buy the item and would not even put it on. Many times the clerks would not let Indian women try on dresses, hats, shoes, and other clothing. If you bought it and paid for it, it was yours, whether it fit or not, and you could not bring it back.

J. T. Lorenzo writes of his conversation with a couple in the airport in Phoenix. They were making light of the proposal in the state to change the name of the infamous Squaw Peak to something else. "The conversation went something like this," he said.

> "Did you hear that they're thinking of changing the name of Squaw Peak?"
>
> "Yeah, it's supposed to be offensive or something."
>
> "Yes, apparently the word 'squaw' means woman; that is offensive to some people (chuckle, chuckle), but I don't know what the big deal is."
>
> "Oh, you never know how far they're going to go ... The next thing you know they'll discover Indian burial grounds on my land, and then I'll have to move out of my home." (chuckle, chuckle)
>
> As I stood there I found myself in a dilemma. As I felt my blood rising, I had a 30-second conversation with myself. "What do I say? Do I have a right to say anything to them? If I turn around and they see that I am a Native person will I be embarrassed? Worse yet, what if they don't care? Will I be embarrassed? Will I even think of something intelligent to say? Shall I just say nothing? No—I can't just stand here and ignore these words! This is offensive to me!"
>
> Before I lost my nerve I turned around and faced an Anglo woman and an Anglo man. I quickly decided that I'd first try to join in on their conversation:
>
> "Actually, the name used to be 'squaw tit' but was changed to its present name."
>
> My intent was not to be funny, but their response was laughter.
>
> "Actually, the word means 'vagina.' It was a French word used to describe Indian women and I think it <u>is</u> offensive," I said as I tried to recall what I had learned about this word.
>
> "Yes, but it just means woman and I don't think it was French. And I don't think it was intended by be derogatory at the time," snapped the woman (as if she knew what the thinking of the time was).
>
> I was unprepared for her indignation. Still, I opted to stick with my be-patient-with-people-who-may-not-know strategy and volunteered more information.
>
> "I believe it is a French-derived word that was first used in the upper Midwest. There was a time when we did not think names like 'Black Sambo' or the image of Aunt Jemima was offensive. If we can change these, then surely we can change names like Squaw Peak."
>
> "Yeah—we should spend our tax dollars on things like that!" replied the man sarcastically.

The Arizona bill to change the name (House Bill 2482) was defeated eight times. Eventually the name was changed to Piestewa Peak to honor the first Indian woman killed in the military fighting for the United States. Her name was Lori Piestewa, and she was a Hopi woman killed early in the invasion of Iraq. She left two little sons behind.

The U.S. Board on Geographic Names voted on April 10, 2008, to make the name change official. Supporters said the state and the board's actions would show the world that "the squaw word is not to be tolerated." In the end, Governor Janet Napolitano and Phoenix Mayor Phil Gordon both supported the name change.

The practice of tribes buying back their lands that have been checker boarded was seriously hampered by a recent decision of the U.S. Supreme Court. In *City of Sherrill v. Oneida Nation of N.Y.*, Justice Ruth Bader Ginsburg, writing for the majority, stated that "A checkerboard of alternating state and tribal jurisdiction in New York State—created unilaterally at the [Oneida Nation's] behest—would seriously 'burden the administration of state and local governments' and would adversely affect landowners neighboring the tribal patches."

Thus does cultural bias and anti-Indian rhetoric reach the highest levels of the federal judiciary. Ginsburg used language that is clearly biased against the Oneida Nation when she referred to "tribal patches." She ignored the fact and distorted history by claiming that the Oneida Nation initiated letting non-Indians gain ownership of Indian lands. In fact, it was the last great Indian land grab, initiated in the 1880s by a senator from Massachusetts, Dawes. The Oneidas let their land go only under heavy threats from the state and federal governments.

Thomas J. Morgan, the Commissioner of Indian Affairs, wrote in a directive on March 19, 1890, "But such names as Flying eagle, Pipe chief, Crazy Horse, Yellow bonnet, Afraid-of-his-enemy, Walk-in-the-water, Rain-in-the-face, Bull-all-the-time, Keeps-his-head-above-water, No-hair-on-his-tail, Bob-tail-wolf No. 3, Kills-the-one-with-the-blue-mark-in-the-centre-of-the-chin, are ridiculous and should not be perpetuated. Such names are uncouth, un-American, and uncivilized."

He and his assistants issued rules on how Indian names should be made. Above all, they should be Christian names, not heathen names. Their rationale was that the allotments that were being made of Indian lands would have to be passed down, and that Indian names would not work.

Some Indians had always refused to take "Christian" names, but they were in the minority. Most went along with the BIA people and used their "white" names. In my lifetime, many Indians have gone back to using their traditional names. Instead of being Robert Jones, they are now called Robert Two Bulls. Today lots of Indians are known with the last names of Two Moons, Two Strike, and my favorite, Bird in Ground. Some of them have had their name changed legally.

- Racial namecalling really hurts. If it is done enough, it can and does lead to alcoholism, abuse of drugs, and in extreme cases suicide.
- Schools need to teach racial harmony to students and staff. Schools need to teach Indian history, culture, languages, arts, literature, and philosophy to students.

FOUR

Indian Mascots
What's the Big Deal?

In 1970 I got my letter of acceptance from the Department of Communication at Stanford. The letter admitted me into the doctoral program for the fall of 1970. I was a 29-year-old senior at UC Berkeley at the time. I was also teaching one class in the Native American Studies (NAS) program and working on the weekends flying C-141 airplanes in the Air Force Reserve at Travis Air Force Base. I didn't sleep a lot.

As soon as I got the letter, I showed it around at the NAS office, very proud of myself. However, several of the male Indian students cut me down to size pretty quickly. "So, you're going to be a Stanford Indian, hah, hah?" they laughed.

I had not given any thought to what the Stanford mascot was. In fact, I may not have even known it was an Indian. I certainly did not know that Tim Williams, Ronald Reagan's in-house Indian when Reagan was governor of California, got dressed up every Saturday in the fall and danced around the football field, putting curses and hexes on the opponents.

A few weeks later, my wife, Toni, and I hopped into our little Volkswagen to drive down to Palo Alto. On the way down, I told her how the NAS students had teased me about becoming a "Stanford Indian."

"That's not right," I told her. "We have to make them change that." Two years later, mainly through the leader of Lorenzo Stars, the president of the Stanford American Indian Organization (SAIO) that we founded, Stanford dropped the Indian mascot and adopted the Stanford Cardinal (the color red, not the bird) as the official mascot. Stanford was the first to change its racist mascot symbol, but many other colleges, universities, and high schools followed over the years.

Lorenzo Stars, a freshman student from Pine Ridge, was the first president of SAIO. It was he who took the fight to the student senate and the rest of the campus. I was too busy trying to survive the hardest year of my life as a first-year graduate student in the Department of Communication. I attended all the Sunday night meetings of SAIO when I was not busy with my Air Force reserve flying or my heavy coursework assignments.

Tim met with us during the fall of 1970. He promised not to conduct a sham religious Indian ceremony where he put a hex on the other team, but he would not stop being the "Stanford Indian." It was like his whole life was taken up with doing his stupid dances after each Stanford touchdown. More specifically, he dressed up in Plains Indian regalia, with the full headdress, the buckskin shirt and pants, and moccasins. The problem with this: he was a Yurok Indian from northern California. The Yuroks have never had a tradition of Plains Indian headdresses.

However, he would not agree to give up being the Stanford mascot altogether. It took a vote of the Student Senate, with the administration sitting on its hands and mostly doing nothing, to make the change happen. The vote by the Student Senate was 18 to 4 to drop the Indian mascot. Richard Lyman, the president, did not object.

Even so, most of us sensed that Lyman felt the same way about the symbol as he did about Native American Studies. At a meeting in the spring of 1971, in response to a question by a freshman female about whether Stanford could have any Indian history, culture, and language classes, Lyman said, "An Indian student coming to Stanford has to accept the same terms and conditions that other students come here under." In other words, there would be no Indian history, culture, language, and art classes. After Lyman left Stanford, the university finally got around to offering some Indian classes.

Finally, in February of 1972, after a year and a half of not much action from the Stanford administration, we presented a petition to the University Ombudsman, Lois Amsterdam, asking for "the use of the Indian symbol to be permanently discontinued ...." The petition stated that the Stanford community was insensitive to the humanity of Indian people. We thought the use of the name of a race on entertainment did not show an understanding of Indian culture or empathy with Indian people. We said the use of the Indian mascot was racist, stereotypical, and offensive. It made a mockery of Indian cultures.

We said the teams would never be called the Negroes, the Jews, the Caucasians, the Wops, the Spics, the Chinks, and any other racially charged ethnic name.

Amsterdam referred the matter to Lyman, and he made the decision later in 1972 to drop the Indian as a mascot. The teams then became the Stanford Cardinal, the color red, not the little red bird. People still often call the teams "The Stanford Cardinals," which is incorrect.

The Indian mascot brings out the worst racist symbols in people. The Atlanta Braves do not know, or do not care, how much they are hurting Indian people when they do their racist tomahawk chop. Neither do the Florida Seminoles fans. If they do know, they apparently don't care.

The fans paint their faces with faux red paint, wear turkey feathers, buy rubber and plastic tomahawks, and do the "Tomahawk chop" at football and basketball games. They wear cheap fake war bonnets, run all over the football field, and use imagined Indian religious ceremonies to put hoaxes on the opposing teams.

Their bands play "Indian" fight songs, which are usually stylized or Hollywood images of Indian drumming. There are allegedly 2,498 kindergartens, elementary schools, middle schools, and high schools in the United States which use Indian symbols.

In the Great Plains, Indian basketball teams who play non-Indian teams off the reservation are frequently subjected to racial harassment on the court or the field. The local students will do what they think is an Indian war hoop, yell out "Scalp the Indians," call the Indian girls "squaws," and do a "tom-tom" chant, or imitation of Indian music. The Indian students cringe at the mention of these humiliating insults. Opponents "go on the warpath" against the Indian students.

The non-Indian students have also been known to chase the Indian students on foot or in cars after games, start fights, and throw drinks and other things on them.

Carter Camp, the founder of the Oklahoma chapter of AIM, writes of an incident in his hometown of Ponca City. The Ponca City high school team, the Wildcats, were going to play another team the following week whose team mascot was the Indians.

"All week long," he wrote on the STAR Web site, "our school bristled with signs and posters calling on all true wildcat fans to; 'scratch, scalp, tomahawk, kill, burn and murder the Indians.' Of course they were not meant to hurt the many Ponca Tribal children who attend Ponca City schools."

"Their barbs penetrate and hurt our children like stray bullets. ... The one and only way to stop opposing teams from using racist portrayals of Indian people is to stop the use of Indian people as mascots."

There are many professional and college teams who refuse to change their racist Indian symbols, and in some cases, they will not even talk about it. These include the infamous **Washington Redskins, the Kansas City Chiefs, the Chicago Blackhawks, the Cincinnati Reds,** and the **Atlanta Braves**. Members of AIM and other protest groups have been arrested for picketing their baseball and football games.

The hated term "redskin" originated from the bloody Indian scalps the colonists paid bounties on. It refers to the bloody skin that was attached to the scalp of a murdered Indian. Famous Indian haters collected Indian scalps; Andrew Jackson, who became president (and whose image is featured on every twenty-dollar bill), collected the noses of Indians he killed.

Other racist team names include **Redmen, Scalpers, Utes, Red Raiders, Injuns, Warriors, Cherokees, Savages, Indians,** and **Squaws.**

The Chicago *Sun-Times* reported that there are 51 high schools in the state of Illinois alone that use racist Indian symbols. They often use "war paint," war whoops, tomahawk chops, and faux Indian "dancing." Their team names include the Redskins, the Indians, the Indianettes, the Injuns, the Blackhawks, the Comanches, and the Mohawks. The last three are actual Indian tribes. To me, "Redskin" is the second worst pejorative that one could apply to Indians. The worst, of course, is the hated word "squaw."

Tim Giago, the founder of the *Lakota Times*, later changed to *Indian Country Today,* has been campaigning against racist team mascots for over two decades. He points out that the National Congress of American Indians and the National Indian Education Association have passed resolutions condemning the practice.

Infamous college mascots include Chief Illiniwek of the University of Illinois and the Fighting Sioux of the University of North Dakota, the latter of which still remains in place. Students at UND have worn T-shirts showing Indians having sex with a buffalo.

Mascots or symbols also feature the names of individual tribes, including the Navajo, the Apaches, the Seminoles, the Choctaws, the Sioux, the Cherokee, the Mohawks, and the Chippewas. The Mazola Indian woman got quite a bit of play on TV advertising in the 1970s; the Mazola people were embarrassed when it turned out the model was not an Indian woman, but a Chicana.

When Charlene Teters (Spokane) got to the University of Illinois in 1989, she found that "Chief Illiniwek" was the mascot of the sports teams. The mascot had been adopted in 1926 by Ray Dvorak, the assistant band director. She immediately started a protest movement which was supported by the National Congress of American Indians, the National Indian Education Association, the National Association for the Advancement of Colored People, Amnesty International, and other groups.

The Illinois state legislature, however, and the university's various governing bodies continued to support the use of the Indian mascot. The actual mascot was always dressed in a Sioux war bonnet of turkey feathers (and not the customary eagle feathers). He was always a non-Indian and with one exception was a male student.

It was not until 2007 that the university dropped the use of Chief Illiniwek. The Fighting Sioux still remains the symbol of UND, but that could change within the next few years. In April 2007, the celebrated author

Louise Erdrich rejected an honorary degree from UND because of the racist mascot symbol.

Her 11 novels have frequently been on *The New York Times* best-seller list. She is from the Turtle Mountain Reservation in North Dakota, and her people are Chippewa.

"I hate to do something like this," she said. "It goes against my grain. But I do feel strongly about this symbol."

One of the early protesters against Indian mascots developed a poster similar to the one below. I probably got the team names different from what he had, but I hope you get the idea.

WHAT'S WRONG WITH INDIAN MASCOTS?

SUPPOSE YOU HAD THE FOLLOWING TEAM NAMES:

The Los Angeles Spics
The Cleveland Niggers
The Miami Greasers
The New York Kikes
The Boston Micks
The San Francisco Chinks
The San Diego Blacks
The Georgia Sambos
The New York Wops
The Mississippi Yahoos
The Washington Redskins
The Atlanta Braves
The Kansas City Chiefs
The Chicago Blackhawks

Would they be acceptable?

NOW YOU KNOW HOW INDIANS FEEL!

Most of the Indian mascots and symbols were adopted between the 1920s and the 1950s. People assumed the stereotype about Indians was true—that we had all disappeared, or had been confined to reservations, or had been "assimilated" into the Anglo culture and were not Indians any more, or had just disappeared.

In May 2007, the Tennessee House of Representatives passed a bill 71 to 20 with six not voting to prevent state agencies to impair or prohibit the use of logos by public or private institutions. The Commission on Indian Affairs had earlier passed a resolution opposing the use of Indian mascots and logos and asking for their discontinuation by schools that were using them. The Tennessee House disagreed. Their vote prohibits any state agency from interfering with a team's name. Sports teams in Tennessee are still free to call themselves any racist name they want.

Marquette University changed its symbol from the Warriors to the Golden Eagles in 1994. Mankato State College dropped its racist Indian symbol in 1971. Stonehill College changed its symbol from the Chieftain to the Skyhawk out of respect for Native heritage. Ypsilanti High School in Michigan dropped its Braves name in November 2007 and is looking for a new one.

According to Jay Rosenstein, a professor at Illinois, other colleges and universities that have dropped their racist Indian names and mascots include Dartmouth, Dickinson State University, the University of Oklahoma, Eastern Washington University, Syracuse, Southern Oregon, St. John's, Siena, St. Mary's, Montclair, and Bradley. He produced a film on the subject called *In Whose Honor?*

The Dallas public schools and the Los Angeles public schools have eliminated the Indian mascots from their schools after protests from Indian parents and students. Wisconsin and Minnesota have also recommended that public schools eliminate the use of mascots, symbols, and logos that are offensive to Indian people.

The United States Civil Rights Commission called in 2001 for an end to the use of Native American team images and names by non-Indian schools. It stated that many denigrating terms for African Americans have been eliminated since the civil rights era of the 1960s, but that many schools continue to use denigrating team names based on Indian themes.

Despite the many changes of Indian mascots, the elimination of some of the demeaning practices, and the understanding that having a stupid grinning symbol such as Chief Wahoo of the Cleveland Indians denigrates a people, every year some Stanford people want to bring the Indian symbol back. Just as sure as the sun comes up, some alumna or alumnus will write to the Stanford magazine and reminisce about the old days when they were free to make fun of Indians on the football field.

Sports Illustrated and other publications attack the attackers. They ask, "Will the fighting Irish of Notre Dame and the Minnesota Vikings have to change their names?"

The reactions of the University of North Dakota fans are even stronger. If you do away with the Fighting Sioux symbol, one writes, we should do away with the Indian scholarships as well. Another says that having an Indian symbol is actually a way to honor Indians, and that no bad intentions are meant. Actually, many of the Stanford alumni and UND alumni say the same thing. Indians strongly disagree. Indians say "You can't call me a racist name and make me like it."

Montana passed a law in 1999 outlawing the word "squaw" for its rivers, mountains, parks, lakes, and landmarks.

Dr. Lorenzo Stars is now a physician in Wagner, South Dakota, specializing in internal medicine. Charlene Teters was graduated from the Institute of American Indian Art (IAIA) in Santa Fe in 1986. She finished her B.A. at the College of Santa Fe in 1988 and entered Illinois that fall. She is now a professor of art at IAIA. Peter Jennings featured her as "Person of the Week" on *ABC News* in 1997.

Finally in 2005 the National Collegiate Athletic Association (NCAA) forbade teams with racist Indian mascots from hosting NCAA events. This ruling put tremendous pressure on the University of Illinois, which in March 2007 finally retired the racist symbol. The diehards, just as at Stanford and elsewhere, still maintain that the mascot and symbol are not racist but in fact honor Indian people.

Sheena Crystal Hale, the daughter of former Navajo Nation President Albert Hale, got upset in the fall of 2007 when the Sigma Nu fraternity at Stanford University held a "Wild Wild West" party. "There were multitudes of people dressed in the stereotypical 'Indian' regalia complete with feathers and war paint," she reported. "I was not prepared for seeing people with headdresses and war paint."

Ten Native students showed up and got a shocking greeting. They approached one of the Sigma Nu students in an Indian costume and told him his dress was not appropriate. He did not want to listen.

The Indian students talked to the Sigma Nu president the next day, and he expressed surprise that their actions had hurt the feelings of the Indian students. He apologized and said they would not have such a party again.

In 2005, after 35 years of contention, protests, arrests, tear gassing, police clubbing people over the head, and other symbols of unrest, the National Collegiate Athletic Association (NCAA) finally banned the use of offensive Indian stereotypes for school and college sports teams. Even with the ban, however, some universities are still fighting it.

- All schools and colleges should refrain from using any racist symbol that demeans a race of people, including Indians, Asians, Swedes, Chicanos, Blacks, Polish, Italians, Russians, and any others.

FIVE

Fake Indians

Perhaps no one causes more confusion and muddies the water more than fake Indians. We used to call them wannabe Indians, affirmative action Indians, Johnny-come-lately Indians, census Indians, and other names.

They mislead the public. My uncle Tom Godwin, who is an electronics genius, worked for Martin Marietta in Denver for 30 years. During that time he built the lunar lander, was the chief tech rep for the Titan missile sites, designed and built the Little Red School House satellite communication system, and built the $2 billion launch pad at Vandenberg Air Force Base.

But when the affirmative action thing came about in the late 1960s, somebody looked on his records and saw that he was Indian. He was immediately given the additional duty of identifying and working with other Indians at Martin. All of a sudden people who had never claimed to be Indian said they were. They thought it would help them with promotions, job opportunities, and advancement. Some of them were obviously not Indian.

In 1976 I met with the two gentlemen at Lockheed in Sunnyvale, California, who were in charge of affirmative action. I was working for the Indian Center of San Jose at the time, setting up an education program. During the meeting they told me Lockheed was the largest employer in the Bay Area. They proceeded to pull out this big computerized log book (they were using the old IBM 360 in those days) of several hundred "Indians" who worked there.

I was amazed. As we went through their list, I recognized none of the people they had listed. By that time I had been in the Bay Area for eight years and had met most of the urban Indian leaders in San Jose, Oakland, San Francisco, and outlying cities. I had served a term on the board of the Intertribal Friendship House in Oakland, worked as the Mainland Coordinator for the Alcatraz occupation, taught for three years at Cal State Hayward, and worked at the Indian Center for several months. I still wonder about the real ethnicity of the people at Lockheed who were claiming to be Indian.

The affirmative action managers were happy. They had met their quota of Indians, and in fact had exceeded it. Meeting the quota was a federal requirement. Almost all their funds came from the federal government for defense contracts. However, to be a Lockheed Indian, all one had to do was check a box.

Most of the fake Indians are little people, just trying to get hired, to get a scholarship, to get promoted, and the like. In some cases, however, they have tried to do what my mother used to call "get above their raisings." Several of them have written books that were best-sellers, making them rich and famous. Ultimately, however, some nosy Indian started looking at their genealogy and their credentials and found them out.

Some of these fake Indians have risen to national prominence on the strength of their fake Indian credentials.

Jamake Highwater: (He pronounced it "Juh-MAH-kee.") He claimed starting in 1969 that he was a Cherokee. However, when he was born in the 1920s (the date is disputed), he was named Jay Marks or Gregory J. Markopoulos and was Greek. Under that name he finished high school at Hollywood High School and attended a few years of college in Los Angeles. He then lived in San Francisco for several years.

He later moved to New York and wrote books under the Highwater name. He also obtained a huge grant from the National Endowment for the Humanities, allegedly $840,000, to produce a controversial PBS documentary called "The Primal Mind."

He died in 2001, with his name still in controversy. Hank Adams researched his life and published an expose about him before his death. Joe De La Cruz, the late leader of the Quinault Nation and president of both NCAI and NTCA, condemned his fake Indian credentials and the pap he was pushing. Highwater carried out his Indian charade successfully for over 30 years.

Carlos Castenada wrote a series of books about a mythical Yaqui medicine man he allegedly met in Mexico. His first book, *The Teachings of Don Juan,* became a best-seller and earned him a doctorate in anthropology from UCLA. It now appears he made the whole thing up. There was no Don Juan, there were no long stays in Mexico, and there was no apprenticeship in what Castenada called "sorcery." The anthropology department later stripped him of the doctorate because of his fictional accounts, which he made up instead of doing actual ethnographic research.

Even so, he got away with it, in a real sense. His 12 books sold over eight million copies, making him a rich defrocked academic. They are unfortunately still selling well, leading many novitiates down a false path toward obfuscation about Indians.

Later it was documented that Castenada had even lied about his birth date, having been born in Cajamarca, Peru, in 1925. He claimed to have been born in Sao Paulo, Brazil, in 1931. He died in 1998 with his name and his books still embroiled in controversy.

Hyemeyohsts Storm: He claims to be an enrolled Indian of the Cheyenne Tribe, and a Breed, or mixed-blood person. After his book *Seven Arrows* came out in 1972, he was reviled by people from the Cheyenne Tribe and other tribes for misinterpreting their sacred practices. He has also been accused of not being an Indian.

Ward Churchill: In May 2005, after he had called some of the victims of the 9/11 attacks "little Eichmans," Churchill caught hell from many quarters. His comparing the victims of the World Trade Center bombing to one of the leading Nazi villains of World War II was sure to bring him notoriety, which he craves.

One of those responding was the United Keetoowah Band of the Cherokee Nation. George Wickliffe, the Chief, said "Mr. Churchill is NOT a member of the Keetoowah Band." Churchill has also claimed over the years to be Creek, Cherokee, and Metis.

He got himself hired at the University of Colorado in 1978, without a doctorate, and within two decades had gotten promoted to be the Chair of the Ethnic Studies department. Over his career, he has had 14 books published on genocide against the American Indian, racism, and the boarding school experience of Indians. His books are filled with left wing cant, and he clearly supports AIM. He was a member of the Colorado chapter of AIM for many years.

The University of Colorado, after a lengthy investigation, fired him in July 2007. He had been charged with improprieties in research methods, fabrication of his Indian heritage, and falsifying his academic credentials. Professors Barrie Hartman, Marianne (Mimi) Wesson, and Eric Iliff were on the committee that reviewed the charges. They concluded that seven of the nine allegations against him warranted looking into. The charges of his ethnicity and his possible copyright infringement were not related to the conduct of research.

He was charged with plagiarism, misuse of the work of others, falsification, and fabrication of authority. His comments about the 9/11 victims were ruled to be protected under the free speech provisions of the Constitution.

Roxanne Dunbar Ortiz replaced me at Cal State Hayward when I resigned in 1974 to finish my doctorate. Shortly thereafter she came out with a book on Indian land tenure that has been reprinted once or twice. When we hired her (I was part of the process) she claimed to be Cheyenne. However, Hank Adams alleged later that she was actually part Anglo and part Mexican.

When she came to Hayward she was married to the poet Laguna poet Simon Ortiz. They were divorced a few years later, but she has continued to use his name.

She stayed at Hayward for over 30 years and recently retired. Hank Adams and others challenged her Indian identity in the early 1980s, with little challenge coming back from her. They alleged she had previously been either an Okie or a Chicana, but they were not certain which.

Terry Tafoya was for a time on the faculty at Evergreen College in Washington in the Department of Psychology. He claimed to have a Ph.D. from the University of Washington, a claim that later turned out to be false. In the meantime he traveled around the U.S. telling "Indian" tales and claiming to be a mental health worker as well as an Indian traditionalist.

He even got himself on the board of the famous Kinsey Institute. He claimed to be from Taos Pueblo, but later admitted he was not, after the tribe's enrollment clerk, Alicia Romero, stated she had never heard of Terry Tafoya.

He has also claimed at various times to be Apache and from Warm Springs, Oregon, which has three tribes living on it. However, he has no proof of enrollment in any of these tribes, either.

His cousin Jack says they grew up in Pompano Beach, Florida, and that Terry was born in Trinidad, Colorado. Thus, there is a good chance that he is Hispanic; much of the population of Southern Colorado is Hispanic. He claims to be a licensed therapist, but does not have a license from the state of Washington.

He admitted in a deposition in 2005 that he did not earn a Ph.D. from the university. He also earns $100,000 or more a year in speaking fees and is represented by the American Program Bureau. He also claims to be on the "National Teaching Faculty" for the American Psychological Association, but they say he is not. Ruth Teichroeb, a reporter for the *Seattle Post-Intelligencer,* published a long expose on Tafoya on June 21, 2006.

Phil Stevens was a man who apparently left South Dakota for California at an early age. He told Harry Smith of *CBS News* that he grew up in the East Los Angeles ghetto in the Depression and that he knew little about his Lakota heritage.

After allegedly making millions in the electronics business, he decided at an advanced age to "help" his people. The biggest controversy at Pine Ridge after the killing of 300 Indians at Wounded Knee in 1890 is the return of the Black Hills.

When they signed the Treaty of 1868, the Lakota people still owned the Black Hills. However, within less than a decade this sacred treaty had been broken, and they were forced by the Army to move south and east to two smaller reservations at Pine Ridge and Rosebud.

George Custer had helped in finding gold in the Black Hills in 1874. When the word got out, prospectors, miners, traders, and their camp followers swarmed over the area. Custer was attempting to remove the Indians from the area when they killed him and his men in 1876.

After fighting a battle since the 1920s over the land, the tribes were about to have a settlement made that would have returned part of the Black Hills to them. They had won a land claim earlier for $105 million, which has now grown to $800 million. However, they refuse to take the money.

Senator Bill Bradley, after he visited the Pine Ridge reservation, agreed to sponsor a bill to return 1.3 million of the contested 7.5 million acres to the Lakota people. However, along comes Phil Stevens, and he gets another bill introduced. He muddied the waters so much that Sen. Bradley withdrew his bill.

Indeed, there has been no other bill introduced to fix the Black Hills problem. Thanks a lot, Phil Stevens.

Princess Pale Moon is the name self-chosen by a woman 35 years ago as her "Indian" name. She claims to be a Cherokee and founded an organization in the 1970s called the "American Indian Heritage Foundation." They are headquartered in Falls Church, Virginia. Her husband, Wil Rose, is the operating head of the foundation, which raises money for poor starving Indians. Unfortunately, not much of the money actually gets to the poor Indians.

According to Bunty Anquoe, writing in the *Lakota Times* in 1991, Pale Moon's real name is Rita Ann Suntz. After starting in the Bay Area, she moved east after Ronald Reagan became president and used his coattails to pull in millions of dollars. Supposedly her organization is raising at least $21 million a year.

Her biggest coup after moving to Washington was to latch on to Ronald Reagan's eminent fund raiser, Richard Viguerie. An expert at direct mail, Viguerie raised the art of political solicitation to new levels when he raised big money for Reagan's two terms as President. After some fits and starts, during which she allegedly stiffed some printers and mailing houses, Pale Moon found her groove with Viguerie running her operation. She perfected the "save the poor Indians" theme to new levels.

One of her claims to fame was singing the national anthem at Washington Redskins games. She heavily defends the former owner, Jack Kent Cooke, and his use of the racist name and by implication insinuates that people who protest the use of the name are just troublemakers.

Iron Eyes Cody was the "Indian" name of a man who was probably the biggest and most successful fake Indian in history. He was the "Indian" who cried a tear in the environment commercial where people threw trash at his feet after he beaches his canoe. In addition, he played Indian roles in the movies for over 40 years, appearing in over 200 movies with John Wayne, Roy Rogers, and Richard Harris.

He was born in 1904 in Louisiana with the name Espera de Corti. His parents were Francesca Salpietra and Antonio de Corti. He died in 1999 and is buried in Hollywood. While he was never Indian, he obviously really wanted to be. He rarely left home without his beaded clothing, his Indian wig, and his moccasins.

Asa Carter, also known as Forrest Carter, wrote a memoir which, while fake, has become a classic. *The Education of Little Tree* is about him growing up in the hills of North Carolina as the grandson of a Cherokee couple. The grandfather was supposedly a moonshine maker.

Carter was later exposed as a member of the Ku Klux Klan from Alabama. He had never lived in the hills of North Carolina. He had long been a white supremacist and speechwriter for the segregationist governor of Alabama, George Wallace. Instead of being raised in North Carolina, he was raised in Alabama (see Browder, 1997).

William Least Heat Moon is the adopted name of William Trogdon. A former English professor in the Midwest, he one day woke up and realized he was part Osage. After the college let him go and his wife left him, he went all over the United States and wrote a book on his experiences called *Blue Highways.* With the input of his Indianness as a major ingredient, the book became a bestseller in 1982.

Rigoberta Menchu won the Nobel Peace Prize in 1992 and became an international symbol of repression of Indians in Guatemala. However,

David Stoll let all the air out of her balloon a few years later when he documented that large parts of her horrifying story were false.

The brother, Nicholas, whom she allegedly watched starve to death is alive and doing well in a village in Guatemala. While she was allegedly working as a political organizer on coffee plantations, her sister Rosa says, she was actually a scholarship student at a Catholic school for girls. Her father did not organize any peasant revolutionary armies. She did not engage in political action as a teenager, but was in school. But even with the condemnation she got from *The New York Times,* Menchu has continued to sell her books and lecture all over the world.

Douglass Durham was the security head during the Wounded Knee occupation in 1973. At the same time, he was an FBI agent and provocateur reporting on the American Indian Movement (AIM) from the inside. He was allegedly one of the last people to see Anna Mae Aquash before she was murdered by two AIM people. He claimed to be one-quarter Chippewa, but apparently was not. He died several years ago.

He was also allegedly the last person to be seen with Jancita Eagle Deer before she was hit by a car in northern Nebraska and killed. Bill Janklow, the Indian-baiting former Attorney General of South Dakota, Governor of South Dakota, and Congressman from South Dakota, was tried on the Rosebud Reservation *in absentia* for the rape of Jancita while she was babysitting his children. Janklow was the Legal Aid lawyer on the reservation at the time. He was banned from the reservation but managed to hold on to his attorney's license.

Brian Brown, now listed a former president of National Relief Charities (NRC), has been raising millions of dollars and keeping large parts of it for himself for over a quarter of a century. The overhead for the organization is 57%, compared to 20% to 30% for similar organizations.

Brown does not claim to be Indian, but claims to raise money that directly benefits Indians, mainly Lakotas (Siouxs) and Navajos. The newspaper publisher Tim Giago, founder of *Indian Country Today,* exposed him over and over in his publications. The NRC spends more than 90% of its income on fundraising and administration, with only between 5% and 10% of total income actually going to Indians.

Charity Navigator, one of the five leading nonprofit accreditation agencies in the United States, gives them a low score of only 37 points out of 100. Brown's salary is listed at $208,260, but this does not include perquisites such as rented cars, travel, hotel rooms, and entertainment. The organization reported a total income of over $17 million in 2004.

The organization uses high-pressure tactics to squeeze money out of people. These include direct mail sales and boiler rooms. They say people are starving to death, about to freeze to death, and other dire things. In addition to NRC, the organization also operates the American Indian Education Foundation (AIEF) out of Rapid City. Despite the millions NRC raises, AIEF only gives $300,000 a year in scholarship funds.

In the past 20 years, the organization has been chased out of Pennsylvania, South Dakota, Arizona, and Oregon. It has been sued by the states of Connecticut and Pennsylvania. Its uses other names, including American Indian Education Foundation, Council of Indian Nations, Navajo Relief Fund, Sioux Nation Relief Fund, and Southwest Indian Relief Council.

Sacheen Littlefeather is the actor who turned down the Academy Award for Marlon Brando in 1973. Brando, at the top of his form after starring in *The Godfather,* turned down the Oscar because of the treatment of Indians by the film industry over the years. Brando supported many Indian causes, from the fish-ins in Washington State to the occupation of Wounded Knee by AIM, over the years.

Sacheen later reported that the producer told her she had only 45 seconds to make her little talk. Brando had given her a 15-page speech to read, but, she says, the producer told her he would have her arrested if she went long. The Oscar show allegedly adopted a policy of no proxies to accept awards after that.

Her path had crossed mine in a way. A few days after Sacheen stood in place of Brando, one of the professional students at Cal State Hayward told me, "That's not her real name. Her name is Maria Cruz. When she was here, she hung around with the Chicano students." He had been a student there at the same time Sacheen had been.

A few years earlier she had been a student at Hayward, where I taught from 1972 to 1974. Sacheen was born and raised in Salinas, a little town near the California coast. She started using the Indian name after she dropped out of Cal State to try to make her way in acting and TV work. By the time I got to Hayward, she was long gone and married.

She appeared nude in Playboy in October 1973, surprising a lot of us with a chest we knew nothing about. A blowup of that picture graced the walls of several Indian bars in the Bay Area for years.

On her Web site, Sacheen maintains that she is Native American, not Mexican, but gave herself the Indian name when she was an adult. She says her father was part Yaqui and Apache. She won small parts in a dozen movies over the next few years after standing in for Brando, and now resides in the Bay Area, where she leads a prayer group. For many years she was a healer using nativist methods.

The list of movie actors who have played Indian roles and who were not Indians runs into the thousands. In starring roles there have been only a few, but in supporting roles there have been many, including these (see the "Fake Indians" Web site):

> Rudolfo Acosta, Judith Anderson, Michael Ansara, Joey Bishop, Robert Blake, Delle Bolton, Neville Brand, Henry Brandon, Pierre Brice, Charles Bronson, Jeff Chandler, Linden Chiles, Chuck Connors, Alex Cord, Pearly Cristal, Jacob Daniel, Michael Dante, Frank de Kova, Kevin Dillon, Aimee Eccles, Paul Fix, Robert Forster, Eduard Franz, Audrey Hepburn, Howard Keel, Michael Keep, Burt Lancaster, Martin Landau, Jorge Luke, Paul Lynde, Nick Mancuso, Tina Marquand, Elsa Martinelli, Joaquin Martinez, Mike Mazurky, Mindy Miller, Ruben Moreno, Simon Oakland, Debra Paget, Jack Palance, Anthony Quinn, Donna Reed, Carlos Rivas, Gilbert Roland, Kathrine Ross, William Shatner (that's right, Captain Kirk), Larry Storch, Robert Taylor, Irene Tedrow, Robert Tessier, Corinne Tsopei, Lee Van Cleef, Sam Waterston, Rachel Welch, Robert J. Wilk, and Lana Wood

Lynn Andrews, a Beverly Hills actress, wrote a book about her supposed experiences in becoming an Indian medicine woman. The book, published in 1980, was the first of four of her books that made *The New York Times* best-seller list. She has written many other books as well.

Her former live-in companion, David Carson, sued her in November 1988 for fraud and misrepresentation. He said, "As a result of our personal relationship, she and I composed a series of literary works that includes *Medicine Woman, Flight of the Seventh Moon, Jaguar Woman,* and *Star Woman.*"

After her success with the books, Andrews took off on a cross-country tour selling her brand of Indian religion. She had almost a decade of success before Carson exposed her. (The two of them had split up in the meantime.) Andrews bilked unsuspecting and naïve non-Indians out of hundreds of thousands of dollars to attend her fake Indian rituals and ceremonies.

Sun Bear, real name Vincent LaDuke, founded his own tribe 50 years ago. They were mostly hippies and New Agers. They had their own farm and compound outside Spokane, Washington. Vincent was a Chippewa from White Earth, but he spent his whole adult life with non-Indians, promising them they could be like Indians.

When he visited us at Berkeley in the late 1960s, I quickly learned that he was illiterate. Despite the fact that he is alleged to have written several books, I believe he talked them through to his wife, Waubun, who wrote them out.

His daughter, Winona LaDuke, went to Harvard, returned to her father's home at White Earth, and founded a group working for the return of Indian land and for Indian environmental concerns. Her main claim to fame was running for vice president of the United States with Ralph Nader in 2000. Their run ensured that George Bush would win over Al Gore. Nader wanted Bush to win. He wanted the environmental movement to be mobilized and activated the way it had been when Ronald Reagan was president.

Vincent charged non-Indians to attend his Vision Quest ceremony and made quite a bit of money. He died in 1992, but his organization still exists.

Harley "Swift Deer" Reagan, he of the fake "traditional" Cherokee sex ceremony, claimed that he was a distant relative of Ronald Reagan. That may have been the tiniest of his white lies. He claimed to have been raised on a Cherokee reservation in Texas, which has never existed. The nearest Cherokee reservation is several hundred miles away in Oklahoma.

He claimed (falsely) that the Cherokees killed every man of another tribe when they went to war, which never happened. However, he said, the Cherokees had maintained peace for 6,000 years! He had dozens of terms that he apparently made up, such as Wah-Kawhuan for the supreme deity, which is probably a distortion of the Lakota term for the Great Spirit, Wakan Tonka.

He claimed to have a Ph.D. and to have studied 15 years with a Navajo medicine man. He even claimed to have studied with the same medicine man about whom Carlos Castenada wrote in his hoaxed-up books. Castenada's made-up medicine man was supposed to be a Yaqui from Mexico. Reagan's made-up medicine man was supposed to be a Navajo from northern Arizona. That is, he was a fake claiming to have learned from a fake of the wrong tribe!

Reagan made a lot of money. He charged people $1,200 for a weekend of exploring their "Native American sexuality," according to Buchanan. After he appeared on a segment of an HBO sex show in 1992, claiming to be teaching Cherokee sexuality, Wilma Mankiller, the Vice Chief, threatened to sue the network. Dr. Richard Allen of the Cherokee Nation says Reagan is one of about 200 fake Cherokees about whom the tribe receives complaints.

There is no mystic Cherokee sexuality, says Dr. Allen. "We learn about sex like everyone else does," he said, "behind the barn."

I suppose it does no great harm for someone to claim to be Indian and not be. However, at the least it possibly deprives an Indian of that job. The claims of the little people, who never became famous, are but minor pin pricks compared to the ones who had the gall to pass themselves off as Indians and become famous for it. The misrepresentations of a Princess Pale Moon and an Iron Eyes Cody do nothing to erase the stereotypes of Indians that plague us today.

All these fake Indians, and others as well, are hurting Indians. If nothing else, they are presenting a false stereotyped image of Indians. Tafoya constantly gets comments on how much he acts like an Indian. Dunbar Ortiz is often on the lecture tour or the book promotion tour.

The fake Indians often take jobs away from legitimate Indians who deserve them. I am amazed every time I run into a person with blond hair and blue eyes, who had an Indian grandmother. Interestingly, it is never a grandfather, who would have been a savage warrior and rapist and killer of women and children. Approximately 90% of the time that grandmother was a Cherokee.

This short list does not include the many non-Indians who have claimed Indian jobs. Their exploits could fill this whole book and several more besides. We had them at UC Berkeley in the 1960s, at Stanford, at Cal State Hayward, at Bacone College, and all over the place. I hope these folk can sleep at night.

Beware of folk claiming their Indian ancestry too strongly. They just might be fakes.

SIX

Border Towns

Gallup, New Mexico, the "Indian capital of the world," is the leading border town in the United States. It has five reservations—Navajo, Zuni, Ramah, Hopi, and Acoma—feeding into it. They bring it well over $400 million a year.

The things that are applicable to Gallup are pretty much applicable to 150 or more towns that border on Indian reservations. They include Flagstaff, Farmington, Page, Bemidji, Grants, Santa Fe, Holbrook, Winslow, Lumberton, Chadron, Rapid City, and Scottsdale. There are over 500 more, including many large cities that people don't think of as border towns. Included here are Phoenix, Oklahoma City, Tulsa, Seattle, Denver, Chicago, New York City, San Diego, and Portland and Salem, Oregon.

Gallup is the most successful of all the reservation border towns. It has the most millionaires per thousand people in the world. New York City, San Francisco, Los Angeles, Boston, and Singapore all have fewer millionaires per thousand than Gallup. It has 350 or more millionaires in a population of less than 20,000.

When my friend and boss Boyd Hogner first told me that in 1986, I did not believe him. However, ten years later, when Forbes Magazine and Channel 7 television in Albuquerque ran stories.

How do they make their money? Off of Indians. Gallup gets at least 60% of the money generated on the Navajo Reservation. It gets this money in the first cycle of spending. There is no slaughterhouse on the reservation, for instance. Families who do not have their own flocks, which are most Navajo families these days, buy almost all their groceries from Gallup. The largest Ford truck dealership in the world, Gurley Motor Company, is located in Gallup.

There are 80 Indian jewelry manufacturers in Gallup. Many of them pay wages below the federal minimum wage. They get away with it by paying piece rates. The ring they buy from someone for $15 took the maker three hours to make, plus materials, meaning the person is making $4 an hour. They then re-sell the ring for between $30 and $45.

I have been working in Gallup and visiting it for 35 years, mostly recruiting scholarship students. I worked four years as the evaluator for the Indian Education Act program of the Gallup-McKinley County Schools in the 1980s and 1990s. I spent several hundred hours a year on site and visited all 29 of the Gallup schools twice a year.

The dropout rate in the Gallup schools is 65% for Indians. When a young Navajo teacher said this at a school board meeting 25 years ago, she was promptly blackballed. She told me she could never get a job teaching in the Gallup schools, and I believe her.

When I said the same thing in a letter to the State of New Mexico in 1988, the deputy superintendent, Harry Hendrickson, called me on the carpet. He told me I was not authorized to make those kinds of statements. Only he and the superintendent, Ramon Vigil, were authorized to make them.

"But Harry," I told him, "I got the data from the reports you send to the state!"

"It doesn't matter," he said. "Only Ramon and I are authorized to release that information." I knew that he meant if I did not toe the line that I might never get a contract with the school district again.

The schools are not interested in improving. They want to keep Indians in a poverty condition. They do not want to admit they have any dirty laundry, and will go to great lengths to hide it.

The school district, which is larger than the state of New Jersey, does not have a truancy officer. No one is there to try to get kids to go to school. Instead they have a Hearing Officer. His job is to kick kids out of school.

The school district policy is that students have to go to school 170 out of 180 days. If an Indian kid misses 11 days, they call a hearing and kick him out. They kick kids out as young as 12 years old, despite the state law that says they have to go to school until they are 16. The tribal law says they have to go until they are 18 or are graduated from high school, but no one enforces either law.

When Frank Kattnig, who is half German and half Hispanic, was hired as the JOM Counselor at Tohatchi High School in 1984, he set out to do something about it. I know Tohatchi because my goddaughter Tina Benallie is from there. Tina said the college attendance rate in 1984 was about 10% to 20%.

Frank raised it to 55% the first year he was there. In another eight years he had raised it to 90%, and had the kids earning $1.2 million a year in scholarships. He kept that up the whole 15 years he was there and retired in 1999.

However, the second year he was there he got fired. He was accepting collect calls from some of the students that were away at college. They were not getting adequate guidance from the colleges and would call Frank for help.

He stayed fired for about two weeks, but the parents called a meeting with the school district and demanded that he be rehired, and he was. After that he was partly immune from firing.

Unfortunately, in the eight years since he retired, there have been about 10 people in that position. None of them would even talk to me until this year, when the new counselor, Rosa Gutierrez, called me to come to a Career Day she was having. One of her predecessors was fiddling with a new computer program the whole time I was trying to talk to him. I knew he was not listening.

The six high schools in the Gallup-McKinley County Schools put Indians into bonehead tracks. When I checked on the enrollment in Advanced Algebra at Gallup High School 18 years ago, there were only two Indian students in the two sections. Indians make up 65% of the total Gallup population, so if they had been adequately represented, there would have been 40 Indians in those classes.

Gallup brings in over $400 million a year from the reservations. The town gives back little if anything to the reservations. Twenty years ago one of the tribes asked me how to raise money in Gallup. I spent a day giving them a seminar on how to do it. Find the most important person, I said, make friends with his best friend, and get the best friend to ask him to chair a fund raising campaign.

Unfortunately, instead of doing it the way I suggested, the tribe decided to show up at the big man's office with a delegation of people from the tribe. The big man was Pat Gurley, the owner of the largest Ford truck dealership in the world.

When this delegation of five Indians showed up at his office unannounced, and with no appointment, he threw them out. I'm sure both are still mystified about what happened. Gurley thought he had been sandbagged; the tribe had not laid its groundwork properly. Now the members of the tribe think Pat Gurley is an anti-Indian bully, a loud and an insensitive man. What a shame.

People have told me for years that Gallup does not want Indians to be educated. I believe it. The 350 millionaires don't want Indians to be able to escape the wage slave labor they are locked in now. Without them the millionaires, including the 80 Indian jewelry manufacturers, would be much less powerful.

Jewelry is not the only industry, of course. Pawn shops, trading posts, motels, and grocery stores are also big moneymakers. The motel I have stayed in for 25 years is owned by a man from India who owns six motels. I saw him in Earl's Restaurant 15 years ago paying his lunch bill. He pulled out a roll that would choke an elephant.

In the winter things are tight in the motel business. You can get a room anywhere, mostly for under $50. However, in the summer prices double and the places are full. One of the motel managers told me last summer that they were running 98% occupancy. That means that someone is getting rich.

My aunt and her husband owned a motel in Phoenix in the 1960s and 1970s. When they bought it, the occupancy rate was 80%. Within seven years they built it to 98% and sold it for three times what they paid for it. Motels can be moneymakers.

For years the school board in Gallup had four Anglo or Hispanic members and one Indian. He was a harmless old Navajo who never challenged the system. He went along to get along, never pushing the envelope.

Then 10 years ago the National Indian Youth Council (NIYC) won a lawsuit changing the way school board members were elected. Instead of having at-large elections, which let people in Gallup always win, the court ordered the district to go to single-member districts. That meant a district with a large Indian enrollment could elect an Indian. In the next election, the vote put three Indians and two whites on the board.

Within a year the Indians had let the symbol of the old guard, Ramon Vigil, go. He was the boy wonder of his day, being hired as superintendent in his early thirties. When the board let him go after more than a decade in office, Ramon was only 42.

He represented the old families of Gallup. The board replaced him with Bob Gomez, who served for six years. One of the Indian board members switched her vote at the last moment, choosing Gomez over Dr. Joe Martin, a Navajo.

The schools did improve somewhat under Gomez, who was outspoken about things. However, when he retired and moved back home to California, the next person in line, Karen White, was clearly from the old school. Things went back to business as usual. After two and a half years, the majority Indian board let her go in the middle of the year and put in an interim. They are looking for a superintendent now.

The Gurleys, the Tanners, the Ortegas, and the Vigils run Gallup. They select the mayor and the school superintendent, using their people on the city council and the school board. They are just like the five families who ran Muskogee, Oklahoma, when I was president of Bacone College.

When a young man in Muskogee wanted to run for mayor, he told several of his friends about it. One of them went to the leader of one of the five families and told him the young man wanted to run. "How can he run?" the leader asked. "I don't even know him."

This is the same kind of thing Averill Harriman said about Jimmy Carter when Jimmy wanted to run for President of the United States in 1975. Harriman went to his grave disturbed about how Carter could run and win without his blessing. Harriman had picked presidents for decades by that time.

In 1970, a bunch of us from Alcatraz went to Gallup to protest the inhuman conditions under which Indians working in the Gallup Intertribal Ceremonial had to live and labor. The Navajo youth had invited us there; the National Indian Youth Council hosted us.

We spent a week there, during which time we got kicked out of several bars. As soon as we walked into some of them, they would kick us out without serving us. The word had gotten around town.

The conditions did get a little better as the result of our demonstrations. The Gallup ceremonial is still one of the biggest moneymakers for the city, pulling tens of millions of dollars each August to the one-week event.

The population of the city itself is 36.6% Native. Even with this large percentage, there have never been any Native people on the city council. Those seats are reserved for whites and Hispanics.

Gallup is still a little frontier town living off Indians. Maybe sometime they will show some appreciation for the people who support them, instead of throwing them in jail, throwing their kids out of school, arresting them by the tens of thousands every night, and calling them names.

But I know as surely as I write this that somewhere right now there are groups of people scheming to develop ways to keep Indians off the Gallup City Council, on the poverty line, and in debt.

Towns bordering on Indian reservations, or near them, have been allowed to operate in open secrecy for over 150 years. When the reservation system was made the official policy of the United States in 1867, border towns soon established their primacy over Indian Country.

The question emerges how the people in Gallup make their money. Off of Indians, of course. The Hopi, Navajo, Zuni, Ramah Navajo, and Acoma tribes are all within the Navajo service area. I found in a study for the Ramah Navajos in 1986 that the 703 families on that small reservation spent over $5 million a year in Gallup. (They also spent $2 million a year in Grants and another $2 million in Albuquerque.) The main Navajo reservation brings over $400 million a year into Gallup.

The millionaires are trading post owners, auto dealers, Indian jewelry factories, motel owners, and grocery store owners. There are 80 Indian jewelry manufacturers in Gallup, with most of them being millionaires. They operate at a very high markup—100% for each piece of jewelry. The maker of a watch, a ring, a squash blossom necklace, or a bracelet will sell the piece to the factory, for instance, for $50.

The factory will then sell it to a middleman for $100; the middleman will sell it to the customer for $150. The markup is standard. Some factories have their own stores where tourists can buy directly. In those cases, the stores/factories have a 200% markup, which makes the owners a ton of money in a year.

The Indians have no choice. There are not enough hours in the day for them to make the jewelry and then take time to sell it directly to the customer.

Indian reservations are like water flowing through a fish net. Money leaves in the first round of spending, and it never comes back. I was driving back to Gallup from Chinle one day 20 years ago when I met a pickup pulling a cattle trailer. I had talked to the man driving the truck earlier that morning. He was on the Parent Committee for the school.

I asked people in Gallup and Window Rock on the way home if there was a slaughterhouse on the reservation. There was none. So if a person raises cattle or sheep and sells them, that person has to take the stock to Gallup or another border town to sell them. This man had taken 10 head into town that day; he was one of the few relatively well-off people in the Chinle community.

However, what he needed at home—clothes, shoes, tires, the cattle trailer, cars, fertilizer, seeds, haircuts, insurance, school supplies—he had to buy in Gallup. The Navajo reservation spends hundreds of millions of dollars each year, and most of it goes to border towns.

The people who profit from the spending of Indians should appreciate their business. Instead, one sees much evidence of disdain, chauvinism, cultural haughtiness, discrimination, name-calling, and much other evidence of racism in Gallup and the other towns that border on reservations.

The most celebrated reaction to border town violence happened in Gordon, Nebraska, in March 1972. Raymond Yellow Thunder, an Oglala from Pine Ridge, had been stripped of his pants and pushed into the American Legion dance hall on February 12, a Saturday night. He had been drunk at the time. Eight days later, two young boys found his dead body in the cab of a pickup truck in Gordon. An autopsy said his death was due to a cerebral hemorrhage.

At the end of February, four white men and a white woman were arrested and charged with felonies. The police charged two of the men with false imprisonment. The two others were charged with false imprisonment and manslaughter. The woman was charged with manslaughter.

Russell Means was attending the first national meeting of urban Indian centers a couple of weeks later in Omaha. I was there at the press conference when he challenged the whole group to go with him and the AIM members to Gordon to protest the death of Raymond Yellow Thunder.

Gordon lived on the money people from Pine Ridge bring to it, and it still does. At the same time, though, the white residents of Gordon treated Indians as if they were dogs. Until AIM pushed the issue, nothing was done to change race relations in the town.

The Nebraska Indian Commission later reported that in 1975, some 426 Indians were arrested in Gordon. They were 75% of all the arrests in the town for the year. They were 13% of all Indians arrested in the state that year. Out of the 365 arrests for drunkenness and intoxication, 349 or 95.6% were Indians. In the country seat of Rushville, there were 101 arrests for drunkenness, and all of them were Indians (Mason).

The protests and land occupations in Gordon continued through 1973 and 1974. Finally, in 1975, Cathy Merrill, an attorney for Panhandle Legal Services in Scotts Bluff, listed the allegations against the Gordon Police Department:

- Use of excessive force
- Use of verbal threats and conduct
- Selective enforcement of the laws
- Creation and escalation of tensions
- Use of authority outside of their jurisdiction
- Assaulting prisoners
- General harassment
- Illegal conduct
- Engaging in racist, discriminatory, and prejudicial conduct against the Indian community of Gordon by word, attitude, manner, and act in violation of civil rights laws, the U.S. Constitution, and human decency and dignity (Mason).

Bob Yellow Bird, the leading AIM activist in Nebraska during that time, met with the Gordon City Council in November 1975. He demanded that they halt the racist practices. The Council refused to take actions, instead referring him to the Gordon Human Relations Council. He insisted that the Human Relations Council only existed on paper.

Another troublesome racist border town has been Farmington, New Mexico. Navajo leaders have long called the border town in northwest New Mexico "the Selma, Alabama of the Southwest." The small city of 43,000 is

63% white, 18% Indian (mostly Navajo), and the rest Asian, Muslim, Chicano, and a few Africans.

One incident involved William Blackie, a Navajo. He walked out of a bar in Farmington at midnight on a June Saturday in 2006 after his money ran out. He had gone only a few blocks when three young white men stopped and offered him a ride.

The three men, C. L. Carnie who was 20, Freddie Brooks, also 20, and John Winer, 18, told him they would give him a ride if he would buy them some beer. However, they headed out of town instead of toward the liquor store. They stopped just outside town and proceeded to beat and kick him, yelling, "Die nigger! Just die!" They left him bleeding and alone in the desert.

The police identified the three through anonymous tips. They arrested them and charged them with a hate crime—the first such charge in the history of the border town. The police also charged them with felony assault and kidnapping. Carnie pleaded not guilty at his pre-trial hearing in March 2007.

Winer pleaded guilty in March 2007 and faces 35 years or longer in prison. Trials of the other two men have not been held.

Lawrence A. Greenfeld, a statistician with the Bureau of Justice Statistics, authored a study in 2004 that documented the high level of violence toward Indians, much of it in border towns near reservations. The report stated that 10% of Indians had experienced some form of violence, from assault to rape to murder. For his trouble and his work on another report on racial profiling, the Bush administration fired Greenfeld in 2005, ending his 23 years of work for the federal government.

Four white men from Farmington beat and kicked Roy Castiano, a local Navajo, in 1997, leaving him with a severe brain hemorrhage. Blake Redding, one of the men who assaulted Castiano, admitted to police that it was largely because he was Indian.

Donald Tsosie, a Navajo, was beaten to death with a shovel in 1998. A local white thug and his friend killed Betty Lee, a Navajo mother, in 2000, and were convicted of murder. The men responsible for both deaths were later identified as members of the KKK—the Krazy Kowboy Killers.

The former mayor of Farmington, Marlo Webb, carries on the racist traditions. He said of his Navajo neighbors, who surround the city on three sides, "They've culturally not come in to join what we call modern society," he told an interviewer. "They're not, they haven't been educated to do it. They're not equipped to do it. They're very backward."

The most notorious case in Farmington happened in 1974. Three Navajo men, Benjamin Benally, John Harvey, and David Ignacio, were bludgeoned to death, mutilated, and burned in Chokecherry Canyon outside of town. Three white boys who were students at Farmington High School were arrested for the murders. The judge overruled the district attorney and sentenced the three boys to reform school. The district attorney wanted them tried as adults; two of them were 16 and the other one was 15 when they committed the murders.

"We wanted to come in and burn the place," says the local Navajo leader, Duane (Chili) Yazzie. He was the victim of an earlier racist attack. Yazzie lost his right arm to a shooter 30 years ago.

The Navajos wanted to protest the light sentences and applied for a permit to hold a parade. The city denied the local AIM members a permit, and gave a permit to the local posse to parade in Wild West frontier costumes on horses. When the Navajos tried to stop the posse, they were teargassed and 30 people were arrested.

After a hearing by the U.S. Commission on Civil Rights, the county was forced to develop a plan for district elections for the County Commission, which let a Navajo have a shot at being elected. The at-large system in place for years had denied the Navajo people any seat on the commission. The Justice Department sued the county hospital for not treating Navajos. The Equal Opportunity Commission sued the city for employment discrimination and won the case.

In Brandenburg, Kentucky, Jordan Gruver, a Native teenager, was beaten, kicked, spit on, and doused with whiskey by skinheads on July 30, 2006. At the age of 16, he had his jaw, his ribs, his wrist, and his teeth broken. His sin was not being white.

All this happened at the county fair. The Southern Poverty Law Center (SPLC) filed suit against the Imperial Klans of America on his behalf the next year. The SPLC has won several cases in the past three decades against Ku Klux Klan organizations, skinheads, and Tom Metzger's Aryan Brotherhood.

These folk are following in hallowed footsteps. Teddy Roosevelt, who was later President of the U.S., said in 1886, "I don't go so far as to think that the only good Indians are the dead Indians, but I believe nine out of every 10 are, and I shouldn't inquire too closely into the case of the tenth."

My hope is that we will see some improvement in the Gallup schools one day. It is high time to review the state of race relations, health treatment, shopping conditions, and other things in reservation border towns.

SEVEN

Hate Groups

L. Frank Baum, who became famous as the author of *The Wizard of Oz*, earlier had a career as a pioneering newspaperman in South Dakota. He wrote in the 1890s:

> The PIONEER has before declared that our only safety depends upon the total extirmination (sic) of the Indians. Having wronged them for centuries, we had better, in order to protect our civilization, follow it up by one more wrong and wipe these untamed and untameable creatures from the face of the earth. In this lies safety for our settlers and the soldiers who are under incompetent commands. Otherwise, we may expect future years to be as full of trouble with the redskins as those have been in the past.

In the 1970s, following a decade of Indian activism that started with the fish-ins in Washington, the Mohawk land occupations in New York and Canada, the formation of the National Indian Youth Council (NIYC), and the occupation of Alcatraz, anti-Indian "white backlash" groups started to form.

In Washington State they were a reaction to the 1974 *Boldt* decision that stated Indians were entitled to half the runs of steelhead and salmon as guaranteed in the 1854 treaties. Whites who had bought land on reservations also protested having tribal governments exercise jurisdiction over them. In Montana, they formed around protests of tribes exercising jurisdiction over range lands. Many of the hate groups also advocate for the complete revoking of all treaties with Indian tribes. They also resent the rights Indians reserved through treaties to hunt and fish on reservation lands and other public lands.

They maintain that the white race is superior to Indian tribes or Indian individuals. Labeling themselves as "citizen's rights" organizations, these groups barely conceal their hate for Indians in general and their scorn and derision for tribal councils. One of their main planks is trying to assert that they are not subject to the jurisdictions of tribes—even though their property may be in the middle of an Indian reservation.

They maintain that tribes have no jurisdiction beyond the members of their own tribe. They have won some major battles on that issue in the past half century. Tribes no longer have jurisdiction on non-Indians living on reservations.

A decade later, these groups were still organized and had expanded to more states. They are now located in the states of Alaska, Arizona, Idaho,

Michigan, Minnesota, Montana, Minnesota, Nebraska, New Mexico, New York, North Dakota, South Dakota, Utah, Washington, and Wisconsin.

They are made up mainly of people who own property or businesses on Indian reservations and small farmers with land on reservations. They later attracted a substantial number of right-wing professional haters as members. Some people compare the groups to the Ku Klux Klan, the Aryan Nations, and the Skinheads in their ideology and tactics.

The adoption by President Rutherford B. Hayes of the concept of "Manifest Destiny" in the 1880s led to the movement of the U.S. to claim all the land between Canada and Mexico for the U.S., and from the Atlantic Ocean to the Pacific Ocean. This led to the passage in 1887 of the General Allotment Act. Senator Dawes of Massachusetts was the sponsor of the legislation, which detractors denounced as just another way to get to the last Indian land. Despite opposition, the legislation passed, and the Dawes Commission carried out the land giveaway over the next five decades. Indian tribes, of course, were not consulted about the General Allotment Act.

Rudolph Ryser quotes Senator Alfred T. Beveridge as espousing the anti-Indian policy of the time:

> God has not been preparing the English-speaking and Teutonic peoples for a thousand years for nothing but vain and idle self-admiration. No! He has made us the master organizers of the world to establish system where chaos reigns. ... He has made us adepts in government that we may administer government among savages and senile peoples.

As a result of Allotment, almost all Indian reservations today are "checkerboarded." Indian property is next to non-Indian property, which lies next to tribal property, which lies next to Forest Service lands, and so on. The small Navajo reservation at Ramah southeast of Gallup has seven different kinds of land on it.

Under the General Allotment Act, two-thirds of the 150 million acres of Indian lands were lost to the tribes. They were left with 50 million acres, which has slowly been added to in the past 50 years. Kickingbird (1973) documented the history of this illegal selling of reservation lands.

Most of the Indian lands were in isolated areas; some of them were deserts. However, there are also Indian lands that are prime agricultural acreage. Others are prime timber acreage, and still others have petroleum, coal, oil, gas, uranium, and other minerals. It is ironic that the Indian reservations now own about 25% of all the energy producing lands in the United States.

There are now more non-Indians living on Indian lands than there are Indians (Ryser, 1992). Many of them are third or fourth generation ranchers and farmers. They either own the land outright, or they have 99-year leases on it. The second-largest group is absentee landowners who use the property as vacation homes. The third-largest constituent of the groups is sport and commercial fishermen.

The leading Indian hate group these days is the Citizens Equal Rights Alliance (CERA). Dave Lundgren, an attorney, calls them the Ku Klux Klan of Indian Country. Its sister organization is the Citizens Equal Rights Foundation (CERF). In 2002 CERA held a Mother's Day conference in Washington called "Confronting Federal Indian Policy." CERF at about the same time filed an amicus curiae brief with the Supreme Court in *U. S. v. Lara* calling for the Court to find that Congress has no power to recognize the inherent powers of tribes.

Both CERA and CERF are made up of white owners of Indian reservation lands. The CERF and CERA members are the third and fourth generation descendants of the people who profited from acquiring Indian lands. What alarms them these days is that tribes are re-acquiring some of these lands in order to build an economic base for their people again. The hate groups can't stand the idea that Indians would get some land back, no matter how it happens.

The CERA Web site presents a case for doing away with tribal sovereignty:

> Tribal sovereignty diminishes the rights of Indian Americans, hundred-of-thousands (sic) of non-Indians who live on reservations, and millions of others who are affected by tribal governments. Federal Indian policy, modern tribal governments and the concept of tribal sovereignty violated the most basic principles of the American Revolution and also the vast majority of early Indian traditions. We can't grant popular sovereignty to Indian people without reducing the current exalted sovereign status of tribal governments. Fortunately, conveying popular sovereignty to American Indians would also return traditional concepts of Individual (sic) freedom and dignity to Indians. As Judge Randall also noted, "[T]his country, has the power and the legal right to protect any and all parts of Indian identity, culture, tribal assets, self-determination, religion/spirituality that needs to be protected, and yet do it all within the framework of treating American Indians like we treat ourselves, as normal citizens of this state, of this country. The real issue is, do we have the will?" Granting popular sovereignty and equal constitutional rights to reservation residents is the last truly great civil rights struggle in this country.

The "reservation residents" they refer to are the non-Indian farmers, ranchers, miners, and absentee owners of lands on reservations.

Larry Kibbey lists the following anti-Indian groups on his Web site:

- U.S. Farm Bureau, National
- All Citizens Equal (ACE), Montana

- East Slope Taxpayers Association, Montana
- People for the West, National
- North Dakota Committee for Equality
- Equal Rights for Everyone, Wisconsin
- Citizens Rights Organization, Montana
- Cheyenne River Landowners Association, South Dakota
- Concerned Citizens Council, Nebraska
- Equal Rights for Everyone, Wisconsin
- Wisconsin Alliance for Rights and Resources (WARR)
- Trout Unlimited, National
- Protect Americans Rights and Resources (PARR), Wisconsin
- National Wildlife Association
- Citizens Equal Rights Alliance, National
- International Association of Fish and Wildlife
- Interstate Congress for Equal Rights and Responsibilities (ICERR)
- Steelhead/Salmon Protective Association and Wildlife Network (S/SPAWN)
- Western States Coalition.

Ryser says the total list now has more than 50 organizations on it. They claim to have 500,000 members, but Ryser puts their active membership at 10,850. The number of people who give money or write support letters he puts at 34,150, which is a potential force. They are still trying to eliminate reservations, outlaw tribal governments, and declare an end to the "Indian problem."

EIGHT

Racism and Wildlife

When we took over Alcatraz Island in November 1969, the first phone call we got came from Billy Frank, Sr. He called our headquarters at the American Indian Center in San Francisco that first night after he had seen me on television. Mr. Frank was the long time leader of the fish-ins in Washington State. The tribes finally won back their treaty right to hunt and fish, years later.

"Hey, Dean, what are you guys doing down there?" he asked me in his booming bass voice.

"We're taking back some Indian land," I told him. "We're starting with Alcatraz, but we are going to take back some other places."

"Good for you," he said. "It's about time. A couple of carloads of us are coming down tonight."

Sure enough, they showed up the next day. Al Bridges, who would ultimately be arrested over 50 times, and his wife, Maiselle, showed up ready to help. Their daughter Suzette and her husband, Sid Mills, were with them when they came into the Indian Center. Another carload of Washington State people went straight over to the island.

The actions of the fish-in people, including the ideological leader Hank Adams, the Bridges family, the Mills family, the Don and Janet McLoud family, the Frank family, and others, had sparked the revolution standing up for Indian rights in Washington State. According to the treaties they had signed in 1854, they had the right to hunt and fish in the usual and accustomed places.

However, beginning in the early part of the twentieth century, the state game wardens began to enforce state laws on Indian lands. The BIA, which should have stood up for the Indian people, looked the other way. The BIA never sent any law enforcement people or attorneys to help the beleaguered Indians. They were mostly on their own, although the actor Marlon Brando and the Black comedian Dick Gregory both joined ranks to show their support by getting arrested with them. Gregory and his wife both pulled prison terms after being arrested in the fish-ins.

The local non-Indians fought hard, including shooting Indians with rifles and shotguns. Hank Adams got shot in the stomach by a rifle at one fish-in and barely survived. The state law enforcement people, egged on and helped by the citizens and vigilantes, clubbed Indian people, slapped them in handcuffs, threw them in jail.

The *Boldt* decision in 1974 affirmed the right of the Indians to 50% of the salmon and steelhead runs. That decision soon ended the fish-ins and led to the creation of the Northwest Indian Fisheries Commission (NWIFC). For a quarter of a century, the Commission, made up of Indians and non-Indians, has regulated the fishing industry in a manner that has helped the fish to recover. Where the runs of both fish had diminished greatly in the previous several decades, the runs have begun to build up to much higher levels. Maiselle's brother Billy Frank, Jr. is the head of the Commission.

However, the court decision started a reaction by commercial and sport fishermen in the Northwest that is still having serious consequences today. The decision was prompted by the actions of the "fish-in" people from several tribes in the state of Washington. Several of them had been arrested dozens of times when they fished the old Indian way at Frank's Landing.

The 1983 *Voigt* decision affirmed the treaty rights of the Chippewa tribes to harvest off-reservation natural resources in parts of Wisconsin, Minnesota, and Michigan. The decision affirmed the treaties of 1837, 1842, and 1854. It immediately set off a chain of events that are still causing problems today.

By 1987 the anti-Indian groups were very active. The leading groups were Equal Rights for Everyone (ERE), the Wisconsin Alliance for Rights and Resources (WARR), and Protect Americans Rights and Resources (PARR).

The state of Wisconsin also spawned the development of "Treaty Beer." A pizza parlor owner, Dean Crist, started an anti-Indian group in the 1980s. He called the group Stop Treaty Abuse. He organized anti-Indian demonstrations around the state, mainly on the issue of Indians asserting their right to spearfish walleyes. The state had passed a law in 1908 outlawing the practice, but the law did not apply on reservations. Indians, however, had complied with the law almost from the beginning. When they started asserting their right to spearfish again in the 1980s, they became the object of hatred.

When the Anishnaabe (Chippewa) people started to fish the way they had been guaranteed by the treaties, and which the courts had just reaffirmed, they were assaulted on a daily basis. The locals called them timber niggers, welfare warriors, and spear chuckers. They carried signs such as the following, which were also made into bumper stickers:

Save a Spawning Walleye, Spear a Pregnant Squaw

Too Bad Custer Ran out of Bullets

The crowds around the fishing spots were often drunk or drinking. They threw rocks, bottles, and full beer cans at the Indian fishermen. Soon thousands of non-Indians were harassing the Indians every time they fished or speared walleyes, which spawn in great numbers every spring.

They slashed the tires of the fishermen, ran their vehicles off the roads and into ditches, threatened them with death. They rammed their boats while they were fishing, swamped the boats, and blocked them with other boats. They fired metal ball bearings at them with high-powered slingshots. They shot at them from the banks with high-powered rifles. They were assisted by Skinheads, members of the Aryan Nations, and Ku Klux Klan members.

When I was asked to attend a meeting in Hayward, Wisconsin, in 1981, I agreed to go. The Lac Courte Oreilles Chippewa Tribe had asked Frank Blythe, the director of the Native American Public Broadcasting Consortium (NAPBC) to attend. However, he was committed to another meeting, and so he asked me to attend for him.

The issue was the Indian hunting and fishing rights on the reservation. It was in the courtroom in Hayward. I observed for a couple of hours, saying nothing. Then someone asked me to speak. I stood up and said, naively, "If the two sides would just talk to each other, the issues could be resolved."

The white men in the room started yelling, "Throw this guy out." "Who is this troublemaker?"

I sat down, dumbfounded, and said nothing else. I was mystified by the whole experience until 15 years later. The tribe asked me to come up to do a seminar on education, and the federal projects lady was my chauffeur for the two days. She was not a local, but she had spent several years in the school district.

I told her the story, and asked what I had said that had made the white men so mad. "Back in those days," she said, "they didn't think they had to talk to Indians."

The fight between Indians and local whites over hunting and fishing took a bizarre turn in South Dakota in 1999. Page 69 shows a replica of a poster some locals passed out around the state. It was obviously tongue-in-cheek, but its vile contents set some people on edge.

One of them was the senator from Colorado, Ben Nighthorse Campbell. Ben is a Northern Cheyenne from Montana. His dad moved to California as a young man, married, and raised his son and daughter in the foothills east of Sacramento. Ben served six years in the U.S. House of Representatives and 12 years in the Senate—the only Indian in either house the whole time.

Ben asked Attorney General Janet Reno to order an investigation into the poster. "This hate-filled propaganda exhorts hunters to murder human beings," he said in his letter. Senator Tom Daschle of South Dakota joined Ben in condemning the poster. It apparently did not lead directly to any murders, but it inflamed racist passions.

The U.S. Civil Rights Commission announced it was planning a hearing in South Dakota on several deaths of Indians in the state.

When the Makah Tribe of northwest Washington announced it had won a court decision to conduct whale hunting, the people against whale hunting descended on the reservation. Greenpeace and other conservation and environmental groups were opposed to the hunt. The tribe had stopped hunting whales for 80 years, under duress and orders from the federal government. They announced in 1999 that they would go on another hunt.

They got ready to go by training a crew in the ancient techniques. They would hunt in a long boat with the traditional methods. While they were out on the ocean, however, the Greenpeace boat, loaded with a bunch of environmentalists, almost rammed their boat several times.

Nevertheless, the hunters finally managed to harpoon a whale and bring it in to shore. Their culture a hundred years ago was based largely on whale hunting and gathering other types of marine life. Despite the obstacles, they completed the hunt, in the traditional manner.

The U.S. Humane Society and the Sea Shepherd Conservation Society also oppose the Makah hunting whales, despite the fact that the International Whaling Commission allowed them to hunt up to 20 gray whales over the next five years.

The Stroh Brewing Company in 1996 started selling Crazy Horse Malt Liquor in 32 states. At its height, the malt was being brewed at seven different plants. Finally, after protests from the family of the late Lakota warrior leader, the company agreed to stop brewing and selling the malt, and settled a lawsuit with an insulting payment of sweet grass, blankets, tobacco, and seven race horses.

The Klamath Indians in Chiloquin, Oregon, have been under assault in recent years for their defense of the sucker fish. The Klamath, who suffered one of the worst fates under the termination of their treaty in the 1960s, finally had their treaty rights restored in the 1980s. To them the sucker fish is sacred.

They have been the victims of drive-by shootings, intimidation, and violence. The bumper sticker of the hoodlums who defend the farmers who want Klamath River water is "Save a farmer, fillet a sucker fish."

State of South Dakota
Indian Hunting License
Game, Fish and Parks Department Pierre, SD (605) 224-0000
PROCLAMATION

Re: Indian Hunting Season Hunting Fees: Free to first 7,883 hunters/$1.00 thereon

Dear South Dakota Hunters:

The 1999 Big Game hunting season in the state of South Dakota has been canceled due to shortages of Deer, Turkey, Elk, and Antelope. However, this does not mean there will be no hunting. In the place of the big game animals this year we will have open season on the Sioux Reservations. This will entail the hunting of America's Worthless Siounis Pyutus, commonly known as "Worthless Red Bastards," "Dog Eaters," "Gut Eaters," "Prairie Niggers" and "F--- Indians." This year from 1999–2000 will be an open season, as the f--- Indians must be thinned out every two to three years.

IT WILL BE UNLAWFUL TO:

- Hunt in a party of more than 150 persons.
- Use more than 35 bloodthirsty, rabid hunting dogs.
- Shoot in a public tavern (Bullet may ricochet and hit civilized white people).
- Shoot an Indian sleeping on the sidewalk.

TRAPPING REGULATIONS

- Traps may not be set within 15 feet of a liquor store
- Traps may not be baited with Muscatel, Lysol, rubbing alcohol, or food stamps.
- All traps must have at least 120 lb. spring strength and have a jaw spread of at least 5 feet 3 inches.

OTHER RULES AND REGULATIONS

- Shooting length-wise in a welfare line is prohibited.
- It will be unlawful to possess a road-kill Indian; however, special road-kill permits shall be issued to people with semi-tractor trailers and one-ton pickup trucks.
- With such a permit you may bait the highway with Muscatel, Lysol, rubbing alcohol or food stamps.

HOW TO KNOW WHEN AN INDIAN IS IN YOUR AREA

- Disposable diapers litter the street.
- Large lines in front of the welfare office and for free cheese.
- Trails of empty wine bottles leading from the city parks to all city alleys.
- Empty books of food stamps thrown all over.
- Carloads of Indian children waiting outside liquor stores.

REMEMBER LIMIT IS TEN (10) PER DAY. POSSESSION OF LIMIT: FORTY (40).
GOOD HUNTING!

One of the last of the Indian fighters is former U.S. Senator Slade Gorton. When he was attorney general of the State of Washington, he lost the battle in the *Boldt* decision that let Indians have half the salmon and steelhead run. Gorton backed the sport fishermen and wildlife groups who were trying to suppress all rights of Indians to hunt and fish on their traditional grounds. His hatred of Indians deepened to the point of no return.

He later ran for the Senate and won, despite opposition from Indians. In an ironic twist, however, it was Indian votes and money that defeated Gorton in his bid for re-election to the Senate. The Northwest tribes banded together, got some help from tribes outside the area, and defeated him. Ten of the tribes opened offices in Washington, DC, to help in the fight against one of the last remaining Indian fighters with the mentality of George Custer.

Gorton as a consultant is still trying to take away from Indian tribes their immunity from lawsuits. He accuses tribes of using too much of their influence to rule over non-Indians who live on reservations. As a result of his actions, and the actions of others, the tribes have lost huge powers in the past 30 years through Supreme Court decisions. They can no longer prosecute non-Indians for crimes committed on the reservation, for instance. The Supreme Court, after being a wonderful defender of Indian rights for two hundred years, has turned into an anti-Indian body.

- The U.S. needs to live by the terms of the 389 treaties it forced on Indians. Despite the fact that most of them were approved by the Indians only under threat and duress, they still remain binding instruments of U.S. policy. Failure to enforce the terms of the treaties puts the United States on a par with Russia and China in terms of human rights abuses. It makes the United States look almost as bad as slavery and segregation of Blacks in the South did in those evil days.

NINE

Redlining

For decades, the General Motors Acceptance Corporation (GMAC), the largest holder of credit in the world, redlined Indian reservations. That means Indians living on reservations could not get credit from GMAC to buy a car, no matter how good their salaries were or how much money they made. It was blatant racism on a national scale.

Then in 1984 the corporation agreed to a consent decree in federal court in New Mexico. A consent decree to me says, "I wasn't doing anything wrong, but I won't do it any more." It is hypocritical in the extreme. However, sometimes it is the best settlement a lawyer can get for a client.

The Civil Rights Division of the U.S. Department of Justice had filed the action on behalf of Indian clients in the states of Arizona, New Mexico, Montana, Washington, North Dakota, and South Dakota.

The complaint charged that GMAC "has discriminated on the basis of race in extending credit to American Indians." It also said that the corporation had "failed to provide the required written notice of adverse action to rejected loan applicants," which violated the Equal Credit Opportunity Act (ECOA).

The ECOA states that credit should not be denied to Indians or other ethnic groups because of their race or ethnicity. Deputy Assistant Attorney General Daniel F. Rinzel led the civil rights attorneys. They charged that GMAC had "refused credit" to American Indians "on account of race." The groundwork on the case had been done by an Indian attorney, Lawrence Baca.

Transportation is a major matter in Indian Country. In a study I did for the Ramah Navajo reservation in 1986, the 706 households spent 24% of their income on transportation, including cars, trucks, gasoline, insurance, tires, maintenance, and so on. There are few if any Indian reservations with a bus line, train service, airport, steamship, or dogsled that serves them. Indians live in isolated areas. If they are to be able to travel to buy food, clothes, fuel, fertilizer, furniture, or pots to cook in, they must have cars available.

Since GMAC is an affiliate of the General Motors Corporation, the largest automobile manufacturer in the world, its actions affected tens of thousands of Indian people directly. It also affected many more thousands indirectly, by setting trends and patterns that are followed by banks, credit unions, savings and loans, and other lenders nationwide.

The corporation did not want to try the facts in court. So before they got to court, and without admitting any wrongdoing, GMAC and the federal government negotiated a consent decree. The federal district court of New Mexico then accepted the decree. It binds GMAC to approve credit applications from Indians. It cannot discriminate against anyone who lives on a reservation. It cannot discourage an Indian from applying for credit to buy a car. It must provide rejected applicants with written notice of why they were rejected.

It also is obligated to advise all its employees of the law, train its supervisors in the law that forbids discrimination in granting credit, and test its employees annually on their knowledge of the law.

The officers of GMAC also have to file a report with the Justice Department every six months detailing the number of Indians and non-Indians who have applied for credit, how many of each have been approved and denied, the location of any of its offices that have opened or closed, the outlines of any litigation it is involved in with regard to Indians, and any complaints it has received.

This consent decree raised many questions in my mind, more than it answered. How many Indians did GMAC turn down over the years? We will never know; the decree means the facts of the case will never be tried in court.

Is GMAC still discriminating in other states, such as Oklahoma, California, Montana, Washington, Nevada, Minnesota, Wisconsin, Idaho, Kansas, North Carolina, Florida, and Nebraska, where large numbers of Indians live? We will probably never know the answer to that question, either, since the Department of Justice is not likely to file a separate lawsuit for those other states (it has not to date).

Are other lending institutions discriminating against Indians because of their race when they try to buy a car? Are other lenders turning Indians down in applications for houses, boats, farms, and businesses?

Are there "patterns and practices" of discrimination against Indians in these areas? How serious are they? Is there anyone out there with the legal knowledge, the skilled and trained people, and the sense of outrage necessary to investigate these questions? Does anyone care, except Indians?

How willing are Indian people generally to fight for their civil rights, including voting, housing, loans for cars and for businesses, freedom of association, and so on?

Indian people need to thank Mr. Rinzel and Mr. Baca for doing the legwork. They need to thank Mr. Thomas Keeling, head of the section that filed the case, who works in the Justice Department in Washington, DC.

We ought to thank them publicly, with letters and tribal resolutions. However, we ought to ask our Indian leadership to put these questions forward for more public debate and discussion. I suspect there is more discrimination against Indians than anyone wants to admit.

Banks also stick Indians with higher interest rates than non-Indians pay. The First National Bank of Gordon, Nebraska, agreed to a settlement in May 1997 to pay $275,000 to Indians whom it had charged higher interest rates for consumer loans. The U.S. Justice Department had sued the bank in 1996 under the Equal Credit Opportunity Act and the Fair Housing Act.

"Every community needs fair access to credit, including American Indian reservations," said Isabelle Katz Pinzler, the Acting Assistant Attorney General for Civil Rights. "No one should be charged a higher rate for credit just because of the color or his or her skin."

The bank, which made most of its loans to Indians to the citizens of the Pine Ridge Indian Reservation, was charging considerably higher interest rates to Indians than it was to non-Indians. This is a violation of federal fair lending laws.

The settlement was the second one going in effect in South Dakota in less than five years. This was also a consent decree. In 1994 the Blackpipe State Bank of Martin settled a lawsuit in which the bank allegedly refused to make secured loans where the collateral was located on a reservation (*United States of America v. Blackpipe State Bank).*

It also placed credit requirements on Indians that it did not place on whites. It allegedly had no Indian employees. It avoided loans that might be subject to tribal court jurisdiction. It required higher collateral of Indians than it did of white people. It charged higher interest rates to Indians. It had redlined the entire Pine Ridge and Rosebud Reservations. The bank, though, denied all these charges.

The bank created a fund of $125,000 to compensate victims of the alleged discrimination. It was required to maintain records of all loan applicants and to report the information to the federal government.

In Rapid City, Mark Koehn, an attorney, filed a class action lawsuit in 2005 against J. D. Byrider and members of the Nelson family, all car dealers. The suit, representing 25 Indian people, alleged that Byrider and the Nelson dealers sold Indians cars, but only if they could sign a payroll deduction agreement in advance. That way, the dealer was going to get paid as long as the Indian person had the job. To show their appreciation, the car dealers also added a couple of thousand dollars added to the price of the respective Indian's car.

The lawsuit charged the dealers with deceptive sales techniques, higher than normal interest rates, beefed-up vehicle prices, and unfilled warranty promises. The promises by the dealers that they would help people improve their credit ratings never came true, the suit said.

Aegis Mortgage Corp. of Houston settled a lawsuit in July 2007 agreeing not to redline Indian reservations for home loans. The twentieth-largest mortgage provider in the United States, the company had made $8.5 billion in mortgage loans in 2005. It had made only $51 million in loans on reservations, making it 77th in loans to Indians. However, Aegis had redlined some people living on reservation lands. The lawsuit cost the company $475,000 to settle. The lawsuit had been brought by the National Community Reinvestment Corporation (NCRC).

The year before, Ameriquest Mortgage settled the largest lawsuit ever over redlining on reservations. The settlement cost it $325 million. The Securities and Exchange Commission (SEC) had brought that lawsuit.

NCRC has filed lawsuits against five other lenders for the same issue—redlining. They are NovaStar Mortgage of Richmond, VA, Guaranteed Rate of Chicago, Franklin Bank Corp. of Houston, ComUnity of Morgan Hill, CA, and Hyperion Capital of Lake Oswego, OR. NovaStar has said the lawsuit against it has no merit and the company will fight it.

The new practice of banks and mortgage companies has been reverse redlining. Instead of drawing a red line around a ghetto, a barrio, or a reservation, the mortgage companies make mortgages to the minority people, sometimes eagerly and greedily. However, instead of making mortgages at the prime rate, they classify the minority people as being in the sub-prime category, regardless of their income.

Thus, the borrowers have to pay several points above prime for their mortgages. Part of the reason for the mortgage crisis of 2008 was that when things got tight, these folk paying sub-prime rates could not afford the payments and lost their homes.

First Nations Development Institute published a research report in May 2003 (Smith) on how Indians are gouged by lenders on a regular basis. Some of the most common methods of "predatory lending" are tax refund loans, pawnshop transactions, payday loans, car title loans, and housing mortgage loans.

They reported that an astounding 73% of respondents at a housing conference had reported that predatory lending practices were a problem in their communities. Indian people are charged high interest rates, high equity, excessive fees ("packing"), repeated loan refinancing ("flipping"), large payment amounts ("ballooning"), penalties for paying off the loan early, high credit insurance, the sale of unaffordable loans, and terms designed to trap borrowers. Some of the interest rates for payday loans run as high as 300% per year!

These payday lenders are clustered around the edges of Indian Country. There are more of them than there are mainline banks in these border town areas. The report stated that twice as many Indians as non-Indians get these sub-prime lending rates. Indians often do not get the complete information on the terms of loans. They may lose their homes or their automobiles if they do not keep up with their payments.

In 2003, Indians were 193% more likely than whites to have become victims of a sub-prime home lending scam. Some 26.5% of home loans to Native Americans were from sub-prime and manufactured home lenders; this number compares to 10.4% of loans to white borrowers. The most extreme case was New Mexico, where in 2000 some 79% of home loans to Native Americans were from sub-prime and manufactured home lenders.

Indians may pay as high as 25% for housing loans, the report stated. Many banks and other lending institutions will still not consider making loans to Native people, in effect redlining whole reservations.

Banks are often not available to Indians living on reservations. And "non-bank" lenders use the fact of tribal sovereignty to their advantage. Since banks and credit unions often will not make loans to Indians living on trust land, it leaves the market open to shady lenders who use unscrupulous methods to hook Indians into taking out costly loans.

Tribal governments have not kept up with the extent of these sharp lending practices, Smith (2003) stated. He estimated that 32% of tribes had not yet acted to curb predatory lending practices. The most common tactic used by tribes was trying to educate tribal members about sharp lending practices.

- The BIA and the states need to review the practice of mortgages and loans to Indian people and report the results to the public.
- Congress needs to pass a law making it a crime to conceal the terms of interest on mortgages and loans, and to set penalties for lenders who violate the fair use of loans.

TEN

Racism and Murder

The most infamous murder of an Indian person in my lifetime was when Michael Morgan shot and killed Richard Oakes. Morgan shot him on September 20, 1972. Richard was the charismatic leader and organizer of the Indian occupation of Alcatraz Island in San Francisco Bay in 1969.

He was a Mohawk and had married Annie Oakes, a Kashia Pomo woman, several years earlier. Richard had worked in high steel with his fellow Mohawks for almost a decade before he decided that he needed an education.

Mad Bear Anderson, the Tuscarora medicine man, told me one time of how Richard had sneaked onto the bus when the leaders of the Iroquois Confederacy were going to Washington, DC, to try to get some help with their problems at Akwesasne, St. Regis, and the other reservations in upstate New York. Richard was 12 years old at the time.

Richard and I spent six months at the Pit River Tribe in 1970, trying to help them get some of their land back. We would drive up on a Sunday afternoon and stay for one or two weeks, then drive home to get clean clothes on a Friday. We drove up in my little yellow Volkswagen every time. I had just gotten married, and Richard left Annie and their five kids at home in the student housing at San Francisco State.

We occupied the PG&E campground first, followed by occupations at Mount Lassen and other places. There were arrests, bailing people out of jail, serenades by Buffy St. Marie outside the Shasta County jail, and more demonstrations and protests. The Pit River people had been demeaned, murdered, and stolen from since 1850. Their numbers had shrunk from 7,000 to only 600. Mickey Gemmill, Richard's friend and a fellow student at San Francisco State, was the Tribal Chairman.

Three years after the Alcatraz occupation, Morgan shot and killed Richard in a dispute over a horse. The horse had gotten loose from the reservation and had wandered onto the YMCA camp next door. When Richard went to get it, he mouthed off to Morgan, who pulled a pistol and shot him. Richard died soon afterward. The most ironic thing to me was that Morgan ran the YMCA camp for the city of Berkeley, supposedly one of the peace-loving places in the world.

It is also ironic that Richard got killed this way. He had survived a beating a year before, when some Samoans beat him in the head with a pool cue. They were in a bar in the Mission District when it happened. The Samoans had a beef with Richard over something that had happened in the summer of 1969, when Richard was working as a community organizer in the Mission. The severe beating, which fractured his skull and left him in a coma for weeks, almost killed him.

Morgan was only charged with involuntary manslaughter. A jury in Santa Rosa found him not guilty. At that time, in Northern California, killing an Indian was not a big deal. After all, the great-grandparents of some of the white people living in that area had hunted Indians for sport back in the period from 1850 to 1900. None of them was ever charged with murder or any other crime. They killed thousands of Indians with impunity. The Indian population of California dropped from 100,000 in 1850 to only 15,000 in 1900.

Robeson County, North Carolina: My family has had its share of murders. We had half a dozen "rough" families in our large family. Fighting, cutting, shooting, and murder were too commonplace. Two of my cousins, brothers, were vying for the affections of a young lady back in the 1940s.

The young neighbor across the branch also had his eye on her. One day when they were putting in tobacco, he came across the branch with his gun and shot both the brothers, one in the chest and one in the leg. Clemmie Lowery lost his leg, but his brother Footie lost his life.

Javie Locklear shot my cousin Stoney Godwin in the head in 1970, in front of a half-dozen witnesses, despite the fact that Stoney was on his knees begging for his life. Javie had been going with Stoney's wife. He got two years; it was one Indian killing another one, which is still lightly punished in Robeson County, North Carolina.

Aubrey Locklear had just gotten back from Korea in 1956 when he got killed. He had only taken his uniform off the day before. He and some of his buddies went into town for a sandwich. They got into an argument with my cousin Grady Godwin, Stoney's brother, and some of his friends, including Boots Jacobs, at a joint called the Seaboard Grill.

Somebody allegedly said, "I'm gone go get my gun," and the whole place cleared out. Half an hour later these crazy city boys and country boys were shooting at each other in front of the joint. A .22 bullet hit Aubrey in the chest and he keeled over dead.

I was in class that afternoon with Aubrey's brother. I walked by the joint on the way home, and the police were everywhere. No one was ever charged in that murder. It was just one Indian killing another one. Boots Jacobs went on to an illustrious career on the other side of the law, wearing a gun and a badge, which he is still doing. He worked at the college for 30 years and then went to work for the county.

One of my cousins shot and killed one of his neighbors when they were 21 years old. They had gotten into an argument over a cow. The killer went to trial and the jury found him not guilty. Then 35 years later his son got into a beef with a boy in town and came home with his tail between his legs. His daddy put him in the truck and they drove back to the place. The son pointed out the other boy, and the daddy shot him dead. The jury also found him not guilty in that killing. So far: two killed, no time served.

The U.S. Civil Rights Commission reported in 2005 that the murder rate for Indians is the highest for any ethnic group in the United States. Indians get killed at a rate three times higher than the national murder rate.

Red Lake, Minnesota. Jeff Weise, 16 years old, killed nine people, including his grandfather and the grandfather's girlfriend, before turning the gun on himself. Seven of the victims were at Red Lake High School. He had recently relocated back to Red Lake after living with his mother in the Twin Cities. He was obviously a troubled young man.

White Clay, Nebraska: Wilson Black Elk, Jr., 40, and Ronald Hard Heart, 39, were found murdered on June 8, 1999, outside White Clay. They had been brutally beaten to death. AIM member Tom Poor Bear, a brother of one of the men, said, "I will say who ever murdered them had a lot of hate. They were chopped up pretty bad with an ax or a hatchet." No one has yet been charged in their murders.

Roberts County, South Dakota: Justin Red Day, 21, was walking along a highway near the Sisseton Reservation in March 2000 when Mark Appel, 17, a local white, ran over him. He was unsure of what he hit, so he backed up. He again ran over Red Day, crushing his ribs. He then put Red Day into the back of his pickup. He drove with the wounded man for several hours before delivering him to the Sisseton Public Health Hospital, where he died. Appel was charged with DUI and sentenced to 30 days in jail and a $330 fine. An Indian life in South Dakota is very cheap.

Indeed, the double standard in South Dakota is so severe as not to be believed. Justin's mother told a newspaper, "If my son had been driving, rather than the victim, he'd be serving 20 years."

Melanie Seaboy, an Indian woman, collided with a white motorist at an intersection while he was on his way to work, killing him. She had been drinking. She was not charged with DUI but with vehicular homicide and was not given a slap on the wrist as Appel had been. She was sentenced to 14 years in prison. Her father, David Seaboy, hired a lawyer and found that in 10 comparable cases, the maximum sentence was five years. The only female defendant in the 10 cases pleaded guilty to vehicular homicide, but received a suspended sentence of five years, David learned. The sentence for an Indian woman in a vehicular homicide case in South Dakota is three times the sentence of a white man.

And Bill Means's daughter Kimberly was killed by a drunk driver while she was participating in a spiritual run from Porcupine to Sioux Falls. The driver was only charged with DUI and sentenced to serve 15 days in jail. "Had the situation been reversed and I ran over and killed his daughter, I'd still be in prison today," Means said. Bill is Russell Means's brother and an organizer of the International Indian Treaty Council.

Mobridge, South Dakota: A Lakota man, Robert "Boo" Many Horses, was found dead in Mobridge on August 2, 1999. He suffered from fetal alcohol syndrome and was small in stature. He had been beaten to death. His body was stuffed into a trash can. Four local rich white male teenagers were charged with the murder. Their bond was set at $250,000 each. They were charged with murder, but they were released the same day. The charges were later reduced to first degree manslaughter. The autopsy concluded that Many Horses had died of alcohol poisoning.

The district attorney initially charged four teens with murder in the case. However, on October 1, 1999, a local judge, Tony Portra, dismissed the charges against all four, saying the police had failed to make a case against them. The lead defendant was Layne Gissi. Jody Larson, Ryan Goehring, and Joy Lynne Hahne were also initially charged with murder, but Judge Tony Portra also dismissed their charges.

The case led many Indian people to conclude that racism was part of the reason none of the four people was charged and tried. The fact that the victim was Lakota and all the other four were white is alleged to be the main reason. The Many Horses family brought a lawsuit against the four, which was settled out of court.

Rapid City, South Dakota: A total of eight bodies were found in Rapid Creek in this city between May 1998 and July 1999. All but two of the men were Indians. All were between the ages of 33 and 56. No one has yet been charged with any crimes as the result of the deaths.

- The first body found was that of Paul Benjamin Long Wolf, 36, of Martin. He was found on May 21, 1998, under a bridge. He had moderate swelling in his head, but his death was ruled an accident.
- The body of Dick Bartling of Gregory, a white male, was found in the creek on May 29, 1999, near downtown Rapid City. His blood alcohol was 0.288%, three times the level to bring drunken driving charges. His death was ruled a drowning as the result of severe intoxication.

- May 31, 1998, saw the body of George Hatten, Jr., 56, a transient, found in the creek near a drainage ditch. He had marks around his neck, but his death was ruled an accident.
- The body of a white male, Allen Hough, 42, was found on July 4, 1998. He was from Rapid City. There was no evidence of foul play; his cause of death was listed as drowning.
- Randelle Two Crow, 48, from White Horse, was found dead on December 8, 1998. The police say he died the night before while he was asleep under the bridge. His death was ruled as an extremely high blood alcohol level of 0.515%. His death was also ruled an accident.
- Loren Two Bulls, 33, from Rapid City, was a local Indian artist. His body was found on December 9, 1998, a half block from where Two Crow was found the day before. His cause of death was listed as severe alcohol toxicity with his blood alcohol level at 0.531%.
- Timothy Bull Bear, Sr., 47, of Allen was found in the creek on July 8, 1999, by the Dive Rescue Team. There was no apparent cause of death. The investigators say they are unsure of how his body got in the creek.
- On June 7, 1999, the body of Arthur Chamberlain, 45, from Lake Andes, South Dakota, was found near downtown Rapid City.

When Howard Pretends Eagle tried to report an incident where a carload of white youths tried to chase him with their car, the police tried to arrest him! "It doesn't do any good to report crimes against the homeless," he said.

Rick Afraid of Hawk said, "When I've made reports to the police department, they tell me it didn't happen."

So the authorities still don't see the hate crimes, the assaults, the murders, the rapes, and other felony crimes against Indians. U.S. Attorney Ted McBride said a total of three hate crimes had been reported in the whole state in 1999. One was an assault and two were vandalism crimes, all racially motivated. "Many crimes may not be reported as hate crimes, but it doesn't appear to be a big problem in South Dakota."

Farmington, New Mexico: "The Selma, Alabama, of the Southwest" has seen a series of murders of Navajos in the past three decades. Three Farmington High School students killed three Navajo men in 1974. They tortured, mutilated, and bludgeoned the three elderly men in what was for a while a rite of passage in the border town. They then dumped the bodies in a canyon and set them on fire.

The three teenagers were sentenced to reform school for the murders. The Navajo protesters the next day were denied a parade permit, leading to dozens of arrests when they paraded through downtown Farmington anyway.

"Rolling Indians" has become a rite of passage for some teens in this town that borders the Navajo Reservation. The Southern Ute, Ute Mountain, and Jicarilla Apache reservations are within easy driving distance. Much of the town's income is from Indian spending. Interestingly, though, much of the Anglo population is from Texas and Oklahoma and brought their anti-Indian attitudes with them. Oil production is one of the big industries as well.

In 2000 a Navajo woman, Betty Lee, was murdered by two casual acquaintances. One of them was Robert Fry, who is now on death row. He was tried and convicted in her death. Fry was also suspected in the brutal killings of three other Navajos and in the disappearance of a Navajo man, Donald Tsosie. Apparently the two murders he committed were racially motivated. His friend said he was mad at the world, and liked to roll Indians. He was also tried for killing two non-Indians in a robbery of a store.

In 2001 a teenage Navajo boy was killed in Colorado by a white Farmington man in what was a hate crime, a gay hate crime, or both. Farmington was also where two teenagers used a shopping cart to kill a Navajo man.

The **Wounded Knee occupation** of 1973 was initially a protest about the oppressive conditions the federal government had forced upon the people who killed George Custer and his cavalry regiment in 1876. It quickly became about the high murder rate on the Pine Ridge Reservation. In this case, reactionary tribal leaders cooperated with biased federal agents and local vigilantes to subject the reservation to a reign of terror.

In a period of less than a decade, more than 60 people were murdered at Pine Ridge. The leading cause of death was thought to be the tribal government, which was led by Richard (Dickie) Wilson, a half breed who was a violent power-hungry person. He cooperated with the BIA and the FBI in trying to suppress the AIM insurgency that had started earlier and came to a head at the occupation of Wounded Knee in 1973. He called the AIM members Communists and agitators, and agreed with William "Wild Bill" Janklow that they ought to be shot. Janklow was the attorney general of South Dakota at the time. The difference between Wilson and Janklow is that Wilson carried out his threats, while Janklow only mouthed his.

Wilson's enforcers were members of a quasi-police force he called "Guardians of the Oglala Nation," or the GOON squad for short. Since they were the police and were alleged to have murdered most of the people who were killed, it is no wonder they failed to carry out any investigation in most cases. Churchill in his rebuttal to the official FBI report on the murders says a third of the Pine Ridge police were in the GOON squad.

A number of the GOON squad members went on to greater fame and fortune. Among them were Delmar Eastman, Gerald Janis, Manny Wilson, Duane Brewer, and Benny Richards.

Richards was the chief of police at Duck Valley Reservation in Nevada when AIM member John Trudell's family and his mother-in-law were killed when a faulty gas line on their house blew the whole house up. This made AIM members more paranoid and convinced that Richards had something to do with the deaths.

Art Manning, Tia Trudell's father, told me a few months after the tragedy that the gas line had faulted, and it had blown up the house, killing everyone in it. He had been away selling cattle at the market, or he would have been killed in the explosion and fire. Thus the allegations by John Trudell and others that the family was killed on orders from the FBI or the BIA have little credence, but many paranoid AIM members still believe them.

Eastman, a Crow, was the chief of police at Pine Ridge during the Wounded Knee occupation. He was allegedly the boss of the GOON squad, the quasi-legal enforcement arm of the Dickie Wilson government. The GOONs maintained law and order on the reservation in a manner similar to the way the Ku Klux Klan maintained segregation and separation of the races in the pre-civil rights South. The police were the visible arm of tribal government, but the GOONs were the other arm that enforced things. Much of their effort was pointed toward AIM, whom Dickie Wilson hated. He blamed all the reservation's troubles on AIM.

The FBI and the BIA backed Wilson's corrupt regime with money, personnel, and arms, including machine guns, rifles, grenade launchers, and armored personnel carriers. The FBI was seemingly intent on eliminating the presence and influence of AIM on the reservation. It sent an undercover provocateur, Douglass Durham, into Wounded Knee; he ultimately became head of security for AIM.

Another FBI provocateur, Johnny Arellano, was responsible for trapping political activist Hank Adams after he volunteered to find missing papers after the AIM occupation of the BIA headquarters in Washington. Other informants and agents included Leroy Little Ghost (Hunkpapa Lakota), and a couple from the South, Gi and Jill Shafer.

Almost all the persons killed were autopsied by Dr. W. O. Brown, the man who failed to find a gunshot wound in the head of Anna Mae Aquash. (Her family demanded and got a second autopsy by Dr. Garry Peterson, who found the gunshot wound to the back of her head.) In most cases, Brown reported they were inebriated, died from exposure, accidents, explosions, and suicide. All except two of the people murdered were enrolled members of the Oglala Sioux Tribe (OST).

The events of the decade at Pine Ridge and the surrounding area were the subject of a comprehensive book by Hendricks published in 2006. The AIM Web site says that the 61 people killed at Pine Ridge, if projected to the whole United States, would have raised the total murders in the United States from 20,000 per year to 340,000 per year.

The murder rate at Pine Ridge in the 1970s was 170 per 100,000. During the same period, the murder rate in Detroit, the "murder capital" of the U.S., was 20.2 per 100,000. The national rate was 9.7 per 100,000. Thus the rate at Pine Ridge was 1752% higher than the national rate.

Furthermore, the national rate of prosecutions for murder, which is usually 80% or higher, was below 50% at Pine Ridge. The FBI, which was supposed to investigate the killings, was too busy building portfolios on AIM people to investigate the murders of them.

The U.S. Civil Rights Commission in 1999 held hearings on the murders in South Dakota and issued a report on them. Gov. William "Wild Bill" Janklow, then known as South Dakota's chief Indian hater, called the report "garbage."

"I haven't read the report, because I don't read garbage," he said in a radio interview on South Dakota Public Radio. "I'm so sick of these people that badmouth my state."

Janklow told reporters in 1974, "The only way to deal with these AIM leaders is to put a bullet in their heads." It appears that several people in the state took him at his word.

After serving as governor, Janklow ran for Congress and won. Ironically, in 2003 he ran a stop sign in a rural area near Trent, South Dakota, at 70 miles an hour or faster and killed a man riding a motorcycle, Randolph E. Scott. A jury convicted him of second degree manslaughter. He was sentenced to 100 days in jail—an extremely low penalty even for manslaughter. He was forced to give up his seat in the U.S. House and face humiliation and disgrace for the rest of his life. However, he was released in 2004 and won back his law license in 2006.

Also very ironically, while he served as the attorney for the Rosebud Sioux Tribe in the late 1960s, he and Russell Means used to dress up in Santa Claus costumes and deliver toys each Christmas to poor kids on the reservation. He ran legal services on the reservation.

In 1974 the tribe charged him with raping a fifteen-year-old girl, Jancita Marie Eagle Deer, in 1969. He was tried *in absentia* and convicted. So, theoretically, if he ever shows up on the reservation, he could be arrested and sent to federal prison. He could have been arrested, theoretically, all the time he was attorney general, governor, and congressman. Even so, he is still free.

Jancita said that Janklow forced her to have sex with him while he held a gun on her. She was later killed in a hit and run auto accident. The last person known to have talked to her before she died was an FBI agent.

After being convicted of rape, Janklow ran for state attorney general and won. Then he ran for governor and won. Then he ran for Congress and won. All the time he was spouting anti-Indian and anti-AIM rhetoric. He became a rabid anti-Indian to win office, and he is still playing that game today.

"The FBI and its Agents in South Dakota can only operate effectively where we have the trust and help of the American people," Douglas J. Domin, the Special Agent in Charge of the Minneapolis office of the FBI said in a report issued in 1999. He did not say why it took the FBI 25 years to make a response, but he claimed he did not have the names of the dead people until a hearing in 1999 by the U.S. Civil Rights Commission. The FBI maintains that most of the deaths were not murders, but were caused by exposure, alcohol intoxication, accidents, and suicide.

The following AIM people and AIM supporters were killed at Pine Ridge between 1972 and 1999 (there may yet be others not reported), which both AIM and the FBI agree on. The FBI, however, has a different interpretation on almost every case. In the following list, the AIM claims are in regular type and the FBI reports on each case are in italics. The FBI reports are direct quotes from the report:

- Raymond Yellow Thunder, 1972, Gordon, Nebraska, killed by Melvin and Leslie Hare, Anglos. They were initially charged with assault and battery and released without bail. The charge was later changed to second degree manslaughter, and they were convicted and served one year each in jail. This case and the follow up by AIM instigated the long seizure and occupation of Wounded Knee the next year. The demands of Indians for prosecution of the Hares and others who killed Indians and got away with it went unanswered in the courts on the reservation and in the surrounding border towns.
- *[The FBI report does not mention Yellow Thunder.]*
- Wesley Bad Heart Bull, 1973, stabbed and killed by Darold Schmidt, Anglo, who served one day after pleading guilty to involuntary man-

slaughter. Sarah Bad Heart Bull, Wesley's mother, served five months for protesting Schmidt's sentence.

- *[The FBI report does not mention Bad Heart Bull.]*
- Frank Clearwater, 1973, killed by heavy machine gun fire at Wounded Knee during the occupation.
- *Frank Clearwater, true name Frank J. Clear, was shot at a road block in Wounded Knee, South Dakota, in April 1973 during a gunfight which started when Federal agents were fired upon. They returned fire. Clearwater died in a hospital on 04/25/73. The facts gathered indicated Clearwater's death was the result of gunfire received from Federal law enforcement officials after 6–8 individuals began firing at Deputy U.S. Marshals at a road block on 04/13/73.*
- Buddy Lamont, killed by M16 fire during the occupation, bled to death.
- *Buddy Lamont, aka Lawrence Dean Lamont (TN), was shot and killed 04/27/73 during a gunfight with Federal officers at a roadblock in Wounded Knee. The facts of the matter, along with the autopsy report, were reviewed by the U.S. Attorney. No charges were filed.*
- Priscilla White Plume, 1973, AIM supporter killed at Manderson by members of the GOON squad, no investigation.
- *Priscilla White Plume was found dead 07/14/73. She was believed to have been struck and killed in a hit and run accident, near Manderson, South Dakota, by a vehicle. On 09/28/76, the South Dakota U.S. Attorney's Office declined prosecution in this matter because there was insufficient evidence to establish a Federal crime. Further, there was inadequate information to identify a perpetrator. In view of the declination, no further investigation was conducted by the FBI.*
- Julius Bad Heart Bull, 1973, AIM supporter killed at Oglala; GOON Bartholomew Long was convicted of second degree murder and sentenced to ten years.
- *Julius Bad Heart Bull was the victim of an assault occurring near Oglala, South Dakota, on 07/30/73. Witnesses to the incident said Bartholomew Joseph Long knocked the victim to the ground with his fist, picked up a 2 x 4 board, approximately three feet long containing several protruding nails, and hit victim in the head several times. Victim died at Rapid City, South Dakota on 07/31/73. Long was arrested on 08/03/73, and charged with Second Degree Murder. On 01/11/74, he appeared in United States District Court, Rapid City, South Dakota and was sentenced to the custody of the Attorney General. On 04/19/74, Long was committed to the custody of the Attorney General for 10 years.*

- Melvin Spider, AIM supporter killed at Porcupine, no investigation.
- *On 09/22/73, a BIA officer requested FBI assistance with regard to Melvin Spider, who was found dead on the road between Porcupine and Sharp's Corner on the Pine Ridge Reservation. Initial investigation suggested Spider was either a victim of a vehicular hit and run or a severe blow to the head. Interviews revealed Spider was drunk prior to his death. An autopsy on 09/22/73 revealed Spider died on 09/21/73, of extensive cerebral lacerations of the brain, which were traumatic in nature, the cause of which was not obvious. Although a suspect was developed, there was insufficient evidence to charge that person with the death.*
- Vernal Bad Heart Bull, 1974, shot and killed in Allen, Nebraska, one year after the death of his brother Wesley.
- *[Vernal was not mentioned in the FBI report.]*
- Phillip Black Elk, 1973, AIM supporter killed when the gas stove in his house exploded; no investigation.
- *On 06/30/73, the private residence of Phillip Black Elk was completely destroyed by a propane gas explosion. Investigation determined that the explosion was caused by a leakage of propane gas within the residence. A thorough neighborhood investigation was conducted which revealed there had been a previous problem with propane gas leakage in the neighborhood over the previous two weeks. Immediately after the explosion, Black Elk advised he entered the residence and attempted to light the pilot light on the hot water heater when the explosion occurred. Black Elk suffered severe burns and was immediately taken to the Pine Ridge Community Hospital, where he was listed in serious condition. Shortly thereafter, Black Elk was flown to Fitzsimmons General Hospital, Denver, Colorado, where he died. Since the injury was accidental and caused by the actions of the victim, no further criminal investigation was conducted.*
- Aloysius Long Soldier, 1974, AIM supporter killed by GOON squad at Kyle; no investigation.
- *On 02/09/77, South Dakota DCI advised the FBI of investigation into the death of Aloysius Long Soldier. He died on 10/07/74. On 02/16/77, a family member requested a review of the death investigation. The BIA investigative file into the death was reviewed. It was the conclusion of the BIA that there was no evidence that the death of Aloysius was anything other than a suicide. The BIA case was closed. In view of the BIA investigative results, and since the family member was*

unable to offer any factual evidence suggesting that the death was a homicide, no further investigation was conducted.

- Phillip Little Crow, 1973, AIM supporter beaten to death by GOON squad, no investigation.
- *On 11/14/73, on the Pine Ridge Reservation, Irby Leroy Hand killed Phillip Emery Little Crow by striking him with his fists. Hand signed a confession. Autopsy results revealed Little Crow died of a skull fracture. On 08/28/74, Hand was sentenced to five years custody of the Attorney General.*
- Pedro Bissonette, 1973, AIM supporter and OSCRO organizer beaten to death by GOON squad, no investigation.
- *Pedro Bissonette was killed on a highway four miles north of Pine Ridge. BIA officers tried to arrest Bissonette on two fugitive warrants, one stemming from his Wounded Knee activities. When Bissonette advanced on the officers with a raised 30.06, he was shot. Five hours prior to the time he was shot, Bissonette had eluded two other BIA police officers. Autopsy results revealed Bissonette was killed by a single shotgun blast in the chest fired by a police officer.*
- Allison Little Fast Horse, 1973, age 15, AIM supporter shot to death by GOON squad, no investigation.
- *Allison Fast Horse, aka Allison Little Spotted Horse, Jr. (TN), was found shot to death on Chadron Road approximately one mile south of Oglala, SD on the morning of 11/23/73. He had been shot in the chest with a .22 caliber bullet. An autopsy indicated death was attributed to the bullet wound. Examination of physical evidence failed to provide any indication as to the identity of any possible suspects.*
- Edward Means, Jr., 1974, AIM member found dead in an alley at Pine Ridge, beaten to death, no investigation.
- *On 01/07/74, Edward Means, Jr. was found dead in an alley behind the Wesleyan Lakota Mission, Pine Ridge, South Dakota. The autopsy determined the cause of death to be hypothermia related to acute alcoholic intoxication.*
- Edward Standing Soldier, 1974, AIM member killed near Pine Ridge, no investigation.
- *On 02/18/74, Edward Joseph Standing Soldier died of a gunshot wound to the abdomen. Investigation by the FBI revealed Standing Soldier died of a .22 caliber gunshot wound fired by Gerald Janis. Investigation revealed that three juvenile subjects, including Standing Soldier, were involved in an armed robbery in Janis' residence at Pine Ridge, South Dakota. Janis shot Standing Soldier with a .22 caliber rifle as a*

result of this armed robbery. The matter was presented to a U.S. Grand Jury on 2/22/74, and no bill was returned resulting in no prosecution and the FBI investigation being closed.

- Roxeine Roark, 1974, AIM supporter killed at Porcupine, no investigation.
- *Roxeine Roark, a teacher at the Porcupine Day School, was shot in stomach with a .357 magnum pistol at her residence in Porcupine, South Dakota. Investigation revealed that Roark and a friend were handling the weapon when it discharged accidentally. Roxeine died en route to the hospital. No prosecution was undertaken due to the lack of sufficient evidence of a crime.*
- Dennis LeCompte, 1974, AIM supporter beaten to death by GOON squad, no investigation.
- *On 09/07/74, the Pine Ridge, South Dakota Police Department officers responded to a fight at the Glenn Three Stars residence, Pine Ridge, South Dakota. Upon arrival, police found children in living room and Dennis LeCompte dead in the northwest bedroom. Three Stars admitted shooting Dennis LeCompte during a struggle after LeCompte stabbed Three Stars' son with a knife. On 06/23/75 Three Stars was indicted by a Federal Grand Jury, Sioux Falls, South Dakota. On 10/15/75, his trial commenced in U.S. District Court, Deadwood, South Dakota. On 10/17/75, Three Stars was acquitted of the charge Voluntary Manslaughter.*
- Jackson Washington Cutt, 1973, AIM member killed at Parmelee, no investigation.
- *On 9/11/73, Jackson Washington Cutt was found dead in front of a residence in Parmelee, South Dakota. Information from witnesses indicated the victim was involved in a fight earlier in the evening. An eyewitness observed a suspect hit the victim over the head with a hatchet. The suspect was arrested on 12/27/73 in Parmelee, South Dakota by the Rosebud Police Department. On 01/29/75 a witness was re-interviewed and advised that he did not actually see the suspect strike the victim with a hatchet. On 01/29/75 the suspect was re-interviewed. He admitted being near the scene but denied involvement and denied knowledge of who perpetrated the crime. An Assistant U.S. Attorney, Sioux Falls, South Dakota, advised that a motion and order to dismiss the indictment in the above captioned matter was filed on 03/13/75. There was insufficient evidence to achieve a conviction.*
- Robert Reddy, 1974, AIM member stabbed to death at Kyle, no investigation.

- *Robert Reddy was found dead on 12/16/1974, near Kyle, SD on the Pine Ridge Reservation. An autopsy revealed Reddy died of two stab wounds through the heart. Although a suspect was identified, there was insufficient evidence to charge and convict the suspect.*
- Delphine Crow Dog, 1972, beaten by BIA police and left in a field to die from exposure, sister of AIM religious leader Leonard Crow Dog, no investigation.
- *Delphine (Crow Dog) Eagle Deer died 12/06/72. The cause of death listed on her death certificate was exposure and sub-zero weather. Other significant conditions included acute alcoholism. More specifically, the death certificate indicated that the injury occurred as the result of "accidental freezing to death," in an open field approximately 2.3 miles southwest of St. Francis, South Dakota, within the exterior boundaries of the Rosebud Reservation. An autopsy was conducted and the findings of the autopsy determined the above-listed causes of death.*
- Elaine Wagner, 1974, AIM supporter killed at Pine Ridge by unknown persons, no investigation.
- *On 11/30/74, the body of Elaine Wagner was found in a creek bottom in Pine Ridge, South Dakota. Autopsy showed Wagner died of exposure. Interviews revealed that at about 4:00 p.m. on 11/29/74, Wagner joined two car loads of persons and drank with several individuals on the evening of 11/29/74. After drinking for several hours, Wagner went to a nearby home. At approximately 10:00 p.m. on 11/29/74, Wagner left the house. Her body was found on the afternoon of 11/30/74 approximately 100 yards from the house. No subject has been developed and all investigative leads were exhausted. From all the evidence, this matter appeared to be a non-felonious death. The U. S. Attorney advised that there was insufficient evidence to charge any person.*
- Leon L. Swift Bird, 1975, AIM supporter killed at Pine Ridge by GOON squad, no investigation.
- *On 01/05/75, Leon L. Swift Bird was killed near Pine Ridge, SD, by Dorothy Iris Poor Bear. Poor Bear stabbed Swift Bird to death with a knife. On 09/15/75, Dorothy Iris Poor Bear appeared in U. S. District Court, Rapid City, South Dakota, and entered a guilty plea to an indictment which charged her with Voluntary Manslaughter in Violation of Title 18, U.S. Code, Sections 1153 and 1112. On the same date, Poor Bear was sentenced to the custody of the Attorney General for a period of three years. Execution of the prison sentence was suspended, and Poor Bear was placed on probation.*

- Martin Montileaux, 1975, killed in a bar in Scenic, South Dakota. AIM member Richard Marshall was convicted in this murder. Russell Means was charged in the murder and acquitted.
- *On 03/07/75, Martin Montileaux died after being shot in the neck in a bar in Scenic, South Dakota. Montileaux's dying declaration was "Russell Means' friend" was the person who shot him. Russell Means and Richard Marshall were arrested by the Pennington County Sheriff's Office for the shooting of Montileaux. Scenic, South Dakota, is approximately 20 miles north of the Pine Ridge Indian Reservation border. The FBI had no investigative jurisdiction in this matter.*
- Stacy Cottier, 1975, ambushed and shot in Manderson, South Dakota, no investigation.
- *Stacy Cotter, true name Stacy G. Cortier, aka Stacy G. Cottier, was found 03/21/75 in Manderson, SD, with numerous bullet wounds. Cortier was shot sometime during the evening or early morning of 03/20/75-3/21/75. Investigation revealed that after apparent arguments and a car being shot up, Jerry Bear Shield may have been shot in the neck by Cortier, and Bear in turn killed Cortier. Jerry Bear Shield was convicted 10/23/75 upon a plea of guilty in U.S. District Court, Rapid City, SD, to an information charging violation of 18 USC, Section 1153 and 1112, Voluntary Manslaughter. Bear Shield was sentenced to one year in custody.*
- Lena R. Slow Bear, 1976, AIM supporter killed at Oglala by GOON squad.
- *On 02/06/76, Lena R. Slow Bear was found dead beside a road near Pine Ridge, South Dakota. The autopsy determined that death was caused by alcohol intoxication and exposure.*
- Ben Sitting Up, 1975, AIM member killed at Wanblee by "unknown assailants." No investigation.
- *Ben Sitting Up was killed in May, 1975, by an individual using an axe. A suspect was identified but was not prosecuted because of impairment caused by a mental condition.*
- Floyd S. Binals, 1974, AIM supporter killed at Pine Ridge by GOONs. No investigation.
- Yvette Loraine Lone Hill, 1974, AIM supporter killed at Kyle by "unknown" party or parties, no investigation.
- *On 12/25/74 Floyd Sherman Bianas, age 16 months, was killed at the residence of Marion High Bull. High Bull stated he fell with Bianas. No one else was present. The body of Yvette Lorraine Lone Hill, age 7, was discovered on 12/28/74. Lone Hill had scars and bruises all over her*

body and had obviously been beaten. A witness advised he observed Marion High Bull hit Yvette Lone Hill. On 12/30/74, Marion High Bull was arrested by FBI agents. Marion Allen High Bull was tried by a jury and on 10/08/75 High Bull was found guilty of one count of voluntary manslaughter (Title 18, USC, Section 1112) and one count of second degree murder (Title 18, USC, Section 1111). On the same date he was sentenced to 10 years count 1 and 20 years count 2, sentences to run concurrently.

- Edith Eagle Hawk, 1975, run off the road by a white vigilante, Albert Coomes, who was also killed in the automobile accident. Her four-month-old daughter and three-year-old grandson were also killed in the accident.
- *Edith Eagle Hawk died 03/22/75. She died as a result of a two-car automobile accident four miles north of Scenic, South Dakota, in Pennington County, outside the exterior boundaries of the Pine Ridge Indian Reservation. Her injuries described on her death certificate indicate the immediate cause of death was a crushed chest. This matter was not investigated by the FBI because it occurred off the reservation, outside of federal jurisdiction.*
- Jeanette Bissonette, 1975, AIM member killed by sniper at Pine Ridge. No one was charged in the shooting.
- *Jeanette Bissonette died 03/26/75, as a result of being shot about eight miles north of Pine Ridge, South Dakota, when her car broke down. No positive identification was developed to identify the individual responsible.*
- Richard Eagle, 1975, the grandson of AIM supporter Gladys Bissonette, was killed while playing with a loaded gun kept in the house as protection from GOON squads.
- *Richard Eagle died of a gunshot wound to the head which occurred on 03/30/75. Eagle was shot with a .22 caliber sawed off rifle that he and other children were handling at a relative's home on the Pine Ridge Indian Reservation. The South Dakota U.S. Attorney's Office declined to prosecute the case which appeared to be accidental.*
- Hilda R. Good Buffalo, 1975, AIM supporter stabbed to death by GOON squad at Pine Ridge, no investigation.
- *Hilda R. Good Buffalo was found dead 04/04/75, in her home in Pine Ridge. She had a superficial stab wound on her neck and there had been a small fire in her home. The autopsy determined the cause of death to be carbon monoxide poisoning, acute alcoholism, and other*

factors. There was insufficient evidence of a crime to support filing of criminal charges.

- Jancita Eagle Deer, 1975, AIM member beaten and run over by car, no investigation. She had earlier (1966) charged former attorney general, governor, and Congressman William Janklow with rape, for which he was convicted *in absentia* at Rosebud. She was last seen in the company of federal agent and provocateur Douglass Durham. No investigation.
- *Jancita Eagle Deer died near Aurora, Nebraska, on 04/04/75. She was the victim of a car/pedestrian accident, and her death was reported as an accident. Since her death occurred outside the jurisdiction of the FBI, no investigation was conducted by the FBI. However, a motor vehicle accident report from the State of Nebraska indicated that Eagle Deer was standing in a lane of traffic at night and was hit by a driver who did not see her. The driver stopped, called for an ambulance and police assistance at the time of the accident.*
- Delphine Eagle Deer, 1974, AIM member and sister of spiritual leader Leonard Crow Dog, allegedly beaten to death by GOONs and left for dead in a field.
- *[Delphine was not mentioned in the FBI report.]*
- Kenneth Little, 1975, AIM member beaten to death by GOON squad, investigation still ongoing.
- *Kenneth Lee Little died on 06/01/75, in Pine Ridge after being struck with a tire iron by Antoine William Bluebird during a quarrel. Bluebird was found guilty in U.S. District Court, Rapid City on 10/14/75, and sentenced on 10/14/75, to 7 years; 6 months probation.*
- Leah Spotted Elk, 1975, AIM supporter killed by GOON squad at Pine Ridge, no investigation.
- *Leah Spotted Elk was murdered near Wolf Creek, SD, on 06/15/75. Her husband, Kenneth John Returns From Scout, was charged. Subject pled guilty on 10/13/75, to shooting his wife while the two were drinking. He was sentenced to 2 years with 5 months probation.*
- Clarence Cross, 1973, AIM supporter shot to death in ambush by GOONs. Although assailants were identified by eyewitnesses, brother Vernal Cross, wounded in ambush, was briefly charged with crime. No further investigation.
- *This was a color of law-law enforcement brutality case involving two BIA police officers who allegedly shot victims during an arrest on 07/11/73, near Batesland, SD. Clarence Cross died and another family member was wounded. The victim's car was stopped by the subject officers and when victims resisted arrest they were shot by the officers.*

Vernal Cross was treated at Gordon, NE hospital and released. Clarence Cross was shot in the stomach and right thigh and ultimately died of complications at Fitzsimmons Army Medical Center, Aurora, CO. An autopsy was performed and the cause of death was linked to the gun shot wound to the abdomen. The U.S. Attorney's Office advised that there was insufficient evidence to charge the officers with a crime.

- Joseph Stuntz Killsright, 1975, AIM member killed by FBI sniper at Oglala firefight, no investigation.
- *Joseph Stuntz Killsright, aka Joseph Bedell Stuntz (TN), was shot and killed 06/26/75, during the RESMURS investigation. Stuntz was seen shooting at FBI SA's Williams and Coler at Jumping Bull Community, and his body was subsequently found alongside the Green house near the edge of the cliff. Stuntz was apparently shot by a law enforcement officer at the scene. When the body of Stuntz was found, he was wearing a SWAT fatigue jacket with "F. B. I." on the back, belonging to SA Coler; it had apparently been taken from the trunk of SA Coler's vehicle after SA Coler was murdered.*
- James Briggs Yellow, 1975, Cheyenne elder was killed by heart attack when the FBI launched an air assault on his home; no investigation.
- *James Briggs Yellow, true name James Brings Yellow, was in the Pine Ridge Hospital at least one day prior to his death and may have been in for five days prior to his death. A review of his death certificate showed that he died of three causes. The three causes were ascending cholangitis, gram negative sepsis, and resulting shock. Other significant conditions included pneumonia and lung shock.*
- Andrew Paul Stewart, 1975, nephew of AIM spiritual leader Leonard Crow Dog, killed by GOON squad at Pine Ridge, no investigation.
- *On 07/26/75, a Bureau of Indian Affairs (BIA) Officer, Rosebud Indian Reservation, South Dakota, advised that Andrew Stewart was dead on arrival at the Rosebud Public Health Service Hospital. Stewart was shot in the head. On 02/05/76, an Assistant U.S. Attorney at Sioux Falls, South Dakota, declined prosecution. The autopsy report revealed the cause of death was probably a self-inflicted gunshot wound. No credible information was developed suggesting that any specific person caused the death.*
- John S. Moore, 1976, a 20-year-old Penobscot from Maine, AIM supporter stabbed to death in Lincoln, Nebraska. With stab wounds through the neck and face, and with other cuts and bruises, death was ruled a "suicide." Eight years later, the "suicide" ruling was changed, but there has been no further investigation.

- *On 12/02/74, Lincoln, Nebraska, Police Department executed a search warrant for the barracks housing the Wounded Knee Defense Offense Legal Committee. The warrant was based on the armed robbery of local residents by four Indian males. Three individuals, Laurence V. Red Shirt, Garrett E. Wounded Head and Larry J. Martinez, were arrested in connection with the robbery. John S. Moore, the fourth suspect in the robbery, was found dead in the barracks. He was fatally stabbed through the neck and the right side of his face. The autopsy report indicated death was caused by suicide. This matter was not investigated by the FBI.*
- Randy Hunter, 1975, AIM supporter shot at Kyle by a GOON named Vern Top Bear; he was charged with second degree murder and acquitted.
- *During the night from 08/25/75 to 8/26/75, Randy Hunter was shot to death in Kyle, South Dakota. Vern Carlin Top Bear was identified through witnesses as threatening victim with a rifle and subsequently shooting the rifle which resulted in Hunter's death. On 10/13/75, Vern Carlin Top Bear was found not guilty by a jury in United States District Court, Rapid City. The indictment had charged him with Second Degree Murder in violation of United States Code, Title 18, Sections 1153 and 1111.*
- Howard Blue Bird, 1975, AIM supporter killed by GOON squad at Pine Ridge, no investigation.
- *On 09/04/75, the Pine Ridge, South Dakota Police Department received a telephone call from an unknown female who reported a fight and stabbing at the Le Roy Apple residence in Pine Ridge, South Dakota. Pine Ridge Bureau of Indian Affairs (BIA) police officers found the victim, Howard Blue Bird, lying in the kitchen. On 09/05/75, a Federal Grand Jury, Rapid City, South Dakota returned a true bill charging Le Roy Apple with violation of Title 18, USC, Sections 1153 and 1112. On 09/10/75, Apple was interviewed and admitted stabbing Blue Bird. On 10/15/75, Apple appeared in U.S. District Court, Deadwood, South Dakota, and pled guilty to Violation Title 18, U.S. Code, Section 113(c), Assault with a Deadly Weapon to Commit Bodily Injury. He was sentenced to one year in the custody of the Attorney General.*
- Jim Little, 1975, AIM supporter stomped to death by GOON squad at Pine Ridge, no investigation.
- *On 09/10/75, James Little was kicked and beaten to death at Oglala, South Dakota. Tom Chief Eagle, Cecil Bear Robe, Fred Marrowbone, and a juvenile were identified by witnesses as having participated in*

the beating death of Mr. Little. The suspects were arrested by Bureau of Indian Affairs (BIA) Officers on 09/11/75. On 10/20/75, a Federal jury sitting in trial in Rapid City, South Dakota, found subjects Thomas Chief Eagle, Fred Marrowbone, and the juvenile guilty of Voluntary Manslaughter, Title 18, U.S. Code, Section 112(a). Cecil Bear Robe was acquitted. On 12/05/75, Thomas Chief Eagle was sentenced to the custody of the U.S. Attorney General for a period of six years; the juvenile was sentenced to the custody of the U.S. Attorney General for a period of four years pursuant to the Federal Youth Corrections Act; Fred Marrowbone was sentenced to the custody of the U.S. Attorney General for a period of six years.

- Olivia Binals, 1975, AIM supporter killed in Porcupine by unknown assailants; the investigation is still ongoing.
- *(True Name Olivia Bianas) On 10/26/75, BIA police contacted the FBI to advise that Olivia Bianas was found dead in her home. An autopsy revealed Olivia died of a brain hemorrhage caused by a severe beating. Witnesses observed Norman Bianas beat his wife on the day she died. On 10/27/75, Norman Bianas was arrested. On 11/13/75, he made an admission of his role in the death. On 01/23/76, Bianas pled not guilty to voluntary manslaughter. He subsequently withdrew the plea on 03/08/76. On 07/09/76, he was sentenced to eight years custody of the Attorney General. The U.S. Federal Appeals Court upheld his conviction.*
- Janice Black Bear, 1975, AIM supporter killed at Manderson by GOON squad, no investigation.
- *Janice Joyce Black Bear died on 10/26/75. An autopsy revealed the cause of Black Bear's death was cerebral contusions. Contributing death factors were acute alcoholism and phenobarb/qualude intoxication. A suspect, George Mitchell Twiss, admitted to spending the evening with the victim. Twiss recalled that he woke up at home and had blood on his arms, shirt, and pant leg. Twiss was arrested by the FBI when they arrived at his home and he was washing his hands. On 07/06/76, Twiss pled guilty to involuntary manslaughter. On 09/03/76, Twiss was sentenced to three years custody of the Attorney General.*
- Michelle Tobacco, 1975, nine-month-old baby killed at Pine Ridge by accident when a bullet shot by GOON squad caused a relative holding her to duck, hitting her head on a table and being knocked out, crushing the baby, no investigation.

- *Michelle Linda Tobacco, age 9 months, died on 10/27/75. A relative of the victim advised that she consumed liquor, tripped, and fell with the baby. When the relative awoke, Michelle was dead. Autopsy revealed victim died on 10/27/75, of acute pneumonitis and hemorrhage to her adrenal gland. The U.S. Attorney's Office declined to prosecute the relative.*
- Carl Plenty Arrows, Sr., 1975, AIM supporter shot to death at Pine Ridge by unknown persons, no investigation. Frank LaPointe, 1975, AIM member killed at Pine Ridge by GOON squad, no investigation
- *At 6:30 p.m. on 12/05/75, Glen Thomas Janis shot Carl Plenty Arrows, Sr. and Frank Claude LaPointe at Pine Ridge, South Dakota. Carl Plenty Arrows, Sr. was pronounced dead at the scene. Frank LaPointe subsequently died at Gordon Hospital, Gordon, Nebraska, on 12/05/75. Janis voluntarily turned himself in to Pine Ridge authorities on 12/05/75. During an interview with FBI agents on 12/06/75, Janis admitted shooting Carl Plenty Arrows, Sr. Janis was also identified by witnesses as the person who shot both victims. On 03/29/76, Glen Janis pled guilty to second-degree murder and voluntary manslaughter (Title 18, USC, Sections 1153, 1111, and 1112). On 06/15/76, Janis was sentenced to 20 years on count II and 10 years on count I, sentences to run concurrently.*
- Anna Mae Pictou Aquash (Micmac Indian from Canada), 1976, AIM organizer killed at Pine Ridge, gunshot wound to the head, ongoing investigation. This is the most famous person killed during the effort to squash AIM. The FBI has tried for 30 years to prove that AIM had her killed. Arlo Looking Cloud, a Lakota man, was convicted in 2004 of killing her; he received life in prison. John Graham, a Canadian Indian and the alleged hit man, is being held in jail in Rapid City awaiting trial after fighting extradition from Canada for over a year. Anna Mae had been accused by some jealous AIM members of being an FBI informant, a charge that appears to be groundless.
- *In September, 1976, Anna Mae Pictou Aquash's partially decomposed body was discovered in a remote area in the northeastern part of the Pine Ridge Indian Reservation, South Dakota. The cause of death was determined to be a gunshot wound to the head. The Aquash murder has been linked by media reports to the RESMURS investigation. In June, 1975, FBI SAs Jack Coler and Ron Williams were ambushed and killed execution-style on Pine Ridge. The ensuing major case investigation, RESMURS, resulted in the trial and conviction of Leonard Peltier, and the trial and acquittal of two other individuals. Some attention had*

been focused on Aquash for her possible knowledge of the slayings. Rumor circulated that Aquash cooperated with the government and was an FBI informant. These rumors were untrue. The coroner, who died shortly after performing the autopsy on Aquash, was not deposed. The Aquash murder has not been solved.

- Lydia Cut Grass, 1976, AIM member killed at Wounded Knee by GOON squad, no investigation.
- *On 01/05/76, Lydia Cut Grass died at a residence in Wounded Knee, SD. Initial information suggested that Cut Grass may have died as a result of a beating that took place three weeks prior to her death. An autopsy revealed her death was not linked to the prior beating, but was a result of over-consumption of liquor.*
- Byron DeSersa, 1976, AIM member killed by two men at Wanblee. Dale Janis and Charlie Winters served two years of a five-year sentence for manslaughter. Charges were dropped against GOON leaders Manny Wilson and Chuck Richards.
- *Byron DeSersa was shot and killed 01/31/76 while driving his motor vehicle on the outskirts of Wanblee, SD. The defendants were acquitted by a jury on 03/2/77. Codefendant Charles David Winters pleaded guilty to being an accessory after the fact to second-degree murder and was sentenced to 5 years in prison. A juvenile defendant was tried on second degree murder charges and found guilty by a federal jury and was sentenced 05/16/77, under the Federal Youth Corrections Act, 18 U.S.C. 4219.*
- Lena R. Snow Bear, 1976, AIM supporter killed by GOON squad at Pine Ridge, no investigation.
- *[Lena Snow Bear is not mentioned in the FBI report.]*
- Hobart Horse, 1977, AIM member beaten, shot, and repeatedly run over by car at Sharp's Corners, no investigation.
- *Hobart Kenneth Horse died on 03/27/77 from multiple gunshot wounds. Roger James Cline was charged with the death on 03/28/77, and found guilty of voluntary manslaughter on 09/08/77. Cline was sentenced to 10 years.*
- Cleveland Reddest, 1976, AIM member killed at Kyle by unknown assailants, no investigation.
- *Cleveland Reddest died 3/26976 (sic, no doubt 3/26/76), as a result of a hit and run accident 18 miles east of Kyle, South Dakota. Evidence points to Reddest lying in the road before the accident. Two suspects were identified. One of the individuals acknowledged driving the car.*

The case was not prosecuted because there was insufficient evidence of criminal conduct.

- Betty Jo Dubray, 1976, AIM supporter beaten to death at Martin, no investigation.
- *Betty Jo Dubray died 04/28/76, approximately three miles north of Longvalley, South Dakota, on Highway 73, in Washabaugh County, as a result of a brain injury in an automobile/truck accident. Her death was the result of an automobile/truck accident, and no investigation was conducted by the FBI.*
- Marvin Two Two, 1976, AIM supporter shot to death at Pine Ridge, no investigation.
- *Marvin Two Two died in Portland, Oregon on 01/02/93. David Martin Two Two died 05/06/76. A review of death certificates in all surrounding counties in South Dakota and Nebraska reflect no record of his death. The FBI had 27 Agents assigned to Pine Ridge during that time and would have addressed this case if Two Two had been murdered on Pine Ridge.*
- Julia Pretty Hips, 1976, AIM supporter killed at Pine Ridge by persons unknown, no investigation.
- *Julia Pretty Hips was found 05/09/76, near the public school at Pine Ridge. An autopsy was performed. The cause of death was attributed to tetrachloride poisoning which led to pneumonia. No signs of trauma were observed on her body. Since there was no evidence of a crime, no charges were filed.*
- Sam Afraid of Bear, 1976, AIM supporter shot to death at Pine Ridge; Churchill states that Rudolph Running Shield and Luke Black Elk, Jr. were convicted of second degree murder in this case. Investigation ongoing.
- *Sam Afraid of Bear was discovered on the Pine Ridge Reservation on 05/20/76. He had been beaten to death. Two subjects were identified. Rudolph Running Shield pled guilty in 07/77. Luke Black Elk, Jr. was found guilty in U.S. District Court of 2nd degree murder and sentenced to serve 15 years on 2/09/78.*
- Kevin Hill, 1976, AIM supporter killed at Oglala by unknown assailants, no investigation.
- *Kenneth Mansfield Hill, a resident of Los Angeles, was hitchhiking in Oelrich, SD when picked up by four individuals. He was stabbed 19 times, presumably for his money, by a 17-year-old Indian youth. The juvenile was convicted of second degree murder on 10/12/76 in U.S. District Court. He was sentenced on 01/03/77, to 15 years in prison.*

- Betty Means, 1976, AIM member killed by GOON squad at Pine Ridge, no investigation.
- *On 07/03/76, Betty Lou Means was found dead along Highway 18 several miles east of Pine Ridge, South Dakota. She was apparently hit by vehicle. Investigation revealed that an individual was driving a vehicle which struck the victim. Investigation also reflected that the passenger, Arlene Good Voice, grabbed and jerked the steering wheel which caused vehicle to hit Ms. Means. On 12/02/76, the U.S. Attorney's Office, Sioux Falls, South Dakota, declined prosecution of the driver. Although he left the scene of an accident, his actions were not a violation of Federal law. On 07/07/77, Arlene Good Voice pled guilty to Assault, a violation of Title 18, United States Code, Sections 1153 and 113(d). She received a sentence of 18 months probation on 08/22/77, in United States District Court, Rapid City, South Dakota.*
- Sandra Wounded Foot, 1976, AIM supporter shot in the head at Sharp's Corners by BIA policeman Paul Duane Herman, Jr. He pleaded guilty to voluntary manslaughter and got a ten-year sentence.
- *On 08/16/76, Sandra Ellen Wounded Foot, age 16, was found shot in the head in a remote area of the Pine Ridge Indian Reservation. Suspect Paul Duane Herman, Jr., who was a Bureau of Indian Affairs Investigator, was believed responsible for the murder. The victim was last seen alive with Herman in the early morning of 08/14/76. On 08/16/76, a Federal Grand Jury for the District of South Dakota, Sioux Falls, South Dakota, returned a true bill charging Paul Duane Herman, Jr., with violation of Title 18, U.S. Code, Sections 1153 and 1111. Herman was arrested on 08/24/78, at Fort McDowell, Arizona. On 12/19/78, Herman pled guilty in U.S. District Court, Rapid City, South Dakota, to a suspended information charging him with violation of Title 18, U. S. Code, Sections 1153 and 1112, Voluntary Manslaughter. On 02/09/79, he was sentenced to ten years in the custody of the Attorney General.*

An analysis of the 61 deaths, according to the FBI report, reveals the following causes:

- Indian person killed someone, 24 cases
- Accident, six cases
- GOON killed someone, five cases
- Police killed someone, four cases
- Unknown, four cases
- Exposure, four cases
- Suicide, three cases

- Car crashes, two cases
- White person killed someone, two cases
- Sickness killed someone, two cases
- Alcohol killed someone, one case
- Explosion killed someone, one case.

Of the 24 Indian cases, 20 were solved, three were unsolved, and one had no charges brought. The average sentence for Indians was 9.14 years, for GOONs it was 6.0 years, and for whites it was substantially no time.

In 1994, police in Saskatoon, Saskatchewan, Canada, arrested John Crawford for the murder of a young Indian woman. In time they learned he had killed at least four Indian women. He would not just kill them. He would brutalize them, rape them, and then kill them. He rightly concluded that few people in Canada would care if Indian women showed up dead. The victims ranged in age from 16 to 35.

The facts that came out during his investigation and trial were astonishing. It seems that in five years, from 1990 to 1994, over 500 Native women in western Canada had been reported missing. Most of them never showed up and were never found again.

Crawford was convicted and sentenced to three consecutive life sentences for the killings. He turned out to be Canada's most prolific serial killer. The author of a book on the cases, Warren Goulding, pointed out that the media barely covered the missing women. However, white women who disappeared received huge coverage.

Police brutality is an ongoing thing in Indian Country. In 2004 the Yankton Sioux Tribe protested the rehiring of Jeremiah Nelson as police chief in Lake Andes, South Dakota, according to David Melmer in *Indian Country Today*. He had left a year before, under some suspicion of bad behavior, after he admitted hitting a local tribal member in the head with his flashlight. The wound required seven stitches to the head of 21-year-old Keeler Hopkins.

The city cleared Nelson of charges of police brutality, although Hopkins said Nelson hit him with the bottom of the flashlight, requiring him to have to go to the hospital to get the cut sewn up. The tribe accused Nelson of countless charges of racial profiling, unjustified stops and searches, and cases of excessive force and brutality while he worked in Lake Andes previously.

In 2000 police officer Michael Atwood was accused of choking a 12-year-old Indian boy in a park in the small reservation town. The incident sparked protest marches from the Indian community.

Charon Asetoyer, organizer of the 2004 protest, also accused Nelson of pulling a gun on an Indian couple in their home. The wife is director of the Women's Resource Center in Lake Andes, but Mayor Merritt Stegmeier stuck by his decision to rehire Nelson.

In 2007 police in Duluth, Minnesota, were accused of beating and killing an Indian man. David Michael Croud was arrested by police and charged with public drunkenness. According to the Lake Superior Social Action newspaper, he died six days later, after lapsing into a coma. The newspaper said many such incidents had happened in the past, but most Indians, it said, had not reported them for fear of retaliation.

Police brutality, racial profiling, and hate crimes permeate Indian Country. South Dakota, Arizona, New Mexico, and California probably lead the states in rates of violent crimes against Indians. However, at least 35 of the 50 states are culpable, and hardly anyone ever does anything about it. Rape in Indian Country is at least three times as high as it is for non-Indians. Sentences for Indians harming whites are outrageously high, while whites who harm Indians often get off with probation or time served. There is something wrong with a justice system that tolerates such an imbalance. It is strongly tinged with racism, and it needs to be fixed.

ELEVEN

Racism in Education

The newspaper man Tim Giago has written movingly of his experiences in a Catholic boarding school. The founding publisher of *Indian Country Today* says in his book *Children Left Behind* that he was beaten, starved, and humiliated during his ten years at Holy Rosary Mission at Pine Ridge.

When he could no longer understand why he was so depressed at times as an adult, he started healing himself by writing about his treatment at the hands of the priests. Later he submitted these writings to Rupert Costo, publisher of the Indian Historian Press, who published them as a book, *The Aboriginal Sin.*

The treatment that Tim and tens of thousands of Indian kids received in the BIA and mission boarding schools developed a love/hate relationship that is so deep in Indian Country that outsiders cannot understand it. While Indian parents **know** their children need to have an excellent education, their own experiences at schools make them leery of even being on the campuses.

Teachers and principals are constantly amazed at the low turnout on Parent Night. They expect to see huge numbers of parents to show up, but only a few do. In fact, the ones who do are the few who have been visiting the school already. The vast majority of Indian parents never set foot in the school—except maybe for a basketball game. The parents are still feeling the effects of the racist treatment they received a quarter of a century earlier.

A meeting in Rapid City in October 2007, one of the first of its kind in that state, had people reporting that racism is alive and well in the public schools of the state. South Dakota is often called the "Mississippi of the North." The non-Indians of the state still hold a grudge over the defeat and massacre of George Custer in 1876, and they take it out on Indians whenever they can.

Martin Reinhardt, a research associate at Colorado State University, said racism prevents the tribes from having access to information on their students, while the states have full access to all student records.

Indian students are the lowest performing ethnic group in the United States. Test scores for fourth or eleventh graders are typically between the 15th and 20th percentile, meaning that even the top Indian students are below the 50th percentile, and the lowest students are down around the fifth percentile.

Dropout rates for Indian high school students nationwide run about 50%, but with a variation from a high of 90% for San Diego County, California, to a low of 25% or so for a few places. The Phoenix area has rates in the area of 85%. South Dakota dropout rates hover around 80%. The rate in Albuquerque was determined by an outside research group eight years ago to be 67.2%, quite a contrast to the district's "official" figures, which they said were 19% to 23%. The lower figures had been reported for years by the research arm of the district.

The Albuquerque Public Schools researchers have no qualms about reporting dropout rates of 20% to 25% for Indians. However, when an outside agency reported the rate as 67.2%, nary a peep came out of them.

Most people do not want to believe it. A decade ago, in a public hearing, I reported that the dropout rate was 65% for Indians in Albuquerque. Joe Carraro, though, a state senator from Rio Rancho who is now running for Congress, argued with me for ten minutes that it could not be.

"I believe the rate is 19% to 23%," he told me. "But it is impossible for it to be 65%." A year later, when the independent study came out, I copied the graph and sent it to him as proof, but he never answered me.

Schools and districts often try to hide or disguise the real dropout rates, which happen over a four-year to six-year period. They will give, as Albuquerque does, a one-year rate, stating it as a fact, without explaining it. Few school districts with Indian students, in fact, try to determine what the four-year rate is.

A dozen years ago I computed the following figures to compare the actual production of Indian college graduates and non-Indian college graduates. It shows there are 20 non-Indian college graduates for every Indian graduate. Since 1970, the gap has gotten larger, when most folk probably assumed it has gotten smaller.

College Completion Rates, Indians and National

	High School Completion Rate	College Entrance Rate	College Dropout Rate	College Completion Rate
Entire U.S.	81%	67%	46%	54%
Indians	50%	17%	82%	18%

Only 17% of Indian students finish high school and enroll in college the next year, compared to 67% of all students in the United States. Thus there is a huge gap of 50% between Indians and non-Indians who are starting college. However, the huge dropout rate from college further widens the gap. Some 54% of all college students will earn a degree in four to six years, but only 18% of Indian students will earn college degrees during the same time period. Taking the 17% entering college and multiplying it times the 18% who finish college yields only 1.5% of Indians finishing college.

There are many reasons for this horrible situation with Indian education and the low numbers of Indians finishing college. The worst side is that there are huge needs and demands for all kinds of Indians—doctors, dentists, nurses, pharmacists, veterinarians, teachers, engineers, computer programmers, writers, biologists, chemists, physicists, hydrologists, and many other types of professionals. The huge demand means that doctors and nurses are not available to treat sick people.

Indian people sicken and sometimes die because of misdiagnosis or lack of treatment for illnesses ranging from diabetes to ruptured appendixes. The Indian Health Service reports that its professional positions are typically 35% unfilled at any given time.

Thus racism in the schools, turning potential doctors and nurses away from medical schools by racist actions, has the long-term effect of denying life-saving medical treatment to sick Indian people. This may seem to some like a stretch, but it is literally true.

It means that teachers are not available to teach Indian kids. And unfortunately, too often the teachers who are available are the rejects who could not get hired elsewhere. In one case, a man with a degree in sociology was trying to teach physics on the Jicarilla Apache reservation. Of course all the kids knew he didn't know the subject, and were bored to death in his classes.

All instruction in most Indian schools is in English only. Fewer than 10% of Indian students have a chance to learn anything in schools in their Native language. In fact, those who do may only have instruction for part of a year to learn a little of their language (Chavers, 1999). The next year they will probably not have a chance. The number of Indian people qualified to teach Native languages is very restricted. Most school people, of course, think Indian children should learn English only.

Indians have to fight like crazy to gain any quality education. The following lawsuits will document the shoddy treatment Indian kids get. There have only been a few dozen such lawsuits filed, and some of them are still pending. Typically the school administrators see nothing wrong with the way they are treating Indian students, even though non-Indians get special preferential treatment while Indians get treated like dirty scum.

Bismarck School District, North Dakota, settled a lawsuit in 1994 to change the ways it placed Indian students into Special Education classes. The enrollment of Indians in Special Education was about 250% higher than their numbers in the school district would predict. The Office of Civil Rights of the U.S. Education Department (ED) told the district it would have to remove the racial bias in its examinations for Special Education by February 1, 1995. The tests they were using were deemed not to be valid.

Navajo students in the **San Juan County School District, Utah,** had no high school available to them within the district. The nearest high school was 80 miles away, with half the distance on a poorly maintained dirt road. High school students in the district were forced to leave home to attend high school elsewhere. Most of them went to BIA boarding schools, some as far away as Phoenix and southern California. Many of them lived with relatives in surrounding communities to attend high school or enrolled in BIA boarding schools off the reservation.

Under a consent decree signed in 1974, the district was supposed to provide educational services to Native people all over the district, but they had not. Sara Krakoff of DNA Legal Services and Eric Swenson, a private Utah attorney, brought suit in 1993 to force the school district to provide a high school education to Navajo students.

The district would admit no obligation to provide a school. It agreed to provide reimbursement to parents to send their children away to high school, and they would not budge on the larger issue of a high school.

Indian parents in **Leupp, Arizona,** on the Navajo Reservation, filed a lawsuit in the U.S. district court in Phoenix in 1994 that charged the Flagstaff Unified School District with intentional racial discrimination against their children. The school is 20 miles out of town on the reservation, and almost all the students are Navajo. The lawsuit claimed that the buildings were unsafe and unsanitary, and that course offerings were inadequate. They made 14 allegations about the inadequacy of the buildings. The maintenance director, Lowell Shira, said in a statement to the press that out of the 14 allegations, only two had not been fixed. The two were no access ramps and no grass on the playground.

The lawsuit alleged that federal funds to pay for Indian education had been allocated improperly. The suit said that the school district had been aware of the problems for some time, but it had taken no action to correct them.

Kent Matheson, the superintendent, denied the charges. He stated that the students in the Leupp School received the same services as students in other Flagstaff schools

One parent on the **Standing Rock Sioux Reservation** in South Dakota was startled by her third grader after school in 1992. The nine-year-old asked her when she got home that day, "Mommy, what's a slut?"

"What?" the mother asked. "Why are you asking me that?"

"Because that's what the teacher calls us Indian girls," the child said.

The mother took her complaint to school the next day, but got no relief. The principal refused to take up the issue with the teacher. So she went to the tribe with her complaint. The tribe asked the school to discipline the teacher, which it refused to do. Then the tribe asked for the teacher to be let go, which the school also refused.

Despite an official letter from the tribe, the school district, McLaughlin, refused to deal with the issue. The teacher, a *wasicu,* or white person, (pronounced "wah-shee-choo"), was the wife of a local rancher.

She had been using the term for years, and she was not about to change. When the students were at recess and she wanted them to come back into the classroom, she would simply tell them, "You little sluts get back in class." And the children obeyed.

Almost all the children in the school district are Lakota (Sioux). The teachers for the most part commute south every day from Bismarck. There is a steady stream of commuter cars headed down Highway 1806 every morning between 7:00 and 8:00. There are a handful of teachers who live in the local area, however, and most are tied into ranching on checkerboarded parts of the reservation. This teacher was one of them. Nothing the tribe did would dislodge her. She is still teaching there.

The tribe then filed a complaint with the Office of Civil Rights of the U.S. Department of Education's office in Denver. The district, which was headed then by Superintendent Tom Frankenhoff, was directed to train teachers about racially loaded remarks, develop a way of discipline that was racially balanced, and keep a log of such complaints. They also agreed to hire more Indian staff and establish a grievance committee of Anglo and Indian members with the same ratio as the student population.

The school district was made up of 80% Indians, but there were no Indian teachers. The total enrollment was just over 500 students. Fifteen years later, there are still few Indian teachers. Three years after the complaint, the OCR found that compliance was still not being adhered to. Out of 104 discipline referrals from January through April of 1995, 96 were for Native students and eight were for Caucasian students. Reforming racially insensitive teachers is obviously a hard job, and one that will take a long time.

Race, class, and gender are social categories and labels as well as social science constructs. They are used to define people in everyday life. They are labels that people can understand immediately—the cunning Chinese, the inscrutable Japanese, the savage Indian, the noble Englishman, the dumb Irishman, the weak woman.

While many maintain that race is an artificial construct, that all races are essentially the same, in everyday social relations race has a distinct meaning. Race, according to Castagna and Dei, "lacks any 'scientific validity.' Yet the concept continues to gain in social currency because of its utility for distributing unequal power and privilege. It has become an effective tool for the distribution of rewards and punishments" (2000).

Chartrand (1992) says that, "Racism is always present in a situation where there is an imbalance of power which permits the 'racist' behavior to have effect. ... Racism only matters if it has the power to hurt." Racism in schools is a way for the dominant teachers, students, and administrators to prove their superiority over minority students.

Indian students are always the "low man on the totem pole." White students and adults just assume that they are the superior race and that Indians are inferior. So anything the white students do to Indians is all right, because they are just Indians. The most unfortunate thing is that many Indian students, after years of this kind of treatment, come to believe that they are inferior. Who cares if they drop out or do well in school? They are just trash anyway, as many of them will tell you.

There is a difference between being racist and being oppressed. The Indian student who is racist himself, believing whites are dumb, mean, and inferior, has no effect on bringing this belief to the forefront. The Indian student is, after all, the oppressed one in the power situation.

Deyhle (1995) found that non-Indian teachers in Utah continue to insist that there is no racial discrimination in their Mormon communities, while the Navajo students try to point it out, but they are silenced by their white peers and the school administrators.

The administrators label students who point out racism as problem students. One of the quickest ways to get relegated to the back of the classroom and to the losers group is to point out instances of racism.

Indian parents often fail to speak out for the same reasons. Deyhle cites one Navajo parent who wishes she had spoken out to the vice principal at the school. She had gone to school with him twenty years earlier.

She wished she had said to him, "You know what it is like for the high school kids. You used to do the same things the kids are doing now against Indians. You remember when you put the pins in my seat? All the things that you used to do to Indians, it is still going on here. You did it, and now your kids are doing it."

The white kids call the Indian students names—when no adults are around. They stick their feet out and trip them. They pull down their dresses and pants, and laugh out loud with their friends. They call them names. If the Indian students ever react, they are the ones in trouble. Reacting is one of the quickest ways to be kicked out of school, and all the Indian students know it. The reservation schools start kicking Indian kids out as early as the age of 12.

In **Red Rock, Oklahoma,** in 1994, the Indian Parent Committee, which had been authorized by the Otoe Tribal Council, brought suit against the Frontier School District. One of the charges was that Indian students were mandated to ride in the back of the school bus. The drivers would not start the bus and move it if an Indian student sat in the front of the bus. The occasional football player who tried it got promptly moved to the back.

School principals cursed the Indian students and called them names like "squaw," "buck," and "savage." Indian students were suspended for three days for minor offenses, while Anglo students who did life-threatening things were not suspended at all. Indian parents were forbidden to visit classrooms or gymnasia. School administrators forced confrontations with Indian parents, and cursed Indian parents. Administrators failed to provide medical attention to an Indian student who broke his leg on the playground. There was instance after instance of namecalling of students by teachers, of cursing Indian students, of labeling students with bad names, of libel, of slander, and of race baiting.

The school also had a jail, two small rooms with one small window at head height. They were called "detention." Mainly Indian students got placed in detention daily. If you got caught chewing gum, you could be sent to detention.

Elections to the school board were on an at-large basis. The same crew of Anglo ranchers had run the school board for decades, successfully beating back attempts by Indians to gain a seat on the board. They worked hand-in-hand with the local election commission to keep voter registration among Indians low.

Teachers and white students regularly called the Indian kids names like Tonto, buck, and squaw. When we pointed out that the word *squaw* refers to a part of the female sexual anatomy, the labia or the vulva, the whites seemed not to care. They could do what they wanted, and no one could do anything to them about it.

One of the incidents that upset the parents the most was that one kid had been suspended for fighting with a white boy. The white boy, who probably picked the fight, was not suspended. At about the same time, a student whose mother was a teacher lit another student's hair on fire, clearly endangering the kid's health if not his life, and the offender was not punished at all!

The school district was 58% Indian, but there were no Indian teachers, school administrators, or board members. The district was the second-richest one in the state of Oklahoma. A huge power plant down the road from the school meant it had a very high tax rate. Only one district in the Panhandle, one with lots of oil wells, had a higher per-pupil expenditure (PPE) rate. The Frontier School District had over $10,000 per student per year to spend, but had very few Indian students finishing and going on to college.

Of the 120 staff in the schools, only four were Indians, including teachers, aides, custodians, administrators, and maintenance staff. There had never been an Indian administrator in any of the schools.

The dropout rate for Indians that year had been 70%. It had been 65% the year before, much higher than the state dropout rate for non-Indians. The teachers and administrators actually force the Indian students to leave school, through harassment, suppression, libelous remarks, and slander.

The district refused for six months to release copies of its Indian Policies and Procedures to the Indian Education Committee, even though the law requires it. The IEC finally got a copy from the Impact Aid office in Washington. The district had never held a public hearing on Impact Aid, which is also required by law.

Indian students were paddled and punished on a racially biased basis, and much more often than non-Indians. Indian students were given much more harsh treatment than non-Indians. They were not allowed to have an Indian Club during school hours. The Indian Club had to meet outside school after school hours.

Interracial dating was forbidden. Indian boys who dated white girls were open targets for harassment, called names, and sometimes beaten up. Indian students were not allowed to make up work when they were absent, while non-Indian students were allowed to make up work.

The Tribe asked for relief on 50 different items. Among the most important were to have 60% of the total staff to be Indians, to withhold Impact Aid funds until relief had been granted, to develop a code of teacher behavior, to forbid the use of corporal punishment, to convert the detention rooms into classrooms, to apply discipline equally, to stop making Indian students ride in the back of the school buses, and to prepare Indian students for college study.

The previous year the first Indian valedictorian had finished high school. When he had asked the counselor to let him sign up for advanced algebra, the counselor had told him he didn't need it. So the kid, who was the son of the Parent Committee chairman, went off to college thinking he had a good high school education. Imagine his surprise when he almost flunked out of college. His father was justly outraged at his son's treatment.

I helped the Parent Committee to file a lawsuit with the Office of Civil Rights (OCR) of the U.S. Department of Education. It was called a "complaint," but it had all the earmarks of a lawsuit.

That fall, a young man came out to the school district from the Dallas OCR office. He told the school officials that they could not keep making the Indian students ride in the back of the school bus. They could not permit teachers to continue calling Indian students bucks and squaws. They had to implement some teacher in-service sessions to teach the teachers what was right and what was wrong in the situation. They had to form a Discipline Parent Committee made up of a majority of Indian parents. Moreover, they had to stop putting Indian kids into the bonehead classes.

On the Omaha Reservation in Nebraska, two school districts serve the tribe's students. One of them is **Walthill Schools.** The district is located entirely on the reservation and has enrollment of 75% Indians, and about 85% of the Indian students are members of the Omaha Tribe. There were no Indian teachers, no Indian administrators, and no Indian school board members, and there never had been any.

The ACLU filed suit in 1994 to reverse a 1979 court ruling that converted elections for the school board from at-large elections. The earlier suit had sought to have district elections, which had been gerrymandered to prevent Indians from winning an election, changed to at-large elections. They had thought that the large Indian majority would finally let an Indian win a seat on the school board.

In practice, the procedure had not worked. Despite the initial optimism, no Indian had yet won a seat on the school board. The 1994 suit sought a reversal, but with the districts not gerrymandered to keep Indians from winning.

Voting in the district has been racially polarized. Indians, even though they are in the majority in the district, have not voted at the same rate as non-Indians, so Indian candidates always lose.

The lawsuit also charged that out of 57 employees in the district, only one was Indian, and she was paid from federal funds. There was no in-service or orientation training for teachers to deal with Indian students. There was no Native American perspective provided in the district. There were no Native American course materials in the curriculum, according to the former Indian Education Act staff person.

As an indication of the total refusal of the school to recognize Indian people, the library did not subscribe to either the Omaha Tribe's newspaper or the nearby Winnebago Tribe's newspaper.

The new superintendent at Walthill, Henry Eggert, had been the principal at Macy High School the previous year. That school made statewide headlines in 1993 when the Associated Press (AP) reported that a full 70% of the students, mostly Indians, had been expelled during the year. Eggert had moved from principal to superintendent in the district next door. Most of the 70% of the 414 total students expelled at Macy were for poor attendance, according to the AP.

The Anglo supporters of the Indian issues in the Walthill schools have been banned, forced to move, and harassed. The Rev. Mark Kemling, a Unitarian Methodist minister, had to leave town after more than half of his 142 parishioners stopped coming to church to protest his support of the Indian cause. He had supported a grant of $250 from the Nebraska Methodist Conference to the plaintiffs in the lawsuit.

When he started a racial reconciliation study group, his parishioners became even angrier, according to the *Lincoln Star*. Charles Merrick, an Indian parent, applauded the efforts of the minister. "Apparently the non-Indians are satisfied to be racist," he told the *Star*.

The former Indian Education Act staffer, Richard Chilton, suffered a similar fate. His landlord asked him to move because of his support for the Indian demands. (He is Dutch and English.) He wrote the press release that made the first announcement about the lawsuit. He was working for the Macy Youth and Family Services department at the time of the lawsuit.

The Omaha Tribe was not a party to the lawsuit but reportedly supported it. The plaintiffs were two parents, Hollis Stabler and Sharon Fremont, and two Indian organizations, the Omaha Tribal History Project headed by Dennis Hastings and the Red Feather Family Services headed by Ms. Terry St. Cyr. The attorney was Michael J. Simpson, who was on the staff of the Legal Aid Society of Walthill. He was assisted by the southern regional office of the ACLU in Atlanta.

In Minnesota the Cass Lake Local Indian Education Committee (LIEC) filed a federal lawsuit in 1994 against the Cass Lake-Bena School District for discrimination against Indian students. It also filed a complaint with the Minnesota Department of Education alleging that the district failed to follow Chapter I parent involvement requirements. The LIEC was one of 12

Exemplary Programs in Indian Education initially identified by Catching the Dream in 1992.

The attorney was Steve Hirsh, who was on the staff of the Anishnabe Legal Services in Cass Lake. He handled both cases. The school district was 65% Native American. Specific allegations in the federal suit, which was filed with the U.S. Department of Justice (DOJ) were:

- The school district had denied Indian students an equal opportunity for education because of their race, in violation of the Civil Rights Act of 1964. Specifically, the district had failed to take action to overcome language barriers, and had segregated ("tracked") Indians into the lowest functioning groups.
- The students speak Ojibwe at home, but they are only allowed to speak English in school. No provisions had been made to teach them adequate English language skills.
- Indian participation in projects and activities that were associated with high academic achievement were much lower than rates for non-Indians in the same areas. Only 5.5% of Indians were enrolled in speech, for instance, but 20% of non-Indians. Indian students were underrepresented in advanced, accelerated, and other high-achievement classes and activities.
- The average Indian student received ten times more behavioral referrals than non-Indians.
- Indian students were overrepresented in Special Education classes.
- Indian students had a higher absenteeism rate than non-Indians.
- Indian students had a higher dropout rate.
- Indian students were disciplined and suspended at a much higher rate.
- There were few Indians on the faculty.

In a separate action, the LIEC appealed to the Minnesota Department of Education in 1994 for help in getting the school district to engage in Indian parent involvement in the educational process. They alleged that the district and the superintendent, James Bottrell, had avoided meeting with parents or Parent Committee representatives.

They had not been involved in planning, annual meetings, hearings, or assessment of the education of their children. Obviously they wanted to improve the poor education their children were getting.

The Department responded in July 1994. It reminded Mr. Bottrell that he had to develop a written policy, make it available, convene an annual meeting for parents, and conduct an annual assessment of the effectiveness of the parent involvement program. Thirteen years later they are still fighting this same battle.

While racism may not be the main determinant of an Indian child's educational outcome, the effects of racism have almost everything to do with it. Racism leads to tracking Indian students into bonehead classes. In some cases, it leads to having nothing but bonehead classes to offer. When I did my dissertation in 1975 at four BIA Indian boarding schools (Chemawa, Stewart, Phoenix, and Sherman), the highest math offering at any of them was General Math. None of them offered even Basic Algebra (Algebra I). The other course offerings were comparably weak.

The typical Indian high school freshman does not take algebra I, but general math. Some 90% of Indian students take less than four years of math in high school; fewer than 10% take the full four years of high school math (Chavers, 1999).

Indian students get placed into "bonehead" classes starting as early as the sixth grade. The placement of Indian students is done by teachers, principals, and increasingly counselors. Counselors in Indian schools mainly have three functions—student schedules, student discipline, and career counseling. Since the principals prefer not to deal with discipline, they are more than happy to pass it along to the counselors, who as a consequence have little time to work with students on career plans.

The counselors look at test scores, attendance rates, and other indicators of academic success. If one asks a counselor why so many Indian students are placed into bonehead classes, the counselor will state that the kids could not handle algebra, or biology, or chemistry. So they will place the Indian students into basic math, general math, business math, and general science. Many Indian students in public schools get tracked into vocational or blue collar types of classes—welding, carpentry, secretarial courses, and agriculture.

Many Indian students have poor attendance; daily attendance rates for Indian students are typically in the range of 65% to 85% instead of 92% to 95%. Schools do little to change this situation. The Gallup-McKinley County Schools, for instance, with the largest Indian student population in the United States, 9,000 students in 30 schools, has no truancy officers.

Their way of dealing with truancy and absenteeism is to kick kids out of school. Instead of a truancy officer, the district employs a hearing officer. His job is to wait until a student misses 11 days of the school year, call a hearing with the student and the parents, and kick the student out of school. Gallup regularly kicks out students as young as twelve years old—creating social problems instead of helping to fix them.

The main growth industry in education on reservations is Special Education. When Education Secretary Dr. Lauro Cavazos stated in a speech to the NIEA in 1989 that almost half of the Indian students were placed in Special Education, I did not believe him. I wrote to his office and asked for a copy of the speech, which cited ED statistics showing that 46% of Indian students were placed into Special Education.

In my 35 years of working and teaching in Indian schools, I have found that the main reason for placing Indian students into Special Education is not academic ability, but the lack of ability to use the English language. As Dr. Magda Costantino pointed out, the typical Indian student enters the first grade with a vocabulary of 1,500 words in English. The typical white student, in contrast, enters first grade with an English vocabulary of 5,000 words. The gap is there from the beginning.

Instead of placing Indian students in Special Education, schools need to place them into English language classes. The main complaint, it seems to me, of superintendents of Indian schools is that they cannot find enough Special Education teachers. I think they have the emphasis on the wrong program.

The main form of racism toward Indians in schools is verbal abuse (St. Denis and Hampton, 2002). Non-Indian students will call students abusive names (see Stereotypes) and if the Indian student reacts, it is the Indian student who most often is blamed.

"We should just send all these kids straight to prison; that's where they will end up anyway," said a teacher from North Junior High School in Rapid City in 1991.

A few years ago at Winner, South Dakota, just east of the Rosebud Reservation, a middle-school student called one of the Indian students a prairie nigger. When the Indian student reacted and the two got into a shoving match, the Indian student got suspended and the white student was not punished at all. The parents of the Indian student are now suing the school district.

The school principal is Brian Naasz, a local man. He had the Native student arrested, but not the white student who started the fight. Naasz claimed that the Native student would "kill somebody next." The student had never been in trouble before.

The ACLU has documented ten cases at Winner High School involving Naasz and two other principals. In all ten cases, the Native students have been arrested and taken to jail. In most cases, their parents or guardians did not know and were not called and told the student was going to jail. In three cases, the other student was also charged and went to jail.

Naasz typically brings the Native student to his office, has him or her sign a "confession," and then calls the police to have the student arrested. A ranker situation of racism in schools will be hard to find. All the ten Indian kids now have criminal records. Their ages have been between 11 and 19 years at the time of arrest.

The reason Mr. Naasz has gained so much attention is that the parents have fought back. In most cases, Indian students and parents "take it." They don't fight back. If they do, they are doubly wrong. So the institutional racism and discrimination continues. The Office of Civil Rights and the ACLU have only stuck one toe into the water. They need to jump in head first and confront the people in the schools who are putting Indian students down.

The Rosebud Sioux Tribe filed a complaint with the U.S. Department of Education in 2006 alleging that the Winner school district uses disciplinary methods that target tribal youths. The district, the complaint said, has an "aggressive and racist practice of seeking the arrest and prosecution of Indian students for minor school misconduct."

Winner superintendent Mary Fisher claimed that the dropout rate of Indian students is not excessively high. However, the tribe alleges that while Indian students make up 25% of the student population in the lower grades, only one percent of the graduates are Indians. They allege that the schools are deliberately pushing Indian students out.

In the 1998-99 school year, a total of 51 Indian students were enrolled in the high school in Winner at the beginning of the year. By the end of the year, the total had dropped to only 11—a 78% dropout rate in one year!

Finally, the U.S. Department of Education stepped in and in 2007 gave the school district 17 things they had to fix. The fixing is still going on. The district is doing all it can to seem to be complying with the ED findings, but avoiding doing anything about them as much as it can.

Michelle Hoffman, superintendent of the Wyoming Indian School District (WISD) in Ethete, Wyoming, said she has witnessed rank discrimination against American Indians. She started teaching at WISD in 1986, intending to stay one year. Despite her intentions, 21 years later she is the superintendent, having filled all positions between classroom teacher and superintendent in the meantime.

Five knowledgeable people predicted she would not win her campaign for Superintendent of Public Instruction in 2006. The reasons: she was a woman, she was a Democrat, and she lived on the Wind River Indian Reservation. She lost the election to Jim McBride, a Republican.

She testified at a trial in 2007 in which five Indian reservation residents sued the county for violations of the Voting Rights Act. The worst incidents, she reported, often came during sporting events. They came from students and parents who called the Indian team members "black Indian boy" and "prairie niggers." They would also yell "Go back to the reservation" and call the students "teepee burners."

The opposing attorney asked her if the derogatory comments at sporting events may be described as "trash talk." It was only fans of one team trying to throw players from other teams off their game, and not overt racist comments, he said. Ms. Hoffman replied that she doubted that fans from two predominantly white schools when they played each other would be using racial slurs in their "trash talk."

Iris All Runner has for years waged a campaign in Wolf Point, Montana, on the Assiniboine Sioux reservation for better treatment of the Indian students. The school district is 80% Indian, but the administration was all white. The school board had one Indian man on it, but he was constantly ruled out of order or drowned out by the white members.

Iris's complaints included no Indian books in the curriculum or the library, an insistence that all students be taught in English only, and that only European and U.S. history would be taught with no mention of tribal or Indian history. Discipline techniques were primitive; they included a padded cell where Indian students were placed.

The typical school curriculum has one day or at the most a few days a year of study of Indian history during the typical school year. The rest of the time the students are studying U.S. literature, English literature, U.S. history, world history, European history, and similar topics.

Costo and Henry identified this problem 40 years ago. Their classic study of public school textbooks found that the typical textbook used in history classes had less than a page of material on Indian history. Other books displayed a similar lack of attention to Indian topics. Indian students know very early along that they are not wanted in the schools, that their history and culture has no value, and that teachers will not try to teach things that are relevant to their lives.

Michelle Hoffman, testified in a trial in February 2007 that textbooks she is forced to use exhibit institutional racism. Out of six state-approved textbooks about American government, history, and social studies, she counted a total of 20 pages devoted to American Indians. They had a half page devoted to Sacagawea, a page or two on tribal casinos, and discussions about how Indians are disadvantaged and live in squalor on reservations.

"I'm embarrassed for my state," she told a group of state lawmakers in 2006. "Ignorance is born of fear, fear of the unknown," she told them, urging them to change to more balanced textbooks. She said that Fremont County, where her school district is, does not have a hand in selecting textbooks.

The state of Montana implemented a requirement 20 years ago for Indian history, language, and culture to be taught in the schools. However, after a few years, with objections coming from non-Indian school people, this requirement was rescinded. Montana has been the only state that ever required minimum competence on the part of teachers to learn something about their Indian students.

So the typical new teacher at an Indian school knows nothing, or next to nothing, or only the stereotypes, about the Indian students he or she is teaching. There is a huge cultural disconnect between this teacher and the students.

The typical teacher in an Indian school cannot even say "Hello" in the local Native language. When I said "Yaht aye," the Navajo word for "hello," to a white teacher at Kayenta in 1987, he looked at me strangely. "Did you just call me some kind of name?" he asked.

"No," I said. "I just said hello in Navajo."

"We don't do that here," he said.

"Why not?" I asked. "Don't you want the students to feel welcome at school?"

"They have to learn our language," he said.

The superintendent of the Kayenta Unified School District at the time, Dr. Joseph Martin, is a Navajo. To his credit, within a year or so they had initiated a Navajo language class. Unfortunately, like so many other school districts in Indian Country, only one Navajo language teacher was hired; he could only teach about 5% of the Navajo students in a typical day. The other 95% got very little exposure to Navajo language in the four schools.

The Port Gamble S'Klallam Tribe sued the North Kitsap School District in 1994 for refusing to let the tribe have access to school policies, for putting Indian students into bonehead classes, putting tribal students into racially separated lower achieving classes, causing high dropout rates and high teen suicide rates, and having few Indian students in the gifted program.

Celine Buckanaga and others brought suit in the U.S. Court of Appeals in October 1986 alleging that the at-large voting system in the Sisseton Independent School District, South Dakota, violated the Voting Rights Act. Some 33.9% of the population was Indian, and 44.9% of the students enrolled in the school district were Indians. Only two Indians had ever served on the board, one being appointed to fill an unexpired term, and the other being the winner in an election. There were nine seats on the board. They asked to have a single-member district plan put into place. The District Court initially ruled that it found no evidence of discrimination against Indians. On appeal, though, the Eighth Circuit of Appeals sent the suit back to the District Court for further actions to fix the problems.

In Walker River, Nevada, the Walker River Paiute tribe brought a lawsuit in 1987 against the principal at Schurz Elementary School, Joel Hodes. He had been at the school almost 20 years. They claimed he had ruined the lives of dozens of Paiute and Caucasian students by ostracizing and blackballing them, forcing them to leave school and go to another school if they disagreed with him.

He caused a dropout rate for Indians of over 60%, mutilated children by acts of carelessness, terrorized the community by following people in their cars to harass and blackball them, desecrated Native ceremonies by declaring native sweet grass to be evil, and called people who follow traditional Indian beliefs "witches," "devil worshippers," and "evil people."

He also practiced racial discrimination on a daily basis, labeling Indian students as slow learners, being told they were just Indians and would never amount to anything, treating Indian students differently from non-Indians, and placing Indian students in a bad light on a regular basis. He also allegedly engaged in sexual abuse, walking in on girls in the shower after physical exercise or after games.

He constantly manhandled students and parents by throwing them into chairs, and putting them forcefully into a van to bring them back to school. The superintendent, Granville Gage, did nothing to correct these abuses, even after parents insisted in writing that something be done.

He had repeatedly told the Indian students they would never amount to anything because they are Indians. They can't or won't learn. They have no future. The girls will get pregnant and have illegitimate children, he said. Neither the girls nor the boys will go to college, and if they do they will flunk out. He told one Cherokee woman who burned sage at an Indian religious ceremony at the school that she would never teach again. She was a witch, an evil person, and a devil worshipper, he said. He harassed her for the next four months, and finally dismissed her in December.

In another case, the new principal of Monument Valley High School in Kayenta, Arizona, asked me to brief him in the fall of 1987 on what I knew about Indian education. His name was Bob Roundtree. He had relocated to Kayenta the year before to teach English, after being a teacher and principal for 20 years in Ada, Oklahoma. He had a few Indian students in the school at Ada, but he had not really gotten to know them.

"I want to pretend I know nothing about Indians," he told me at 8:30 that morning. I had come to make a second site visit for the evaluation of the Indian Education Act Program in the schools, which was run by Gilbert

Sombrero, one of the most capable educators I have ever worked with. Gilbert was a local Navajo who had run the Bilingual and Indian Education Act programs for a few years. When I showed up that morning, Gilbert said, "Bob Roundtree wants to meet with you right away." So we headed to his office.

"I want you to tell me everything you know about Indian education," he said after he had made some brief introductions. "I have all day, and I'll bring in my department heads and librarian from time to time."

I proceeded to give him the longest informal off-the-cuff seminar I have ever given. The department heads and the librarian, Susan Smith, wandered in and out. At noon we took a lunch break and resumed a half hour later. By the end of the day I had convinced Bob that he could improve the school. He could do it if he made sure students were in school every day, that they were reading books outside the classroom, that they had learned how to read, that they were being assigned homework, that teachers should reach out and talk to parents, and that teachers should use more appropriate teaching methods than the lecture method.

That same year the superintendent, Dr. Joe Martin, instituted a college course for teachers on multicultural education. Dr. Donna Deyhle from the University of Utah taught it. The teachers slowly got away from staying in their little ghetto of teacher apartments and started mixing with the community. However, that was a hard one to break. When I came back for the next visit a few months later, Bob sheepishly admitted that he had gotten out of his office and actually visited a Navajo home the week before.

"Why didn't you do that the week after I left?" I asked.

"Well, I was afraid they might scalp me or something," he joked.

In fact, though, he reflected the feelings of other teachers at the high school. Despite that reluctance, the reforms that Bob instituted had the effect of increasing student achievement at the highest level in the history of the school.

Reading scores for seniors went up 2.6 Grade Equivalents (GE) in seven years. Math scores went up 1.7 GE. Language scores went up 2.4 GE. Were these students where they needed to be when they left school? No, but they were ahead of where their predecessors had been.

Bob and I figured that within another five years we would have the seniors at the national norms, 12.8. However, then he got promoted to superintendent. The next principal did away with all the programs we had put in place, and the scores after two years started dropping. Within five years they were back to their 1984 levels. Despite this relapse, we proved that doing the right things could make a huge difference.

The Parent Committee under the leadership of Beverly Pigman had insisted three years before, in 1984, that all the four schools implement a program of truancy and absentee prevention.

Under the direction of Dean of Students Jim Lytle, the daily attendance rate at the high school went from 80-82% to 92% and stayed there for seven years. Julius Young, a local Navajo Home-School Liaison, would get in his truck and go pick up students if they were not at school on time. After a while they just gave up and came to school on the bus. Before, some of them would hide out in the arroyos, get some beer, and smoke some weed during the day, and come home when the bus ran. Their parents were often none the wiser.

The high school had also implemented a Motivation Room for students who were tardy. In an effort to teach them discipline, any student who was not in the classroom and seated when the bell rang got sent to the Motivation Room. There they wrote essays on why they were always going to be a good citizen from then on, or completed homework, or read books. Daily attendance in the Motivation Room was 175 per day at first, but at the end of seven years it had dropped to 30 to 40 per day, and the money for it was reprogrammed into a program to make sure students had the right credits to be graduated on time.

The typical teacher at an Indian school cannot even say "Hello" in the Native language of the students. They are clearly part of the colonial structure, come to convert the heathen savage Indians. They are not taught anything about the culture of their students, practically all of whom are living the biggest part of their lives in a traditional Indian culture. The culture of the students stresses cooperation between people while the schools stress competition and the recognition of the best achievers.

For Indian students, standing out in the classroom, or doing what people in my tribe call "being above one's raisings," is a sure way to bring disapproval, opprobrium, or even beatings to a student.

Indian students who get into fights with white students in school will be suspended or expelled. Nothing will happen to the white students. Steve Hirsh represented two girls at Independent School District No. 36 in Minnesota who had been suspended in November for the rest of the year. On appeal to the state, he got them reinstated as of December instead of being out the whole year.

(Most Indian students who get suspended never get the luxury of having an attorney to represent them. The 50% dropout rate for Indians is mostly "pushouts" instead of dropouts.)

The problem for the two girls was that they reacted to racial name calling by two white students. When the situation resulted in a fistfight, the two Indian students were suspended, and nothing happened to the two white students. The "hearing" called by the Board of Education was a one-sided farce, with the students not being allowed to make certain charges, not being allowed to call certain witnesses, and so on.

In Bishop, California, in September 2007, the Indian parents from the Bishop Paiute Tribe settled a lawsuit against the Bishop Union Elementary School District for discrimination against their children, according to the Associated Press.

The trouble started when teachers reported a 13-year-old Paiute boy was wearing a bandana during recess. The policeman, Glenn McClinton, demanded the boy turn over the bandana to him. The boy resisted, saying it belonged to his grandmother. He was wearing it without her permission.

McClinton then pushed the boy to the ground and handcuffed him, according to the complaint. Pretty soon he pushed three other Indian students and a white student who stuck up for them to the ground.

The bandana wearer was arrested and taken to the police station. He and the other students were suspended for five days. As the result of the settlement, the police presence on the school grounds has been removed.

"Our big fear about kids being over-disciplined is that they stop seeing school as a place where they belong, as an avenue of success for them," said the ACLU attorney who handled the case, Jory Steele.

"There's always room for improvement," said the superintendent, Barry Simpson.

Christine Wilson, one of the mothers involved, said she had been mistreated by the school as a child and that the father of her children had been mistreated as well. "I grew up here, and saw the same thing happen then, how the Native American kids were singled out," she said. "I was seeing the same thing happen with my kids, how they start seeing themselves like they're not worth much, won't amount to much."

The ACLU found that Indian students were disciplined much more than other students. They were also hugely overrepresented in the continuation school, which is for students who have problems in school. Indian students were 17% of the student body, but had gotten 67% of the discipline actions. Indian students were suspended from school for such minor infractions as chewing gum, dress code violations, having candy, and being late to class. The state education code specifically defines suspension as a last resort, said Mr. Steele, and for major infractions.

Part of the settlement was that the students had their records for suspensions expunged. Another part was that the school agreed to participate in diversity training. They also have to keep discipline records for the ACLU to review.

In Montana in 2006, the U.S. Department of Education (ED) identified 33 schools that needed "restructuring" after they failed to make federally mandated adequate progress under George Bush's No Child Left Behind (NCLB) law. The law, which is largely negative, requires schools to make progress over a period of three years, but critics allege that the funding for the law was only half of what schools needed to comply with the law's mandates.

Out of the 69 schools on or near reservations in Montana, 33 failed to make the cut. Linda McCulloch, the superintendent of public instruction, figuratively threw her hands into the air. "The shame is that no one has done much of any research on Native American students' needs," she said.

There are 10 or 15 dozen Indian education researchers, including myself, who were surprised to learn this. I have only worked on this problem for 35 years.

To pass the standard of making Adequate Yearly Progress (AYP), 55% of the students in a school had to pass the reading test at proficient or better. In math, 40% of students had to pass, and have an attendance rate of at least 80%. High schools must have a graduation rate of 80%.

At least one Indian district in the state, Box Elder Unified School District, has been making strong progress. All three of the schools have passed AYP, and the elementary school has won honors for improving outcomes for its students. Dave Nelson, the principal, and Robert Heppner, the superintendent, have completely restructured their approach to education.

Bob, who came out of retirement in 2000 to take the helm at Box Elder, insisted that the schools completely revamp their approaches and return to basics. They emphasize daily attendance, reading, and homework to make sure students continue to improve. Last year all three schools in the Box Elder School District made AYP.

* * *

The worst crimes that happened to Indian students in the United States in the BIA boarding schools will probably never be investigated, documented, or addressed. The staff beat students for speaking their languages. They denied food to students. They handcuffed them to furniture and to beds, allowing them to be vulnerable to other students who had a beef with them and proceeded to beat them up.

Some staff raped students, abused them sexually, and in many cases ruined the psychological health of the students for life. It is no wonder to me that so many Indian parents have trouble raising their kids. They never learned how, and they were physically, mentally, and sexually abused themselves as kids.

Indian students in the BIA and religious schools before 1960 were subjected to many forms of abuse. They had their heads shaved when they came to the school, allegedly to remove lice. However, to many of them, shearing off their hair, which to them was sacred, was a scar they carried the rest of their lives. The staff members also made them stand in line for hours. They often went the whole school year without seeing their parents or other members of their families.

They had to scrub the floors in their dorms on their hands and knees, often with toothbrushes to make it harder and gruesome. They raised crops to feed themselves, and they raised vegetables and fruits for the school kitchens.

They were often forced to work part of the day to pay for their keep, at sometimes dangerous and physically demanding jobs. One of these was working the "mangle," where they often suffered from accidents and sometimes lost fingers in the heavy rollers. This machine, now largely discontinued, was the precursor to the modern day washing machine. It had two rollers and students had to run wet clothes through them to remove most of the water.

They had to march to class and stand at attention for hours. They had to exchange their buckskin clothes for military uniforms.

Ernie Stensgar, the chairman of the Coeur d'Alene Tribe in Idaho, said boot camp in the Army was easy for him after he had gone through Chilocco Indian School in Oklahoma. "I had already in a sense been to boot camp," he said. Ernie was wounded in Viet Nam, but he came home to lead his tribe for many years.

When students spoke their Native language they were either beaten or had their mouths washed out with soap. They often ran away from the schools, and some of them froze to death in the sudden snowstorms and blizzards that often hit the upper Midwest.

Tim Giago, the founder of *Indian Country Today* and the best Indian journalist in the United States, has written a book on the abuse he suffered at Holy Rosary Mission, now called Red Cloud Indian School. As an adult he could not understand the depression he felt come over him. Once he starting writing about it, though, he could cope with it better.

Indeed, some of these abuses reached the modern age. Leon Don Johnson, who was 41 year old, was found guilty in 2000 of ten counts of sexual abuse of a young girl on the Navajo reservation. He had been an elementary school teacher at Chinle for several years. The girl was not one of his students. The abuse lasted from 1996 to 1999.

Reporter Marsha King quoted Genevieve Williams, who was 85 years old, in 2007 on her experiences in Indian boarding schools. "We got to know that strap," she said. "Everybody knew what that strap was for, hanging inside the door."

King attributes the boarding school abuse with most of the social ills that affect Indian tribes today. Women and men who are now grandparents and great-grandparents never learned how to be parents because they were isolated for years from their own parents. They passed this down to their children and the children passed it down to their children. The boarding schools thus caused great social harm by making students deny their heritage, their culture, and their language.

When Stan Jones, the former chairman of the Tulalip Tribes, was dropped off back on the reservation after spending three enforced years at a boarding school, he thought his family did not want him. He went instead to the home of an aunt, who took him in. He realized years later that he should have gone to his dad's. "Actually, I forgot about my home," he told King. "I wasn't sure where I belonged."

Kevin Gover, when he was Assistant Secretary for Indian Affairs in 2000, caused a storm of controversy when he apologized to Indian people for the abuse the BIA schools had heaped on them. He promised that the federal government would never do such things again. He said:

> "The works of this agency have at times profoundly harmed the communities it was meant to serve. From the very beginning, the Office of Indian Affairs was an instrument by which the United States enforced its ambition against the Indian nations and the Indian people who stood in its path," he said.
>
> "In these more enlightened times, it must be acknowledged that the deliberate spread of disease, the decimation of the mighty bison herds, the use of the poison alcohol to destroy mind and body and the cowardly killing of women and children made for tragedy on a scale so ghastly that it cannot be dismissed as merely the inevitable consequence of the clash of competing ways of life. This agency and the good people in it failed in the mission to prevent devastation. This agency forbade the speaking of Indian languages, prohibited the conduct of traditional religious activities, outlawed traditional government, and made Indian people ashamed of who they were. Worst of all, the Bureau of Indian Affairs committed these acts against the children entrusted to its boarding schools, brutalizing them emotionally, psychologically, physically and spiritually. Even in this era of self-determination, when the Bureau of Indian Affairs is at long last serving as an ad-

vocate for Indian people in an atmosphere of mutual respect, the legacy of these misdeeds haunts us."

While the abuse in U.S. Indian schools has been largely passed over by history, in Canada it has become a major issue. It involves thousands of Native students and hundred of priests and teachers. Abuse involved the Roman Catholic Church, the Anglican Church of Canada, and the United Church of Canada. Girls were often sterilized when they went through puberty. Those who were not sterilized sometimes became pregnant as the result of forced sex by teachers and priests.

Thousands of survivors have filed lawsuits in Canada, all since the early 1990s. The costs may well exceed $5 billion. Allegedly over half the victims have attempted suicide. Drug and alcohol abuse are rampant among them.

Recent revelations have turned up a series of mass graves where Canadian Indians were buried after they died or were killed in the Canadian boarding schools. There are supposedly 28 of these mass grave sites. No similar revelations have been made in the U.S., but it is certain that many Indian students died in BIA boarding schools, away from home and family, and were buried without notice to their parents. The students who died at Carlisle, for instance, are buried in a little neglected cemetery on the campus. The cemetery is on ground that used to be part of Carlisle. The campus is now the home of the War College. The families of most students probably lost track of their children and do not know where their children are buried.

Sherwin Zephier, a Lakota who attended a Catholic school in Marty, South Dakota, filed a class action case in the United States in 2004. He told a press conference "I was tortured in the middle of the night. They would whip us with boards and sometimes with straps." His suit claims to represent many other Indian students who were abused by the schools. Their attorneys have interviewed over 1,000 former students who were abused by the schools, they said.

The judge threw his case out of the Court of Federal Claims in December 2004, saying it was not the proper court. It was a tort claim and would have to be filed as an administrative case with the BIA. The BIA/Department of Interior alleged it had handled many similar cases in the past, but that only one had ever been won and been paid money by the Indians bringing the claim.

The FBI arrested teacher John Boone in 1987. He had been teaching at the Hopi Day School on the reservation since 1979. He was charged with sexually abusing 142 Hopi boys, but not even one case had been investigated by the principal. Boone received a life sentence.

In another case in 1987, a teacher from Oklahoma who had been fired for sexual improprieties with students had been hired at Kayenta, Arizona. The school, unfortunately, did not conduct a thorough background check on him. They had no record of his sexual abuse of students in Oklahoma.

He soon became trusted by the students and their parents, who would allow their sons and daughters to spend the weekend with him when they had to travel out of town to ball games and other activities. He was charged with abusing more than a dozen students, both female and male, after he was arrested.

In one of the few cases of racial discrimination filed by a student against a college, David Velasquez, from the Tule River Reservation in California, filed a complaint in 2006 against Central Oregon Community College. He alleged that a former co-worker had slapped him across the face with his own jacket, and that his boss, Jeff Richards, previously had stated in a staff meeting that he believed in "separate but equal" treatment in regard to the races.

"Richards said that he prefers 'separate but equal,' immediately back-peddling when he saw me sitting there," Velasquez reported to STAR. "Since then he never said anything to me ever again, not even said hello to me."

He adds that he was fired immediately. "About the same day I filed the complaint, I lost all of my hours," he continued.

Velasquez is an older student with 20 years of experience in computer technology. He says he was fired immediately after the incident with the other student. He alleges that the campus and the surrounding community of Bend have institutionalized racism in many ways.

Indian students experience discrimination and racism primarily in these four ways:

1. placement in bonehead classes;
2. failure of the school to connect with the home;
3. the lecture method of teaching;
4. low teacher expectations.

Racist Placement: In a study of 5,002 Native students I conducted in 1998, I found the following facts:

- Half of all Indian students drop out of high school prior to graduation.
- Fewer than 10% of Indian students took four years of math in high school. Three out of ten Indian students were taking no math classes at all!
- Only 4.9% of Indian students were taking calculus.

- Almost a third (29.5%) of Indian students were not enrolled in a science class.
- Over half (55.3%) of the high schools responding to the survey had no math lab.
- Fewer than 10% of the high schools were offering tribal government and history classes.
- Indian students belonged to almost no clubs or organizations, including even the Indian Club! Only 6.8% of Indian students were members of Indian Clubs. It was clear that Indians live in one world, on the reservation, and receive their education in a different world, off the reservation (in culture, if not in geography). Even when the school is totally on the reservation, such as Fort Yates and Kayenta, the teachers either commute from off the reservation or live in a compound or "teacherages" on the school grounds.
- Only 17% of Indian students go on to college, compared to 67% for the United States as a whole.
- Only 33.5% of all Indian students were enrolled in at least one college-prep math class. A lot of these (we did not collect data on this) were enrolled in bonehead math classes—General Math, Business Math, and so on.
- Only 76.6% of Indian ninth graders were taking Algebra I.

(The data I collected may be the only ones ever collected on a national level that pertain to Native high school students. There is a definite bias in research on Indian education. Looking at the participation of Native students in the curriculum and co-curriculum has not been done by many researchers. Histories of tribal education, histories of Indian policy, and the effects of Native curriculum on students are frequently studied topics. Student histories, dropout studies, and academic performance of students are very much under-studied.)

Reid Riedlinger, when he was superintendent of the Wellpinit School District on the Spokane Reservation in Washington, got the school board to approve a policy requiring teachers to live in the community. It made a world of difference. Wellpinit schools are some of the best in the United States, and I don't mean just Indian schools. They can compete with Stuyvesant High School in New York City, which sends 30 to 50 kids a year to Harvard. In 2003, Reid had 100% of the graduates go on to college, and had a zero dropout rate! He retired in 2005 after 15 successful years of steady improvement.

It is obvious that Indian students are placed into the easiest classes in high school. At Red Rock, Oklahoma, in 1994, the Frontier School District had three tracks in the school. The advanced track was for white kids who were college bound. The second was for white kids who were going to be farmers. Below these two was a third nondescript track for Indian kids who were not going to amount to anything.

I reviewed the records of nine Otoe students who were then in college to see what their high school education had been like. There were lots of classes on their transcripts in driver's education, wood shop, general math, and other "crip" courses. None of them had taken advanced algebra, geometry, trigonometry, and they couldn't pronounce calcoolus. None of them had taken more than one or two years of basic biology and chemistry.

In my years as president of Bacone College, I reviewed records of Indian kids from all over the United States. One of my adopted "daughters" was typical. She is from the Tohono O'odham reservation southwest of Tucson. She had attended Baboquivari High School on the reservation.

I asked her during her first semester, "When did you plan to come to Bacone?"

"Last June," she said.

"Why so late?" I asked.

"Well, my best friend told me she was coming here, so I decided to apply," she said.

"What courses did you take in high school to prepare you for college?" I asked.

"I took four years of agriculture," she said.

"What?" I said. "You're a girl. Are you planning to become a farmer?"

"No," she said, "But that's where they put me."

"Did you have four years of English?" I asked.

"No, I had two years," she answered.

"What about science?" I asked.

"I had general science," she replied.

"And math?" I asked.

"I had general math and Algebra I," she said.

This girl, who was very bright, struggled through her year at Bacone. She did not return for her second year. She went home and eventually got a job. Then a few years later she went back to college. Eventually she got her LPN license and has worked as a nurse for 25 years, but I still resent how her high school cheated her out of a good education.

In fact, her high school, after making some improvements in the 1980s and 1990s under a progressive principal, has unfortunately regressed back to its earlier days.

The principal had reduced the dropout rate from 42% to 14% and had raised the completion rate from 60% to over 80%. Some of the students were taking five or six years to complete, but at least they were finishing high school. Five years ago when I first started visiting the school, the dropout rate had shot back up again to over 60%. When the dedicated principal left the school after ten years, it went to hell in a hand basket.

Failure to Connect with the Home

The typical teacher at an Indian school is either right out of college, at her first job, or has been in the business for 15 to 30 years. Turnover at Indian schools typically runs between 25% and 50% per year. If I visit a school this year, and don't go back for five years, practically all the teachers will be gone. I won't know a soul, and no one will know me or know anything about the scholarship program I run.

Teachers never set foot in the homes of any of their students, don't know what the parents look like, and have fewer than 10% of the parents ever show up for a school function—except football and basketball, which fill gymnasiums all over Indian Country. Teachers don't learn any of the language of their students.

In one case, I was interviewing all the bilingual teachers at Chinle Unified School District in 1988 for an evaluation of the program. Asking them about their relations with the parents of the Navajo students was not on the agenda, but I was extremely curious. So I asked every teacher, "How many of the parents of your students do you know personally?" There were 30 teachers in the project.

Most answered "One" or "Two." A few said more, but one Navajo third grade teacher, who was from another community, said "None."

"You mean if you were shopping in Eddie Basha's grocery store and you saw the parents of one of your students, and the student was not with him, you would not know who the parents were?" I asked her.

"Yes," she said. "They don't want us to fraternize with the parents. We are supposed to keep it all here at school."

In the Gallup schools, a young Navajo teacher aide who was extremely conscientious decided she would do all she could to help her charges. She started visiting them at home to help them with tutoring after school. When the principal found out about it, he wrote her up for "fraternizing" and made her stop. The Natives are to be left alone once they leave the school. Something from the dirty Native culture might rub off on the school people.

Teachers, as part of the missionaries on reservations to convert the heathens, live in their own little worlds, and not with the people they are supposed to be serving. The teacher compounds and teacherages on campuses are their own little world. They go into towns on weekends, and perhaps they attend church in the nearest border town rather than in the local community. The Indian churches on Sunday will have only Indians attending, and none of the non-Indian teachers, doctors, and health workers, who live and work in the community. There are in effect two communities in the places, one community of Indians and another community of non-Indians. They rarely interact with or reach out to one another.

The teachers are mean to the kids. They yell at them, boss them around, look down their noses at them, and are demanding. They all use the lecture method, a deadly, boring method of teaching. They fail to use hands-on, student-centered teaching, which is much closer to the pedagogic style the students are used to. It is no wonder that Indian students are alienated before they reach high school.

The typical Indian student today attends a public school on or near a reservation, or lives and goes to school in an urban area. BIA schools only get about 6% of Indian students, contract schools get about 5%, mission schools get about 3%, and the other 86% attend public schools. Indian students typically are in the minority in a border town school such as Holbrook, Arizona, Chadron, Nebraska, Ashland, Montana, and Winner, South Dakota.

Border towns are rough on Indian students. The Indian students are marked the day they walk into the border town high school. The norm is for the town students—almost all white—to rule the roost. They are the basketball players, the football players, the baseball players, and the stars of the classroom. In many cases, one can see the segregation in the classroom, with all the white students in front and the Indians in the rear of the classroom.

Teachers and administrators have two sets of rules, one for white students, and one for Indian students. Indian students get harsher penalties for infractions, they are suspended for behavior more often, and they get uneven enforcement of the school rules. The white student might get in-school suspension for an infraction, but the Indian student may get five days of suspension from school for a similar infraction. One of the few times the school will have an interaction with Indian parents during the year is when a parent comes to school to protest some particular punishment the student has gotten, or when parents pull students out of class early to go to the dentist or the doctor or to go to town shopping for the weekend.

Most acts of racism in the schools are denied or silenced (St. Denis and Hampton), which is in itself a racist practice. Few schools have acknowledged racism as a problem and taken steps to retrain their teachers in how to deal with Indian students in non-racist ways. Without acknowledging that there is a problem, it is not likely to be addressed or to go away.

Most solutions, in fact, are based on victim blame. These solutions include programs to improve the low self-esteem of Indian students (which is a very difficult thing to do). They also include drug and alcohol treatment centers, which have proven to be only partly successful in rehabilitating abusers and users. Courses for self-esteem building don't work well because they deal with the symptoms of the problem and not the root cause. We must name "racism" as the root cause of the problems that plague Indian people. Treatment and rehabilitation centers blame the victim; we should be blaming the racists, not the oppressed people suffering from racism.

However, instead of confronting the problem, most Indian schools start the year with a one-day or two-day orientation to the system. In contrast, the outstanding Chugach School District, the winner of the Malcolm Baldrige National Quality Award and the first school to win this prestigious award, spends 30 days each fall before school starts teaching all teachers how to teach and use their new curriculum.

The biggest dropout year for Indian students typically is ninth grade. It is not unusual for 25% to 40% of entering ninth graders not to remain in school all year. My class of 70, which started first grade in 1947, had 35 students who finished high school at Pembroke High School. That's a 50% dropout rate. Only eight of us ever went to college, and only four finished with a bachelor's degree or higher.

Indeed, things have gotten worse in the past 50 years. My friend Robert Locklear's daughter Elizabeth started ninth grade in 2001 in a class of 622, but only 220 of them finished high school in 2005.

The Lecture Method of Teaching

As Swisher and Deyhle, Wolcott, and others have demonstrated, the lecture method for Indian students is deadly. Indian students, to make a broad generalization, do not like to compete against each other, to make each other look bad, to get ahead of each other. The lecture method, in contrast, almost demands these things. Almost never is the utility and worth of the lecture method challenged in Indian Country.

Three people who changed it were Michelle Hoffman at Wyoming Indian School on the Wind River Reservation, Richard DiLorenzo at Chugach School District in Alaska, and Bob Roundtree at Monument Valley High School. They are exemplars of how to do it, and how to do it right. Others can and should take heed of how they accomplished great deeds with Indian students, and follow their lead.

Michelle took her students in only three years from zero competence in math to 65% passing at the competency level. She did it by retraining her teachers vigorously over a period of three years, starting in 2003 when the school board hired her as superintendent.

Michelle has been at WIS for 21 years so far. She has gone from teacher to principal to superintendent. She went there in 1986 for one year, she says, but never left. She has obviously fallen in love with the community, saw the worth of her students, and has become a strong advocate for them. Her testimony on racism in stores and restaurants is reported in that chapter in this book. Her testimony on institutional racism in textbooks is reported in this chapter, above.

Richard was the principal of the high school at Chugach in 1992 when the population grew tired of failure. The district, in southeast Alaska, is in the area where the oil tanker *Exxon Valdez* dumped 11 millions gallons of raw petroleum into the sea after hitting a reef in 1989.

The district, which is made up largely of Native Alaskans, had sent exactly one student to college in the 20 years prior to 1994, and he flunked out. As a group, the whole district decided to start over. They threw out the curriculum and rebuilt the whole thing from the ground floor up. They instituted a massive teacher retraining program, which to this day still requires teachers to undergo 30 days of training each summer before school starts.

It did pay off. In 2002, the district won the most prestigious prize the United States has to offer, the Malcolm Baldrige National Quality Award. Named after the former Secretary of Commerce in the Reagan administration, and the brother of etiquette queen Letitia Baldrige, the Baldrige award is regarded by many as the U.S. equivalent of the Nobel Prize awards and the Deming Prize in Japan. Many U.S. corporations and others compete each year for the prize. Chugach was the first school district ever to win it. The district is still training others how to achieve what they did, and it provides others with copies of their curriculum at the drop of a hat.

Bob Roundtree was convinced when he came to Kayenta in 1985 that he knew next to nothing about how to teach Indian kids. So he set about educating himself on the subject, which was a humbling experience. Most principals, of course, never lower themselves this much. They are, after all, next to God, and know practically everything already. That is overstating the case, but the case can be made for too many principals. I just wish more of them were humble and set about trying to educate themselves, and then their teaching staffs, about how to educate the culturally different Indian student.

In teaching Indian students, it is best to let them work in small groups. The natural tendency of Anglo teachers, to break up the small groups into individual students, is one of the dumbest things teachers can do. However, it is the dominant method of instruction at almost all U.S. high schools and colleges. So naturally the teachers trained in these places bring what they have learned with them to Indian reservations.

Then they fail, and they leave, and a new group of teachers comes in the next year to replace them. Then that group fails, and they leave, and another new group comes in the year after that. It is insanity run wild.

Low Expectations

The teachers have very low expectations of students, as hundreds of people have noted over the years. This is the most racist part of the school culture. Teachers do not demand that students do homework, and students do not do it. Teachers routinely make sure that students do *not* have homework. When I have asked them why they do not assign homework, they constantly tell me that if they do assign it, students won't do it, so they don't assign any.

What they should be doing, of course, is making sure they have a line of open communication going with the parents, and giving students homework every day, at least during and after the middle school years.

Indian students are constantly told they are not going to achieve in school. Low expectations are consistently displayed in the classroom. Students are regularly called derogatory names. After a while it starts to sink in. Students internalize the feelings of low self-worth and low self-esteem.

By the time they are freshmen in high school, they are ready to start taking actions on their feelings. Alcohol and drugs start to become a problem as students abuse them. Unfortunately, a high percentage of Indian students attempt or carry out the ultimate act of self-loathing, suicide. Suicide rates in Indian schools are ten times higher than the national rates of similar age groups. Some schools are suffering from extremely high rates of suicides, and this atmosphere has effects on the whole school culture. In one school where I work, there have been over 50 suicide attempts in the past five years. Several of them succeeded.

The widely reported low self-esteem of Indian students is caused largely by racism in the schools. Students do not want to be identified as Indians because that puts them into a second-class position. They cannot figure out what they are—Indians or something else. They become ashamed of their traditional Indian cultural practices and do not want to participate in them. They wish they had not been born Indian and feel their lives would have been better if they had not been born Indians.

One of the teachers I was initially impressed with in the Gallup schools in 1986–87 was a male math lab teacher. His students were all Indians, even though the district schools all have Anglo, Hispanic, and Indian students. He had developed math exercises from the 100 level to the 700 level. Students would come in, take the next exercise, and work on it until they finished. Then they would turn it in, and he would grade it. No reading was involved—only computation.

His students gained respectably during the year, just a little over one grade level each. However, for ninth graders to move from third grade level to fourth grade level was obviously not enough. When I analyzed the test scores for all nine math lab teachers, however, the female teacher at Gallup High School had her students gaining over two grade levels! And with their progress, in three years, they could have mainly been on track to graduate with adequate math skills. So I was much less impressed with his all-computation approach when the results were in. However, I still thought he was doing a good job overall.

The next fall, though, he took the air out of my balloon. As the teachers and aides were being trained for two days by one of my friends from Window Rock, the male math teacher said, "Well, these kids are just Indians anyway. All they're going to do is pump gas and do beadwork, so any math we teach them is better than they would have gotten otherwise."

To their credit, the others jumped on him for his offensive and racist remarks. He taught there the rest of the year, getting mildly good results again, and left for parts unknown. His comments, though, reflect an attitude that is much too prevalent, and the height of paternalism.

Indian students do no reading outside the classroom. The first time I collected data on this was at the Colorado River Indian Tribes (CRIT). The higher education director, Kenton Laffoon, had asked me to make a presentation to the college-bound students one evening 20 years ago. I asked the students each to stand and tell their name and what they were planning for college.

When that was over, I went back around the room and asked each student to tell us how many books he or she had read outside the classroom during the year. Out of 35 students, only five had read any books, and only two of the five had read at least two books. The other 30 students had read no books at all. I understood clearly why the school, and other Indian schools, had such a high dropout rate, especially in the ninth grade. The students could not understand the concepts they were being taught, especially if they were dealing with abstractions such as the Constitution, basic algebra, and formulas for chemistry.

Teachers can, as has been demonstrated in the past 20 years by some of our Exemplary Programs in Indian Education, learn how to teach without using lectures all the time. Where Indian students are allowed to learn in their own style, using small group work and self-teaching, they have proved they can achieve at higher levels than the national norms!

There are two Indian high schools so far, Wellpinit, Washington, and Navajo Preparatory School in New Mexico, where *all* the Indian graduates have gone on to college and none dropped out of high school. Chugach, Alaska, Mount Edgecumbe, Alaska, and Salmon River, New York, have also achieved very high results.

For the past 17 years, Catching the Dream has made grants to Indian schools for reading. The organization has made 104 of these grants, and about 85 of them have been very successful. In about a quarter of the cases, school officials report back to us that the students have taken really well to reading. They will ask for time set aside to read, they will read on the bus on the way to school and going back home, and they will ask for time during the week to go to the library to check out books. They have gone from being indifferent to books to loving them.

The best of the schools have gone from an average of one or two books per student to as high as 180 per student. Most have gone from near zero to 20 to 40 books per student. In the schools where students increase outside reading substantially, test scores will start to rise during the second or third year. If the schools continue to do it right, in a five year period they typically raise test scores from below the 20th percentile to the 50th (the national level) or higher. In a few cases, test scores have gone above the 75th percentile for whole schools.

But it is difficult for even highly placed Indian people to bring about change. When Montana state senator Carol Juneau (Mandan) sponsored a bill that would teach all students about Montana's Indian tribes, she was attacked by Rep. Ed Butcher. He wrote to retired teacher Dorothea Susag that the program was misguided and was being "propelled by the politically correct crowd of semi-literate proponents."

He said he was "astonished at the naivety (sic) of our educational community in buying into this 'Indian education project.'" He said an accurate picture of historic Indian culture was not possible because Indians were "hunter/gatherer peoples who would have had a limited vocabulary ... and relied upon sign language for much of their communication."

Ms. Juneau, a retired educator with advanced degrees, served for many years as a college president. Butcher still has the audacity to say she is semi-literate.

One of the "experiments" that has not yet been tried in Indian Country, as far as I know, is the famous one done by Jane Elliott of Riceville, Iowa. After the assassination of Dr. Martin Luther King, she divided her class into students with blue eyes and students with brown eyes. She told them that blue-eyed people were naturally smarter than people with brown eyes.

Before the day was out, the students had started acting accordingly. The blue-eyed people starting oppressing the brown-eyed students, talking down to them, and saying how dumb they were. The brown-eyed students started acting accordingly, acting defensively, exhibiting feelings of self-loathing, and even fear.

The next day Ms. Elliott reversed the roles, and the brown-eyed students were suddenly superior. They acted the same way the blue-eyed students acted the day before, putting the blue-eyed students down, making fun of them, and so on.

Several TV programs and films have been made about the Elliott experiment. She has since taken her demonstration to numerous places around the world. It is so obvious to me that this is what happens in Indian classrooms. Only in that case it is the non-Indian teacher using blatant as well as subtle clues who lets the Indian students know they are second-class citizens.

The people of Riceville took great offense at her appearance on the Johnny Carson show, where she talked about the experiment. Her own children were called names and told their mother was soon going to be sleeping with a nigger. Her twelve-year-old son was beaten up. When Mrs. Elliott called the mother of the ringleader to complain, the mother said Elliott's son had gotten what he deserved.

The Pygmalion effect, documented in a study at Stanford, shows that the expectations (and no doubt actions) of teachers are very important in how students will do. In the Stanford experiment, students were "matched" into two groups. In matching, one student with an IQ of 140 is placed into Group A, and another student with an IQ of 140 is placed into Group B.

The subjects are evenly matched all the way down, fifty-fifty. So any effect, high or low, can be attributed to something outside the group.

The two groups were given to two Stanford teacher interns. One intern was told the students she had were very bright, and would probably knock the roof off with their scores. The other intern was told her students were slow, slightly retarded, and would have to struggle to learn.

The results: as expected the "bright" students overachieved, and the "slow" students underachieved. The conclusion: teacher attitudes and expectations are crucial to what happens to students in the classroom.

The attitude of too many teachers of Indian students is "They are just Indians. They aren't going anywhere except the reservation, so anything we teach them is better than they would have anyway." They seldom say that, but they act it all the time.

Extremely Low Reading

I was fortunate to work as a consultant for the Kayenta Unified School District from 1986 to 1993. During that seven years, the high school improved daily attendance from 82% to 92%, raised ASVAB scores from the bottom quartile to the second quartile, and raised SAT scores for seniors from the ninth grade level to the eleventh grade level.

The results of the SDRT ninth grade reading scores for 1987 at the high school are shown below. This is one of the better schools on the Navajo Reservation; other schools have shown even worse results.

Grade	Number in Grade	Percentage
2	14	9.0
3	17	10.9
4	11	7.1
5	31	19.9
6	16	10.3
7	19	12.2
8	14	9.0
9	10	6.4
10	6	3.8
11+	3	1.9
12+	15	9.6
	TOTAL 156	

Below norm = 122 (78.2%); above norm = 34 (21.8%); median = 6.3; norm = 9.1

These are the numbers of students scoring at the various grade levels when they entered the ninth grade. There were 14 students reading at the second grade level out of 156 students, for instance. There were 122 students below the national norms, or 78.2%. The median score was 6.3, meaning the typical student was 2.8 grade equivalents (GE) below the norm, which is 9.1. You can do the same thing with your scores. Don't let them lie in the vault and collect dust. See where your kids are!

When we checked, it turned out that few of the students were reading anything outside the classroom. Library circulation was very low. Few homes had newspapers and magazine subscriptions. Parents read very little, and students followed their example.

One of the fixes for this problem was to teach the students how to read. I told this to the principal, Bob Roundtree, the first time I met him. The first thing you know, he found the money in Title I funds to put in a whole new reading department. It had five teachers whose only job was to teach students how to read. In the first year, one girl went from third grade level reading ability to tenth grade in one year! Both she and her grandparents, who were raising her, were determined to make sure she succeeded.

The results from Kayenta are shown on the following page. It is proof that you can improve an Indian school—if you want to, if you try, and if you are smart.

STANDARDIZED TEST SCORE GAINS
MONUMENT VALLEY HIGH SCHOOL
1984–1991

Reading	84–85	85–86	86–87	87–88	88–89	89–90	90–91	Total
1	1.7	1.5	1.4	NA	NA	NA	NA	NA
2	2.2	2.2	2.1	2.2	1.9	1.8	1.6	–.6
3	3.2	3.1	3.2	3.2	2.9	3.0	2.9	–.3
4	3.8	3.8	3.9	3.9	3.7	3.7	3.8	–0–
5	4.5	4.8	5.0	4.9	4.9	5.0	4.9	+.4
6	5.5	5.4	5.7	5.6	5.8	5.7	5.7	+.2
7	6.6	6.4	6.3	6.8	6.8	7.0	7.1	+.5
8	7.2	7.2	7.7	7.5	7.4	7.7	7.8	+.6
9	6.0	6.3	6.5	7.1	8.5	8.6	8.1	+2.1
10	6.8	6.6	6.7	8.4	9.0	8.7	8.8	+2.0
11	8.3	7.3	7.5	8.9	9.4	10.0	9.0	+.7
12	8.0	8.0	8.3	9.0	10.2	10.9	10.6	+2.6

Math	84–85	85–86	86–87	87–88	88–89	89–90	90–91	TOTAL
1	1.7	1.8	1.8	1.6	NA	NA	NA	NA
2	2.5	2.6	2.4	2.5	2.5	2.4	2.4	–.1
3	3.7	3.3	3.4	3.4	3.3	3.3	3.3	–.4
4	4.3	4.0	4.1	4.0	3.9	4.0	4.1	–.2
5	5.1	5.0	5.3	5.1	5.1	5.2	5.2	+.1
6	6.1	5.6	6.1	6.1	6.0	6.2	6.02	–.1
7	7.2	7.4	6.9	7.1	6.9	7.0	7.0	–.2
8	8.0	8.2	8.5	8.2	7.9	8.0	7.9	–.1
9	7.9	8.2	8.8	9.1	9.3	9.0	8.9	+1.0
10	8.5	8.6	9.4	9.6	10.5	10.1	9.8	+1.3
11	9.1	9.2	9.9	11.0	11.0	11.3	10.3	+1.2
12	9.3	9.6	10.2	10.8	11.3	11.5	11.0	+1.7

Language	84–85	85–86	86–87	87–88	88–89	89–90	90–91	TOTAL
1	1.9	1.9	1.8	1.6	NA	NA	NA	NA
2	2.6	2.6	2.6	2.9	2.4	2.5	2.4	–.2
3	4.3	4.3	4.1	4.2	3.9	4.1	3.9	–.4
4	4.6	4.6	4.6	4.5	4.2	4.5	4.4	–.2
5	5.2	5.2	5.9	5.6	5.5	5.5	5.4	+.2
6	6.1	6.1	6.5	6.4	6.2	6.1	6.0	–.1
7	6.8	6.8	7.2	7.4	7.2	7.3	7.4	+.6
8	7.7	7.7	8.4	8.3	8.8	8.3	8.5	+.8
9	7.0	7.0	7.8	7.9	8.9	9.0	8.7	+1.7
10	7.6	7.6	7.9	8.5	9.0	9.7	9.0	+1.4
11	8.9	8.9	9.5	9.6	10.6	11.5	10.2	+1.3
12	8.6	8.6	9.2	9.6	10.8	11.5	11.0	+2.4

Why do Indian schools not improve? My guess is, first of all, *inertia.* The school systems have evolved as low-performing low-output institutions from the beginning of the boarding schools in 1878. They are not supposed to produce high performance students. My dissertation on social change in BIA boarding schools bore out the slow rate of change in these schools.

After all, their students are ignorant savages. This kind of rhetoric may seem out of place in the twenty-first century, but one can make a case for it.

Second, there is the problem of *high turnover.* Indian schools have turnover rates of 30% to 50% per year, and 70% turnover is not unheard of. I had one principal call me in 1989 from the Navajo Reservation asking me to help him find some new teachers. He had a 90% turnover that year!

Schools are often forced to take anyone they can for a position. People are often trying to teach subjects they are not qualified to teach, and the schools feel they have to hire them out of desperation.

Add to that *low expectations, low attendance, lecture methods, racist placement, low quality of teachers,* and you have the makings of a disaster. The people who are suffering from this now are Indian students.

The United States needs to change its whole system of educating Indian students. Instead of holding on to a failed system that tried to turn Indians into farmers and blue collar workers, the U.S. government needs to embrace a new system for Indian education:

- Apologize for the horrible and dehumanizing effects of the system that has been in place since 1878.
- Announce a new policy in education similar to the Native American Languages Act (NALA), which reversed a policy of extinguishing Indian languages that had been in place for 125 years.
- Announce a new national policy that calls for a superior, full, and complete education for Indian young people, including preparing them fully for college study.
- Launch a new program of excellence in Indian education, starting with recruiting teachers from the top American colleges instead of hiring anyone available.
- Reward teachers with recognition and honors when they succeed at Indian schools, and announce a new federal policy for Indian schools to keep students in school until they are graduated.
- Call for the teaching of Native languages in reservation schools.
- Establish a Native American Teacher Academy to develop Master Teachers for Indian students.
- Develop a series of Native American Preparatory Schools to prepare Indian students for study at the top U.S. colleges and universities.

TWELVE

Racism in Employment

Many folk think that tribal casinos are making all Indians rich. Nothing could be further from the truth. As Pace documented in 2000, Indians are actually poorer now than they were before casinos. The unemployment rate on reservations with casinos has actually risen in the past decade. As tribal administrator Gary Goforth of Fort Mojave says, "Not everyone wants to be a dealer, or a housekeeper, or even a manager in the restaurant."

Jacob Coin, former director of the National Indian Gaming Association, reported that 75% of the jobs in tribal casinos are filled by non-Indians.

The mistake most observers make is putting all Indians together. They expect the tiny handful of really successful tribal casinos to divide their profits up with all other tribes. The word "Indians" is what misleads them. The Lakota people are as different from the Navajo people as Chinese people are different from Latvians.

It is as if one were asking the citizens of Denmark to support the citizens of Nigeria. They are not closely related to each other, do not understand each other, and have no legal obligation to support each other.

One of my friends, Joe Sando, the eminent Pueblo historian, told me in 1994 that in his years of traveling he had never seen an Indian working in the airport in Albuquerque. The airport employees at that time were either airline employees or employees of the city of Albuquerque.

At the time my friend Martin Chavez had just been installed as mayor. He asked me in January 1994 to put together a Commission on Indian Affairs, which I did. It took six months. His Chief Administrative Officer (CAO), Lawrence Rael, took the position that if the City put a Commission on Indians together, the Asians, the Hispanics, and the Blacks would also want their own commissions. This proved not to be true. Lawrence sat on the bill for several months instead of sending it on to the City Council.

Finally, he relented and sent the bill through to the City Council, which passed it immediately. I chaired the Albuquerque Commission on Indian Affairs (ACIA) for the first two years and served on it for another four years.

When the Commission looked at the employment numbers for Indians, we found a disturbing pattern. The employment rate for Indians was about 65% of parity, but all the Indians were at the bottom of the pay scale. There were no Indians in middle or high level management positions. The highest ranking Indian was the head of the truck maintenance department for the Solid Waste Department, which collects the garbage once a week.

The city had passed a Native American Affirmative Action plan back in the early 1970s, but it had little effect. When the National Indian Youth Council pushed for some changes in the 1980s, some things happened, but it will take a huge effort over a period of decades to make any significant improvement in Indian employment with the city, it seems to me. In the meantime, 40% of the homeless in Albuquerque are Indians, and the unemployment rate for Indians in Bernalillo County runs above 20%.

Unfortunately, unemployment rates are high almost everywhere in Indian Country. The Bureau of Indian Affairs (BIA) started keeping records of unemployment on reservations in 1983, but stopped in 1993. The national unemployment rate for Indian Country is 46%, ranging from a low of 15% for the Muskogee Creek Nation of Oklahoma to a high of 85% at Pine Ridge and Hoopa.

The BIA collected these data for seven biennia, 1983–93. The overall numbers for the biennia were:

Indian Reservation Unemployment

Year	Total Unemployment
1983	51%
1985	49%
1987	48%
1989	44%
1991	48%
1993	46%

They then stopped doing the reports. The data were apparently too embarrassing for the national administrations. When we queried them for the 1995 report, they kept sending us the report for 1993.

The chart above shows the unemployment rates for Indians in the 29 states in the United States with large Indian populations. The overall rate for the United States as of 1993 was 46.4%.

(Keep in mind that these numbers are for Indians living on reservations only. It does not count over 200,000 Indians in California who live in urban areas, for instance. And it does not count the 55% of Indians who now live in urban areas because of lack of employment on reservations. In 2003, the U.S. Department of Commerce reported that the national unemployment rate of Indians was 15%, which is three times the national overall rate of unemployment. Their figures are for reservation and urban Indians both, and it unfortunately includes self-identified Indians, over half of whom are bogus, not really Indians.)

The Indian unemployment rate for Minnesota in 1990 was 29.7%. For Minneapolis it was 27.6%. The overall rate for the huge Navajo Reservation is 40%.

Employment is one of the most important issues in Indian Country. High rates of unemployment are associated with all kinds of social ills. Teenage pregnancy rates, high rates of suicide, drug use, alcohol abuse, domestic violence, high dropout rates from school, and other problems are found in communities with high unemployment rates.

Imagine what would happen anywhere else if the unemployment rate were even 20%. There would be riots, protests, and daily turbulence.

The BIA, which is the leading controller of money, schools, police, lands, minerals, jobs, and everything else on reservations, has been the laughing stock of federal agencies ever since its inception. It is riddled with incompetent people, vengeful people, and political appointees. It has deliberately tried to punish Indians on some reservations, for instance, and has succeeded royally at it.

It has tried to break the back of every tribe in the nation, and has done pretty well at that, too. For instance, at Pine Ridge, almost all the range land is leased out to white ranchers. Most of the leases are long term, some of them as long as 99 years each.

When you visit Rosebud or Pine Ridge, the nice houses all belong to the white ranchers, while Indians live in shacks, broken down cars, and even in dugouts and caves. Indians end up being day laborers on "their" own lands.

On the Fort Hall Reservation in Idaho, the tribal people who came back from World War II got started in cattle ranching. However, the BIA in its wisdom decided that cattle were not productive enough and forced the Indian ranchers out of the business. They then leased these acres to potato growers, all of whom are white.

One of them, J. R. Simplot, is the most successful middleman in the world. He has an exclusive franchise with MacDonald's to provide all the potatoes to all its hamburger joints worldwide. Mr. Simplot is a billionaire many times over. The Indians who are fortunate enough to have jobs often are day laborers on the potato farms on their reservation.

The city of Gallup, New Mexico, discriminated against hiring Indians for decades with no one doing anything about it. The city would "lose" applications from Indians, destroy applications from Indians, pre-select non-Indians without allowing Indians to be interviewed, refuse to consider Indian applicants for jobs, and allow discrimination against Indian employees.

In September 2004, the city agreed to sign a consent decree with the U.S. Department of Justice saying it would eliminate these practices from its employee programs. The decree also stated that the city would provide a fund of $300,000 to give relief to Indians who had been discriminated against. It also had to revise its hiring and recruitment policies to eliminate racial discrimination as a factor in hiring.

For a hundred years, a significant minority of Indians have been sidetracked into being cultural attractions. Included here are Wild West Shows, carnivals, jewelry makers, and bead workers. Hundreds of Indians have also become part of the literati, the visual arts, as studio artists, sculptors, carvers, stoneworkers, and painters. The only problem is that these fields of work have very low income levels.

The unfortunate reality is that making a living as an Indian cultural worker is a dicey proposition. One of my friends showed me how an Indian artist in a place like Gallup could be working for wages below the federal minimum wage. Gallup, which has more millionaires per thousand people than any other place in the world, makes most of its money from Indians and tourists.

The Indian jewelry maker working on a piece rate basis could be making a ring for $20 that would take him half a day to make. When the cost of silver and turquoise is taken out, the maker is getting very little, maybe $3 or $4 an hour. The buyer, a middle man, marks the ring up from $20 to $40, and he makes 100% gross profit when he sells it to the marketer. The marketer then adds another $20 and sells the ring to an unsuspecting buyer for $60. All three—middle man, marketer, and customer—have unknowingly collaborated in helping to keep Indians in poverty. The maker, of course, may have no other alternative and is locked into this lifestyle forever.

Furthermore, one of the leading causes of Indian unemployment is racism. Many employers refuse to hire Indians just because they are Indians, and little has been done about this practice anywhere in the nation. There has been little study of the problem, but many people, including this writer, suspect that Indians are turned down often for employment simply because they are Indian.

The emergence of tribal casinos has brought about a whole new arena of labor problems and labor legislation. Tribes as sovereign entities are not subject to several federal laws, including Title VII of the Civil Rights Act of 1964, Title I of the Americans with Disabilities Act, the National Labor Relations Act, and the Workers Adjustment and Retraining and Notification Act.

Only Congress and an individual tribe can waive sovereign immunity, which upsets the anti-Indian forces and irritates them to no end. Tribes are also not in general subject to state laws on employment, hiring, promotion, and retention of employees.

Racism in employment is one of the leading causes of all the other problems found in Indian Country. When it has been solved, it has transformed many of the other problems and made them go away.

One of the most important places where it has been solved has been in tribal casinos and the tribes that have them and are successful. These include some 30 to 50 tribes, out of 557 in the United States. (The number would depend on where one drew the line defining success, and how problems were defined. For instance, the unemployment rate around Foxwoods Casino, owned by the Mashantucket Pequot Tribal Nation in Connecticut, is well below the national rate, at 2%. Clearly MPTN would be above the line on all charts. But would the 50th most successful tribe, which still has 15% unemployment, be above the line?)

Some of the tribal casinos have become world famous, including the Mississippi Choctaws, the Mashantucket Pequots, the Saginaw Chippewas, the Seminoles of Florida, the Viejas Band of Kumeyaay of California, the Sycuan Tribe of California, and the other very successful tribes in southern California. Almost all these tribes have small numbers of members and are located near a major metropolitan area. Fewer than 5% of Indians are affected by the huge success of the most successful casinos. The great majority of Indians still live in poverty and without adequate employment—despite the false accusation of such ignorant people as Andy Rooney of "60 Minutes."

The rich casino tribes do not include the largest tribes, including the Navajo, the Lakota (also called Sioux), and others that have no casinos, or that have very tiny casinos.

The leading cause of Indian unemployment, however, remains the federal government's paternalistic and destructive policies. The taking of Indian land, leasing Indian land to non-Indians, refusal to grant Indians loans to start businesses, and the huge and tragic failure of education for Indians have allowed these conditions to fester.

In the land of plenty that is the United States, conditions like the ones at Pine Ridge should not exist. It is time for the federal government to stop punishing the Lakota people because they killed Custer in 1876. It is time for an Indian Marshall Aid Plan, which Roger Jourdain called for constantly the last four decades of his life. If the United States can rebuild Europe, which is half a continent, it can certainly rebuild Indian Country with its small communities and little reservations.

Unemployment in Indian Country*

State	Total Indians	Total Labor Force	Number Employed	Percent Unemployed
Alabama	1,488	923	440	48
Alaska	163,877	68,670	31,565	46
Arizona	189,845	96,090	54,482	57
California	49,379	23,031	11,531	50
Colorado	3,579	1,658	563	34
Connecticut	155	74	-0-	-0-
Florida	2,731	1,560	495	32
Idaho	9,933	4,886	3,528	72
Iowa	896	393	39	10
Kansas	1,964	1,081	413	38
Louisiana	994	497	100	20
Maine	3,030	1,284	589	46
Massachusetts	646	425	96	23
Michigan	15,334	7,771	3,152	41
Minnesota	23,505	11,384	5,156	45
Mississippi	5,438	2,977	893	30
Montana	39,814	18,793	9,752	52
Nebraska	7,071	3,876	2,849	74
Nevada	10,071	5,215	2,134	41
New Mexico	150,184	77,218	32,717	42
New York	11,055	4,495	2,094	47
North Carolina	10,114	7,097	2,839	40
North Dakota	23,497	10,107	6,020	60
Oklahoma	272,569	109,115	28,453	26
Oregon	13,595	6,522	2,211	34
Rhode Island	2,058	819	371	45
South Dakota	61,500	31,502	24,355	77
Texas	2,624	1,468	315	21
Utah	11,489	4,965	2,132	43
Washington	61,424	29,820	18,149	61
Wisconsin	26,070	12,574	5,726	46
Wyoming	8,038	3,454	2,234	65
TOTAL	1,183,967	549,744	255,393	46.4%

* "Indian Service Populations and Labor Force Estimates," 1993. U.S. Department of the Interior, Bureau of Indian Affairs.

THIRTEEN

Racism in Medicine

One of our scholarship students was motivated to go to medical school because her auntie died. The auntie was misdiagnosed by an intern doctor at the Indian Health Service clinic at Pine Ridge. By the time they got her to Rapid City, she was in acute pain. She died of pneumonia a few hours later. The young intern, on duty by himself, had simply got it wrong. If the auntie had been diagnosed properly, she would probably still be alive.

The niece was determined before she left high school to go to medical school. After she earned her degree at the University of North Dakota, with help from my good friend Dr. Leigh Jeanotte, she was admitted to Stanford University Medical School. She was graduated four years later and has been an MD for the past ten years. Her name is Sarah Jumping Eagle, MD.

Misdiagnoses are just one of the problems at IHS clinics. The major problem is lack of staff. The typical Indian hospital or clinic has 35% vacancies. In fact, this is not just a onetime or short-term problem. It has plagued the Indian Health Service for decades, without letting up.

The main problem is not misdiagnosis, but waiting. It is not unusual for people to have to wait half a day, or a day, or even two days, to see a doctor or a dentist. People have died without getting to see a doctor. The Indian Health Service ratio of doctors to patients is now about one for every 1,500 people. For the United States as a whole, the ratio is about one for every 500 people.

When Dr. Connie Uri (Choctaw) began her practice, she had no idea she was about to become a lightning rod that would expose decades of unauthorized sterilizations of Indian women. She first learned about it in 1972, when a young woman asked her for a "womb transplant." She and her husband wanted to start a family.

The young Native woman told Dr. Uri that when she was having problems with alcoholism six years earlier, the Indian Health Service doctor had given her a complete hysterectomy. He told her she could have the procedure reversed later. She was completely heartbroken when Dr. Uri told her the procedure was not reversible (Lawrence, 2000).

Dr. Uri broke the story in an article in the Indian newspaper *Akwesasne Notes* in 1974. Soon protesters were picketing the Indian hospital in

Claremore, Oklahoma, where hundreds of Cherokee and Choctaw women had been sterilized.

Native women soon charged that 25% of young Indian women in the 1960s and 1970s had been sterilized. In many if not most cases, the procedure had been done without their consent. Sometimes it had been done at the same time that some other medical procedure was being carried out.

They charged that the doctors had:

- failed to provide them with proper information about the procedure,
- used coercion to get them to sign the consent forms,
- used consent forms improperly,
- failed to wait an appropriate time, usually 72 hours, between the time they signed the consent form and the procedure.

The courts have held that for a doctor to perform an operation without the patient's consent is considered an assault (*Schloendorff v. Society of New York Hospital*, 1914). The U.S. Supreme Court later ruled that sterilization laws were unconstitutional (*Skinner v. Oklahoma,* 1942). In 1973 the Department of Health, Education and Welfare, the home of the Indian Health Service, issued regulations barring sterilization on persons who were mentally incompetent. It stated that competent individuals must grant their informed consent before sterilization operations could be carried out.

But IHS doctors were still carrying out sterilizations without the consent of the patients. Senator James Abourezk of South Dakota was soon deluged with letters stating that the IHS was not following the HEW regulations and was still sterilizing Indian women without their consent. He asked, as chairman of the subcommittee on Indian affairs of the U.S. Senate, for the General Accounting Office (GAO) to conduct an investigation into the allegations.

The GAO found that Indian hospitals in three areas, Aberdeen, Oklahoma City, and Phoenix, had performed 3,406 sterilizations during the fiscal years from 1973 to 1976. They found that Indian women under the age of 21 were being sterilized, which was in defiance of the HEW regulations. They also found that the doctors were not following the regulations correctly.

The main reasons doctors gave for performing the sterilization operations were for economic and social reasons. At the same time they were performing high numbers of the operations on Indian women, they were also performing them on African American and Hispanic women.

Most of the doctors were white males who believed they were performing a public service by helping minority women limit the size of their families. The physicians had also increased their personal income by doing the procedure. They did not believe minority women were intelligent enough to use other methods of birth control.

Dr. Uri did her own research and found that Indian Health had sterilized between 25% and 50% of Indian women between 1970 and 1976. A Cheyenne judge found that 52% of the women she questioned had been sterilized. A Northern Cheyenne woman found 34% of women on that reservation had been sterilized (Lawrence).

DeFine reported that the rates of sterilization for women varied with ethnic group:

- Anglo, 15%
- African-American, 24%
- Puerto Rican, 35%
- Native American, 42%.

AIM and other organizations charged that the Indian Health Service was engaged in nothing less than genocide. They charged that huge rates of sterilization led to divorce, disruption of family life, turmoil within communities, alcoholism, shame, guilt, and psychological problems (Lawrence).

After years of meetings, charges, countercharges, and studies, the passing of the Indian Health Care Improvement Act in 1976 put the tribes in charge of health facilities. The rate of sterilization has supposedly decreased, but there is still the possibility that it goes on. The high rates in the 1950s, 1960s and 1970s are still causing psychological and mental health problems in Indian communities.

Despite the high rates of sickness and death on Indian reservations, the Indian Health Service is plagued with high vacancy rates in all its professional positions. The data as of January 2008 show these rates of vacancy:

IHS VACANCY RATES

POSITION	TOTAL	VACANCY RATE	TOTAL VACANCIES
Physician	900	10%	90
Nurse	3,400	18	612
Optometry	200	13	22
Pharmacist	500	11	65
Dentist	300	31	131
Medical imaging	200	24	48

The greatest killer of Indians now is not alcohol, automobile accidents, or gunshot wounds. It is Type II diabetes. I got a call five years ago from the son of one of my friends. The friend and I met in the early 1970s in California. I was a faculty member at Cal State Hayward and he was at Long Beach. We kept in touch all through the years, even after he moved back home to Oklahoma. We did some important work together.

"Dad just passed away," his son told me. "They were operating to amputate his other leg, and he didn't make it through the operation."

"The doctors had removed one leg at the knee when he first got so bad off," he went on. "But they had to amputate the other leg when it got so bad."

As King explains, this condition was unknown in Indian Country in 1940. It first appeared in 1950, and today affects between 30% and 50% of adults in almost all tribes. It is apparently true that obesity and total body weight are closely associated with the disease and that so many of the commodity foods given out on poverty level reservations are high in fat and carbohydrates.

Frybread, one of the most popular foods in Indian Country, may be the most important cause of Type II diabetes. Super sweet soda pop and other foods high in sugar may be highly important causes. However, the vacancy rates for Indian health professionals mean that Indians will never get the medical care they need.

Mental health providers are also in short supply, despite the common occurrence of mental health issues on reservations. I have not been able to establish baseline data for either providers or the seriousness of the problem. Health and social welfare experts in Indian Country have stated for decades that mental health is an issue that is almost being totally ignored in Indian Country.

Alcoholism is a common problem among poor reservation Indians. It is more serious than health authorities, tribal administrations, and county officials will admit. In one case, when I wrote an internal memo after interviewing a math teacher at Zuni Pueblo, the superintendent, who was a member of the pueblo, called me in and fired me. I was a consultant doing the evaluation of their Indian Education Act program.

The young teacher, who was from New York, had told me that 80% of his students were affected by alcoholism. They got themselves up in the morning, made their own breakfast, and got to school on their own. Their parents were often still in bed with a hangover. Even though the memo would only be seen by the administration, the superintendent engaged in a cover up. The tribal administration and the school administration were in denial about the seriousness of the alcoholism problem on the reservation.

Infant deaths on reservations are several times the national rate. The incidence of Sudden Infant Death Syndrome (SIDS) is higher than for any other ethnic group.

The government needs to act to lessen the effects of bad health in Indian Country. Among other things, it needs to:

- Reinstate the loan forgiveness provisions that were removed several years ago for health professionals. Under these provisions, physicians could work on an Indian reservation and remove all or part of the loans for medical school they had taken from the federal government.
- Make it illegal for physicians to sterilize Indian women without their consent.
- Step up the treatment and prevention of Type II diabetes on reservations.
- Research the status of mental health professionals on reservations, with the idea of making sure there are adequate numbers.
- Increase the amount of funding for the Indian Health Service scholarship program that funds the health professions.

FOURTEEN

Racism in Law Enforcement

Indians for a long time were not considered to be human beings. Spanish, French, Italian, and English courts, kings, religious leaders, and proclamations declared that Indians were subhuman. The U.S. Constitution defined Indians as less than human.

Finally, in *Standing Bear v. Crook,* the courts decided in 1879 that Indians were really people after all. Judge Elmer S. Dundy ruled that "an Indian is a person" for purposes of acting on a writ of habeas corpus. General Crook had arrested a group of Ponca Indians who had "escaped" from Oklahoma to Nebraska to bury the son of Chief Standing Bear. They were released immediately.

Violence has become a way of life in Indian Country on a number of fronts. Police violate the rights of Indians, including Indian school children, with impunity. They know they will not be found culpable in an investigation of their actions, so they have no problems beating Indians with night sticks, putting them in handcuffs, and throwing them into the back of squad cars and taking them to jail.

It was a reaction to such police tactics that spawned the American Indian Movement (AIM). They began by escorting Indian men home from bars on the weekend instead of letting the cops arrest them and take them to jail. Cops in St. Paul were sometimes heavy-handed, and cracked a few Indian heads over the years.

Indians are the victims of violence at a much higher rate than they are the perpetrators of violence. Some 70% of violent crimes involving Indian victims are the result of a non-Indian engaging in a crime against an Indian person. These crimes include robbery, assault, rape, and murder.

Indians are 0.8% of the population, but have 4% of the prison inmates—500% higher than the population percentage, or 62,000 inmates in the U.S. The rates of incarceration of Indians at the local level is the highest of all ethnic groups.

Rates of Incarceration (Per hundred thousand)

	Native American	African American	White	Hispanic American	Asian American
Federal	46	39	11	51	6
State	242	716	109	230	40

Cops and corrections people in South Dakota are noted for being some of the worst in the nation. Racial profiling, harassment of people, and physical altercations have been some of the leading causes of tension between Indians and whites in the state since 1880.

Greenfeld and Smith summarize the condition of Indian involvement in violence in three short statements:

- "The rate of violent victimization estimated from responses by American Indians is well above that of other U.S. racial or ethnic subgroups and is more than twice as high as the national average."
- "American Indians are more likely than people of other races to experience violence at the hands of someone of a different race, and the criminal victimizer is more likely to have consumed alcohol preceding the offense."
- "On a given day, an estimated 1 in 25 American Indians age 18 or older is under the jurisdiction of the criminal justice system—2.4 times the per capita rate of whites and 9.3 times the per capita rate of Asians."

They go on to say that "At least 70% of the violent victimizations experienced by American Indians are committed by persons not of the same race ..." They added that "The 1997 arrest rate for American Indians for alcohol-related offenses (driving under the influence, liquor law violations, and public drunkenness) was more than double that found among all races." Chadwick, Day, and Bahr reported 35 years ago that 80% of all Indian males have been arrested at some time in their lives, usually on an alcohol-related offense.

For his trouble in compiling and writing the report, the Bush administration fired Greenfeld after he had 23 years of federal experience. They obviously did not want this type of information out.

Indians call it DWI—Driving While Indian. If you have a nice car, or are playing music too loud, or wearing the wrong clothes, or have on shades, you can be pulled over. If your hair is too long, or if your hair is braided, you can be pulled over. If your windows are tinted, you can be pulled over. If you have feathers or religious objects hanging from your rear-view mirror, you can be pulled over. If you have tribal license plates on your car (a few tribes issue their own license plates), you can be pulled over.

The problem got so bad in that state that the South Dakota state legislature held hearings on racial profiling five years ago. The Indians who testified said the police stopped them for having religious artifacts hanging from their mirrors, for having license plates that identified them as living on a reservation, and just for having a suspicion that something was wrong. Other people got stopped for having a medicine wheel decal on their car, clearly identifying themselves as Indians.

Bennett County was identified as being one of the worst places. Police and sheriff's deputies there stopped Indians and gave them breathalyzer tests without warrant, they alleged. They searched vehicles and homes without having search warrants. They demanded to see driver's licenses and automobile registrations while people were in bars.

Starting in 1940, the percentage of Indians in prison in South Dakota began to increase. In 1890 it was a total of 79 whites and five half-breed Indians. In 1940 the prison total was 505, including 439 whites and 63 Indians (12.7%). By 1950 the percentage of Indians had increased to 23.2%, or 127 inmates out of 547 prisoners. By 1968 the total was 225 Indians out of a total prison population of 608, or 37%. On average, Indians served 619 days in prison, compared to 565 days for whites (Braustein).

A study by the Council on Crime and Justice and the Institute on Race and Poverty at the University of Minnesota found that Indians in the Bemidji area were stopped by police at a rate three times higher than non-Indians. Bemidji is just outside the huge Red Lake Chippewa Reservation and is the home of one of the large state universities.

Bemidji Police Chief Bruce Preece denies any racial profiling, and says the study was flawed. The state legislature authorized the study and paid for it. Myron Orfield, director of the institute, says the study by the university was no more flawed than similar studies.

Indian prisoners are often not allowed to wear their hair long or to have traditional religious ceremonies inside prisons. They are often denied legal representation. Their sentences are longer than for whites, typically 200% to 300% longer. Indians are denied parole at a rate more than double that for whites.

Between 1838 and 1840 the legislature of North Carolina passed a series of laws forbidding Indians and "free persons of color" from owning firearms, serving on juries, the right to vote in government elections, the right to serve in a militia, and other rights. This part of the "Black Codes" was in effect until after the end of the Civil War.

The end of the war saw a wave of "carpetbaggers" and "scalawags" take over state and local government in the South for a decade and a half. This was followed by a period of oppression even more severe than had been the case before the Civil War—after the President and the Congress agreed to remove the army of occupation from the South. The "Black

Codes" applied to free Negroes and the few Indians still living in the South—the Mississippi Choctaws, the Cherokees of North Carolina, the Poarch Creek Band of Creeks in Alabama, the Lumbees of North Carolina, the Seminoles and Miccosukees in Florida, and the four tribes in Virginia.

Joe Sando, the eminent Pueblo historian, has lived in Albuquerque for decades, but his son has trouble visiting him. It seems that Joe lives in a white part of town. Everybody has seen him coming and going for decades, and he has no problems. He usually dresses in suits or in blazers or sports coats. Joe could pass for Hispanic, which in New Mexico is almost all right; 39% of the population is Hispanic.

However, when his son comes to visit, he is often stopped by police and questioned. He is doing nothing more than being in the wrong part of town. The police will pull him over, question him, and refuse to believe that he is in that part of town to visit his parents.

Rosalie Little Thunder lives in Rapid City, South Dakota, and suffers from racial profiling. Her biggest complaint, though, is not the profiling itself. "We have heard different people sitting up there saying there is no discrimination, there is no racism," she said in an interview with STAR. "I've seen that to extremes here. And when we deny it, we don't recognize it. We don't recognize it, we don't deal with it."

In Rapid City even Indian policemen get pulled over—if they are driving civilian cars and wearing civilian clothes. Brad Petersen, an attorney for Dakota Plains Legal Services, told a hearing in Rapid City that Indian drivers are pulled over for such minor things as having an air freshener hanging from rearview mirrors and having bent license plates. "I find it had to believe that investigation of these types of charges would show many non-Indian people being arrested on these types of charges."

There are no Indian police officers in Rapid City, Petersen alleged. Sheriff Russell Waterbury of Bennett County is alleged to have said, "If I see a carload of Indians, I'm gonna stop 'em." Thomas Hennies has been on the Rapid City police force for 35 years, the last 16 as chief. He told a hearing, "I personally know that there is racism and there is discrimination and there are prejudices among all people [and] that they're apparent in law enforcement."

Other places in South Dakota alleged to have racial profiling of Indians as a regular feature of their law enforcement include Sioux Falls, Bennett County, Mobridge, and Martin. A bill to require police to keep racial data on traffic stops was defeated in the state legislature in 2001. The reason: opponents alleged it would cost hundreds of thousand of dollars.

In 2001, Governor William "Wild Bill" Janklow (see his anti-Indian record in the chapter on politics and voting) asked the University of South Dakota to research alleged disparities against Indians in the criminal justice system. The report stated that:

- Indians made up 8.3% of the population and 16.7% of the criminal justice dataset.
- Indians were over-represented in being denied bond compared to whites.
- Indians went from arrest to trial in 229 days, while whites took 266 days, since they fought the system harder.
- Indians are more likely to be convicted at trial than whites.
- Indians were more likely to have court-appointed attorneys (public defenders) than whites.
- Indians were more likely to be convicted of violent crimes than whites.

Janklow condemned his own report after it came out. He obviously thought that it would show no difference between whites and Indians in the state. He later also condemned a hearing and a report issued by the U.S. Civil Rights Commission, calling them a bunch of troublemakers.

There are nine reservations in South Dakota, all of them part of the Great Sioux Nation. The Sioux people are made up of three closely related language groups, the Dakota, the Lakota, and the Nakota. In many ways, the people on these reservations are still prisoners of war from the battle in which they defeated George Custer in 1876. Out of the ten poorest counties in the United States, five are on South Dakota reservations.

Minneapolis, which spawned the American Indian Movement (AIM) in 1967, has seen its share of police profiling and brutality. One case involved two policemen who threw two drunken Indians into the trunk of their Ford Crown Victoria instead of in the backseat.

Specktor reports that Charles Lone Eagle (Lakota), a Viet Nam veteran, and his friend John Boney had passed out in the hallway of an apartment building on April 17, 1993. The two policemen who were called to the scene, Marvin Shumer and Michael Lardy, allegedly hit Lone Eagle in the chest with a nightstick. They then threw the two men into the trunk of the car and carried them to the Hennepin County Medical Center.

Carol Halley, a nurse, made a complaint to the police department after she saw the police taking the men out of the trunk. Both policemen were suspended without pay by the police chief, John Laux, but were not fired, and the county attorney refused to bring criminal charges against them.

Recently, some tribes have reverted to the traditional practice of banishing people as a deterrent when all else fails. Prior to European contact, banishment was the ultimate punishment of many Indian tribes. In some cases, banishment meant death to the person banished, since it is so difficult for one person to live alone in the world.

The Native village of Tyonek expelled two white families in 1982 for failing to follow the rules of the village. Banishment as practiced in recent times has meant forcing non-tribal members to leave a Native village or reservation. It also has meant forcing tribal members to leave when they would not follow the rules of the Native people. Bootlegging, drug smuggling, domestic violence, and public drunkenness have been causes of people being banished in the past 20 years.

The Alaskan native village of Kipnuk in 1997 banished a white man, Jimmy Boan, who was living with his Eskimo girlfriend in the village. Boan had refused to let the village elders inspect his luggage when he came in. They also said he pointed guns at people, smuggled drugs into the village against their rules, and would not follow the rules in the Inuit (Eskimo) village on the Bering Sea on the northwest coast of Alaska.

So far, no state has made a statement that racial profiling of Indians is occurring. Only South Dakota has done a study to determine if Indians are treated any differently by law enforcement. (It may have been authorized because it was anticipated that the study would show no differences in treatment between Indians and whites.)

Indians who are eligible to serve on grand juries and petit juries often find themselves stricken from the jury list, especially when the defendant is an Indian. The practice is so common that few Indians actually serve on juries anywhere. In the case of Jay Spotted Elk (see "Racism and Alcohol"), the coroner's jury was made up of two local businessmen and the rest were policemen!

STAR cites the case of Keith Wright of Rosebud, South Dakota, to make these points, most of which come out of the South Dakota Advisory Committee to the U.S. Commission on Civil Rights:

- Indians do not commit more crimes that whites.
- Indians are charged with fewer violent crimes than whites.
- An Indian charged with a crime is looked at as guilty of the crime, despite evidence to the contrary.
- Indians are more likely than whites to be represented by a public defender.
- Public defenders assigned to Indian cases are likely not to develop a case for the defense, but to tell Indians they should plead guilty.
- "Whites are more likely to get acquitted and to receive a suspended sentence than were American Indians."

- Indians are less likely than whites to get a jury trial, and more likely to be offered a deal, which often is a long prison sentence.

Wright got a life sentence in June 2007 for sexual abuse of several foster children who lived in his mother's house. He brought the life sentence on himself after he wrote his mother a letter following his conviction. In the letter he threatened to retaliate against the victims.

Indians in the courts get perhaps the rawest deal of any other aspect of their lives. While Indians are harassed in the schools, in the streets, in stores, in restaurants, and even in churches, it is only the courts that can take away a person's freedom.

The states need to research whether racial profiling happens to Indians in their boundaries. If it occurs, they then need to determine the levels at which it occurs, in what types of situations, and who is doing the profiling. Furthermore, it needs to determine if the profiling is illegal and unconstitutional. To the extent that it is, the law codes need to be amended to remove the illegal portions.

- States need to research the arrest rates of citizens by ethnic group.
- States need to pass laws forbidding racial profiling, and defining it in plain language.
- States need to develop codes of infraction for officers who violate racial profiling laws.
- Judges, policemen, parole officers, attorneys, prosecutors, and public defenders need corrective training to remove racial profiling against Indians.

FIFTEEN

Racism in Sexual Abuse

Amnesty International reported in its study of sexual abuse among American Indians that the following was a typical case:

> In July 1996 an Alaskan Native woman in Fairbanks reported to the police that she had been raped by a non-Native man. She gave a description of the alleged perpetrator and city police officers told her they were going to look for him. She waited for the police to return and when they failed to do so, she went to the emergency room for treatment.
>
> A support worker told Amnesty International that the woman had bruises all over her body and that she was so traumatized that she was talking very quickly. She said that, although the woman was not drunk, the Sexual Assault Response Team nevertheless "treated her like a drunk Native woman first and a rape victim second."
>
> The support worker described how the woman was given some painkillers and some money to go to a non-Native shelter, which turned her away because they also assumed she was drunk. "This is why Native women don't report. It's creating a breeding ground for sexual predators."

American Indian women are two times more likely to be sexually abused and raped than other women. This has been reported to range from 12% of Indian women to as high as 49%. The overall rate of sexual violence against Indian women is reported to be 350% higher than the rate for the rest of the population. Most of the time, the women are young. About a third of them are between the ages of 18 and 24. A high percentage of Indian females report being assaulted before they turn 18.

At least 86% of the cases of rape against Indian women involve a male from another race. This finding contrasts with the situation for white women, where white men are the perpetrators in 65% of the cases. For Black women, the perpetrators are Black men in 90% of the cases. These data seem to say that white men target Indian women for sexual attack.

The usual ways of reporting data include domestic violence, domestic sexual abuse, stranger sexual abuse, and rape. Rape may be committed by a person known to the woman or by a stranger. One of the conditions that frequently goes along with rape and sexual abuse is drinking. An Indian woman who has been drinking is more likely to be classified as a drunk than a rape victim, and be treated accordingly.

One out of ten Indian women report they have been stalked at some time in their lives. The rate of stalking in Indian Country is much higher than it is in the rest of the nation.

A lot of people in authority look the other way. A check of the Indian Health Service Web site finds no listing for domestic violence, for rape, and for sexual abuse. McEachern says that Indian women with a history of domestic violence often "provoke rape and battery in order to satisfy [their] needs ...." McEachern is an IHS physician; her remarks were in a government-sponsored journal. Her remarks and her conclusions are outrageous. Most experts on sexual abuse, of course, do not blame the victim but the perpetrator.

For a variety of reasons, most of the instances of rape and sexual abuse do not get reported. Research shows that at least 70% of rape cases are never reported by the victim. The women report that staff persons of domestic abuse shelters do not understand them, use confusing terminology, and use racist and stereotypical epithets.

In many cases, there is confusion about which police department or court has jurisdiction of a particular Indian tribe, reservation, or community. Indian women are thus not sure they will be able to bring a perpetrator to justice.

Many Indian cultures have rules that discourage the disclosure of intimate sexual relations, of whatever type. Thus, partners and acquaintances take advantage of this knowledge to victimize, knowing that the woman will probably not report the incident.

The close knit nature of small rural Indian communities, where everyone knows everyone else, is a barrier to reporting; the women often do not want other people to know about the rape and its demoralizing effects.

Women fear that the attacker may bring retaliation on her if he is not convicted and put in prison. Many Indian women fear and don't trust any federal authorities, including medical staff at hospitals, police, prosecutors, and attorneys.

The lack of staffing at Indian Health Service hospitals is a barrier to reporting. Many of these facilities do not have adequate facilities to deal with sexual abuse. The high rate of vacancies for doctors, nurses, psychotherapists, and mental health workers is a strong barrier. People have been known to have to wait for up to two days to be seen at an Indian hospital! Most of the cases of sexual assault occur close to home, usually on a reservation.

As a result of sexual abuse, Indian women are especially susceptible to sexually transmitted diseases (STDs). Chlamydia, syphilis, gonorrhea, and HIV/AIDS are running rampant in some Indian communities. They are a problem in almost all Indian communities.

The Southwest Center for Law and Policy in Tucson reports that one of the newest trends to emerge in Indian Country is prosecution of Indian women who are victims of abuse themselves! If they allow their children to be abused, even if the women themselves are abused, they can be prosecuted for failure to protect their children. The law now expects them to leave an abusive relationship, and may hold them accountable if they stay in the relationship!

An abused woman whose child is killed by a spouse can also be prosecuted for murder. Isn't this a fine mess they have gotten us in? Despite the seeming unfairness of this type of prosecution, the reality is that Indian women are being held accountable for domestic abuse, sexual abuse, and other crimes that involve their children.

- Tribes need to take positive actions to protect their female members from sexual abuse and assault. They need to put education programs in place to let women know they should report abuse.
- And they should have safe places for women to go when they need to get out of an abusive relationship.
- Tribes also need to be strong advocates for Indian women who have been attacked. Often these women have to face cold-hearted police, uncaring prosecutors, social workers with heavy loads, and hospital staff who are overworked and overloaded with patients.
- A woman with a rape case takes a back seat to a shooting or stabbing victim. The obvious answer is to have all medical staff positions filled at Indian Health Service hospitals, to have adequate numbers of attorneys in the office of prosecutors, and to have all social worker positions filled.
- The federal government, especially Justice and Indian Health, need to sponsor some research on the rate of all types of sexual abuse in Indian Country. The research needs to focus on the types of abuse, the rates of reporting and non-reporting, and the types of treatment or lack of treatment that victims receive.

SIXTEEN

Racism in Housing

Most people in the United States first became aware of the shameful conditions of Indian housing in the 1960s. Several exposes showed Indians living in abandoned cars, broken down trailers, and even caves. However, it was not until the 1970s that the U.S. Department of Housing and Urban Development (HUD) got around to building houses on Indian reservations. Indians were still living in their traditional homes, such as chickees in the Everglades and roundhouses made of mesquite and willow for the Pimas of Arizona. The Pueblos still lived in their traditional stone buildings. The Navajos still lived in their traditional hogans.

HUD understood very little about Indian concepts of houses. They proceeded to build a one-size-fits-all type of cheap house all over Indian Country. The houses were better than nothing, but not by much. The ceilings were cheap. The doors didn't close right. The floors split and buckled. Indians moved into them, but took little pride in them. They quickly became ghettos.

They upset the balance of power in many Indian and nearby communities. In Elko, Nevada, the city council recently allowed a wall to be built between the Indian HUD homes on the Elko Indian Colony and the exclusive area next door, Ruby View Subdivision. The latter is filled with local business and government executives, while the former is filled with local, mostly poor, Indians.

While the council did not pay for the cyclone fencing that keeps the Indians from driving onto the street where their well-off non-Indian neighbors live, they paid for the labor and some other materials. Their rationale: Indian dogs were coming into the Ruby View area.

When my wife, Toni, and I moved with our three daughters to Albuquerque in 1985, I found on the first day a beautiful home to rent. It was brick, and had very thick walls, which I like. I went back to the motel and told Toni and our neighbor from Oklahoma, Dick Woodby, that we would rent the house the next morning. Dick had graciously driven the rental truck with all our worldly goods while I drove the car.

However, when Toni and I went back the next morning, the owner met us, took one look at Toni, and said he had already rented the house. Toni is Chicana, and looks more Indian than I do. We went farther north and found another house in a couple of days. Even so, I have thought longingly of that house ever since, and regretted that the little white man who owned it would lie like that.

A study by the U.S. Department of Housing and Urban Development (HUD) found that Indians were the most popular group to discriminate against by housing landlords. Indians got turned down 28.5% of the time, compared to 25.7% for Hispanics and 21.6% for African Americans. Asians came in fourth at 21.5% (Melmer).

HUD conducted the study in New Mexico, Minnesota, and Montana in 2003. Non-Indians were sent in to inquire about apartments for rent, and had few problems finding vacancies. However, when Indian women came to the same apartment later to inquire about renting it, they would be told there was nothing available, or that the apartment had been rented already. In some cases, the rental cost went way up for Indians—if they were lucky enough to be able to rent an apartment at all.

In most western cities, Indians coming from reservations under the Relocation program in the 1950s and 1960s ended up in Indian ghettos. San Francisco, Oakland, San Jose, Los Angeles, Denver, Phoenix, Dallas, and Seattle all ended up with their Indian ghettos. In San Francisco it was the Mission District, specifically the area around 16th and Mission, where the Indian Center was located. In Oakland, it was the east side of town just past Lake Merritt. In Los Angeles, it was downtown near where the Indian Center was located.

Trying to find a place to live outside the Indian ghetto was not impossible, but it was difficult. Indian people who came to San Francisco typically found a family member or a school mate to live with at first. Then when they got a job and got settled, they would move out to a place of their own, something they could share with one or two others and be able to afford. The ones who could not find a job, or who could not fit in socially, in many cases ended up moving back home. Over two-thirds of the Indians relocated to the cities went back home. Russell Means, one of the most famous people who relocated, went on the Relocation program four times—to Oakland, San Francisco, and Los Angeles.

Years after the Roosevelt administration started building public housing in the large cities, the Johnson administration got around to providing HUD housing on Indian reservations. Before this happened in the 1960s, Indians were living in old cars, in unheated homes, and even in caves on reservations such as Pine Ridge.

The HUD housing has never been adequate. The major consequence of a shortage of Indian housing is overcrowding. Indian young people get married and start families, but are still living at home with their parents. It is not uncommon for Indian couples past the age of 30 still to be living with one of their parents. Today, the condition of Indian housing is much worse than the condition of housing for the rest of the United States.

Parents are living in homes with two or three grown children, several grandchildren, and possibly some cousins, nieces, and nephews. Many Indian homes on reservations are still without the basic amenities. They do not have electricity, telephones, running water, paved roads, central heating, and hot water.

Buying or building your own home is still a major problem for Indians. Banks routinely turn Indian loan applicants down. So one of the most frequent places Indians can get loans is "non-bank" lending institutions. These institutions often charge two or three times the going interest rate on loans to Indians. The poorest people pay the highest prices for housing loans.

Loza reported in 1996 that 73% of applications for housing loans in Shannon County, South Dakota, on the Pine Ridge reservation were rejected. Of the loans made, some 78% were sub-prime loans made at onerous rates. "Prime" loans would have been made at the going interest rate of 7% to 9%. Indians ended up paying as high as 25% interest for housing loans. Many of them were at rates so high that the borrowers were likely to lose their homes.

The housing of choice on the reservation is mobile homes. They are relatively cheap, easy to transport and set up, but end up costing the Indians two or three times what they would cost someone else.

"Predatory lending is alive and well in Indian Country," housing expert Jane DeMarines told an Indian housing meeting in Las Vegas in 2002. Over 65% of Indian respondents stated they had to pay exorbitant rates to get housing loans, some as high as 25%, she reported.

Craig Nolte, who worked for the Federal Reserve Bank in San Francisco, told the same meeting that predatory lenders can be identified by some warning signs. They include:

- Lenders who target vulnerable homeowners who have a lot of equity in their homes but little income.
- Loans based on the amount of equity in the home, rather than the ability to repay.
- "Packing": adding costly and unnecessary items in the loan package, such as single-premium homeowners insurance.
- "Stacking": high origination fees added to the mortgage note.
- "Flipping": refinancing a home several times in a short time span to build origination fees, thereby stripping the homeowner's equity.

- A "balloon" feature that requires a homeowner to refinance several times, instead of at the end of the customary 30 years.
- Excessive penalties for prepayments.

The National American Indian Housing Council (NAIHC) reported in 2003 that 70% of the respondents to a survey it had taken said that predatory lending was either a big problem or somewhat of a problem on Indian reservations. Over 35% of the respondents stated they knew someone who had been foreclosed on. They overwhelmingly said that racial discrimination played a major part in mortgage lending on Indian reservations.

The conclusion was that mortgage lenders were taking advantage of Indians. More than half the respondents stated they had been the recipient of a "high cost" mortgage or knew someone who had been, according to *Indian Country Today.*

The average loan rate reported was 15.3%. The highest loan rate reported was 30%, while the national average was 5.21%, according to Freddie Mac, the federal mortgage agency. In New Mexico, 63.8% of Indians, but only 9.6% of whites, got high-cost housing loans. In South Dakota, 34.8% of Indians got the highest loan rate, three times the number of whites in the state.

Indians got rejected for home loans 33% of the time in North Dakota in the Fargo-Moorhead area. This rate was the highest for any ethnic group.

Because of poverty and redlining, Indians live in some of the worst housing in the United States. The National American Indian Housing Council (NAIHC) reported that 32.5% of Indian housing is overcrowded, compared to 4.9% for the rest of the United States. Young Indian people get married, have two or three kids, and are still living at home with mom and dad. Finally, when they are 30 or 40 years old, they are able to get a place of their own. That will probably be a single-wide or double-wide trailer.

The alternative is for Indian young people to leave the reservations and disappear into a city or suburb somewhere. When that happens, the grand plan, originally called "Grant's Peace Policy," is the winner. When all Indians disappear, there will be no more "Indian problem." The only problem with that thinking is that the Indian population is now growing rapidly, and will not go away.

There is a huge need for Indians to have adequate housing. The present barriers of predatory lending and redlining need to be dealt with through state and tribal legislation.

- Tribes and states need to have ways to monitor the predatory lending practices of banks and non-bank lending institutions.

- Tribes and states need to set limits on the interest rates and all accompanying costs of home loans, applicable to all citizens, and with stiff penalties for violations of the law.
- States and tribes need to outlaw stacking, flipping, packing, and ballooning.
- States and tribes need to require potential home buyers to become educated about home buying, which the proposed rule from USDA in March 2006 would do, if passed.
- Builders need to be educated in the culture of the Indian people. The current practice of building "cracker box" houses needs to stop. Houses need to reflect the culture of the Indian people, which is different for every tribe.

SEVENTEEN

Racism in Child Stealing

William Byler (1974) found that 25% of Indian children were adopted by non-Indian parents. Since he was head of the Association on American Indian Affairs (AAIA), a long-standing Indian advocacy organization, his testimony before Congress led directly to the passing of the Indian Child Welfare Act (ICWA) in 1978. Its avowed purpose was to preserve and strengthen Indian families and Indian culture.

Like the American Indian Religious Freedom Act (AIRFA) and the Native American Languages Act (NALA), it was intended to reverse a U.S. policy of long-standing, and right a series of wrongs that the United States had sanctioned, promoted, and condoned since 1867.

I was working at one of the schools on the Navajo Reservation 25 years ago when I saw several Greyhound buses driving around the reservation. They were the buses the Mormons sent from Utah each fall to collect Navajo children to take back to Utah. Some of these "placements" were voluntary, forced upon a family by the circumstances of poverty. But some involved coercion and arm twisting.

For years the Mormons have taken Navajo children away from Arizona to educate them in Utah. A few of these children have done really well. One of them became a high official in the Mormon Church but was later excommunicated from the church when he spoke up for Indian rights. However, many of these children have suffered from an identity crisis throughout their entire lives.

Many well-known Indians were adopted. Buffy Sainte-Marie is a Cree from Canada who was adopted by a white family in Massachusetts. Former Senator Ben Nighthorse Campbell of Colorado was placed in a foster home for part of his childhood. Olympic gold medal winner Billy Mills lost both his parents by the time he was 12, and spent part of his teenage years in a foster home before enrolling at Haskell Indian School and later at the University of Kansas, where he earned his degree.

These three did really well. Buffy earned her Ph.D., Ben earned a master's degree, and Billy earned his B.A. degree and is a very successful insurance executive.

The intent of BIA and state social workers before 1978 was to destroy the Indian family by any means they could. Social workers, judges, attorneys, and teachers all thought of the Indian family as a bad thing. Indian children raised by Indian parents were likely to go "back to the blanket," even if they got an education in white schools and were forbidden to speak their languages.

Indian parents for decades were forbidden to visit the schools their children attended, which by design were often several states away. The best way to get rid of Indians was to make white people out of them. The parents were thought to be hopeless cases, but the minds of young Indian children could be formed within the context of European and English culture and thus saved from a fate worse than death—living as an Indian.

In the period before 1978, Indian families were broken up at the whim of BIA social workers, law enforcement officials, and courts. The preference for foster care or adoption for Indian children was for them to be placed with white families. If a social worker visited an Indian home and found the mother or the father drunk, there was a real danger of their children being taken away and placed into foster homes or adopted by another family. If there were flies in the house, or if the parents were not home, the social workers could take the children away.

In some cases, the parents never saw their children again. Extreme poverty, poor health conditions, environmental contamination, dirty living conditions, sickness, and disease were all conditions that led to the breakup of Indian homes. Only one percent of Indian children were removed from their homes because of physical abuse; the other 99% were removed for "social deprivation," for "neglect," and for "emotional damage" (see Richland).

Stories abound in Indian Country of families being broken up for much less valid reasons. Seeing dirty kids, or kids with raggedy clothing, was enough to launch the social workers/God's workers on a path of saving Indian children. They were to be saved by placing them with a family outside the tribe, someone with the ability to raise the children "properly."

In Minnesota in 1971 and 1972, one out of seven Indian children was in some kind of placement. The total was 1,413 children. Non-Indian homes had gotten 91% of the adoptions. During the same period, in North Dakota, South Dakota, and Nebraska, one out of nine Indian kids was in a foster home, adoptive home, an institution, or a boarding facility.

The consequences of "trans-racial placement" were sometimes debilitating. The children had psychological problems. They were confused about their identity. They had low self-esteem. In extreme cases they turned to drugs and alcohol. In very extreme cases they attempted suicide, and were sometimes successful.

Adopted Indian children grew up with little or no knowledge of their families. They could not speak their Native language, so if they tried to go back to find their families years later, they would often not be successful. One Navajo woman of my acquaintance lost her mother at the age of two. Her family had been reduced to poverty by the circumstances. When her father became incapacitated when she was seven, she was adopted by a white missionary from Georgia.

She moved with her adopted mother from New Mexico to Georgia and was raised there. She later got married and had four children. Then they moved back to New Mexico. In her middle years she decided to try to find her Navajo family. It only took a few months, and she looked forward with great anticipation to the "reunion."

However, her Navajo family—aunts, uncles, cousins—did not want to have anything to do with her. Her Anglo husband was not welcome at any of their homes; her half-Anglo kids were not welcome either. She now has almost nothing to do with her Navajo family, and she is very unhappy about the situation.

Another young lady I knew who had been raised by Mormon parents went the other way. She had completely adopted the aggressive, competitive, domineering culture of her adopted family. She was asked to judge a beauty pageant one time, a major national pageant. When she got to the pageant, she took a look at the entrants and decided, she told me later, "I can beat these girls." So she entered the pageant herself and won it, never looking back. She had no bad feelings about crossing over from judge to contestant.

After the Indian Child Welfare Act (ICWA) was passed, it took years for it to take effect. In fact, there are still thousands of social workers, court workers, attorneys, and teachers who do not know of its existence.

Social workers by and large do not know of its existence, and if they do, they ignore its provisions. If a social worker visits an Indian home, especially in an urban area, and does not know the children are Indians, they still ignore or violate the provisions of the Act. If one parent is Indian and the other one is not, this can lead to the social worker and the courts treating the children as if they were not Indians. Consequently, Indian children stay in foster care on the average for seven to 10 years, compared to two years for non-Indian children.

Indian social workers formed the National Indian Child Welfare Association (NICWA) three decades ago, largely around the new law. They hold an annual meeting and conduct training around child welfare.

There are many Web sites active that promote the adoption of ethnic minority children, including American Indians, Blacks, Hispanic, Chinese, and other children from around the world. They are still going despite the strong restrictions ICWA placed on non-Indians adopting Indian children.

The main requirement of ICWA is that the tribe of the child has to be involved in the adoption. If an investigation into charges of child abuse or neglect leads to a hearing, the tribe has to be notified whether the child is removed from the home or not. The tribe can then determine if it wants to intervene or not.

When a young couple from the Mississippi Choctaw Tribe left the reservation for the birth of their twins, the tribe intervened. The couple tried to give the children away through adoption, but the courts said the tribe had the authority to intervene, even though the babies were not born on the reservation.

There is no ban on adoption of Indian children by non-Indians, but the tribe and its courts have to take all the circumstances into consideration before they make a decision. Despite this requirement, there are still many instances where Indian kids are adopted by non-Indians because no one involved knows the kids are Indians.

Michael Dorris (Modoc) wrote a book about the two boys he adopted when he was a young single professor at Dartmouth. Unfortunately, both boys had suffered from the effects of fetal alcohol syndrome (FAS), which is impossible to detect in babies. Their mothers had drunk alcohol before they were born, leaving them with permanent effects. He and the woman he married a few years later, the Anishnaabe writer Louise Erdrich, did a yeoman's job of raising the two boys correctly, but it was impossible to overcome the effects of FAS.

One of our donors to Catching the Dream wrote to me for several years. She and her husband had adopted an Indian boy under the same circumstances. They had many problems with his development and his actions when he was a teenager. He fought other children, got into trouble at school, and even got into trouble with the police. I felt helpless to tell her anything that would help her, but I wrote answers to all her letters anyway. I hope she got some relief. After five years she stopped writing.

In one case in South Dakota, the mother had her children taken away by the BIA social workers several times. She was also arrested by the police in Winner, South Dakota, just east of the Rosebud Reservation and had her ribs and tailbone fractured when a policeman sat on her for 20 minutes.

She claims the BIA social worker has been stalking her, that police and social workers walk into her house unannounced, and that they have taken her children away with no warrants. They cited the fact that she was Native

American as one of the cultural issues bearing on whether the children should be allowed to stay with their mother or be taken away by the courts.

In another case, when a woman in Kentucky found her husband in bed with another woman—in their house—she fought with him and kicked him out. The social workers proceeded to hold that against her, saying she was a violent person. She responded that the one incident was the only time she had ever been involved in an altercation. The social workers and friends of her ex-husband tried to have the children placed with the husband's family, because they allegedly would be better off. The fact that the mother was a Native American was a detriment to her raising her children.

The police raided the woman's house; they claimed they smelled marijuana. When they searched, they found no marijuana, only a wine cooler she was drinking with her friend. They still took the children away from the home. One of the reasons they cited for taking them was that they were Indian. The reporter covering the story stated that the mother was committing a social crime—Parenting While Indian (PWI).

Indians make up 6% of the total population of Montana. Even so, some 33% of Indian children in Montana are still being adopted out to non-Indian families or placed in foster homes. The ACLU suspects that Nebraska, South Dakota, and Minnesota have similar rates.

Christine Rose of STAR has investigated numerous instances of Indian parents being shadowed, threatened, followed, and harassed by social workers. "Social workers are the most egregious offenders of civil rights in the country," she says. In a case in Winner, South Dakota, a Lakota mother had her children taken away from her several times. The charges were that she was abusing drugs (which she denied), that she drank and went to parties (which she also denied), and that she failed to feed her children (which she denied).

"Southern Plains Social Services started to stalk me," she said, "and they were showing up at my door several times a week unannounced and would enter my house without knocking. The Southern Plains agent, Michelle Keller, kept telling me there was a court order that allowed her to visit whenever she wanted to, but she never produced it. When I walked down the street, a Social Services agent would follow behind me or drive by me several times."

The ACLU has been one of the leading agencies that have brought lawsuits on behalf of Indian parents. Their efforts, however, are not enough. They need to be strengthened and added to by local poverty law offices, law school professors, and others.

Indian kids are so popular to adopt that the efforts will never stop. However, adopting a child is one thing. Harassment over different standards of care, nutrition, child rearing, and schooling is another thing entirely. It is this harassment that needs to be dealt with now.

My daughter is a social worker, so I am not picking on the profession. However, there is a conspiracy underfoot to take as many Indian kids away from parents as possible. That is what we need to guard against. Even though the law changing the federal policy from breaking up Indian families has changed to a policy of keeping families intact, the system is slow to react. It still wants to follow the old rules mandating the death of the Indian family.

- Tribes need to enforce the provisions of ICWA. They need to stand up for their members in the settings of schools, stores, courts, workplaces, and other places that continue to discriminate against Indians.
- The tribes need to have control of the money involved in settling court cases, not the local governments or social agencies.
- Social workers handling Indian cases need training in the law and procedures involved in Indian cases, including referring cases to tribal courts, following tribal law and custom, and working across state boundaries.

EIGHTEEN

Racism in Sports

If you want to get a crowd in Indian Country, put on a sporting event. Baseball and basketball are the big ones everywhere. Football and rodeo come in as strong seconds, but with some parts of Indian Country not having enough bodies or enough means to field football teams.

Bacone College, the oldest Indian college in the nation, won the national junior college football championship in the early 1950s. However, by the time I became president there in 1978, the football team was long gone. Several years after I left, the college enrollment doubled, and it now has football again. When I was there, football and baseball were the big sports.

Bacone played only other local junior colleges, all of which were integrated by 1978. Bacone was integrated as well, but it was still identified as an Indian college. I never heard racial remarks during a game when I was at Bacone. However, since I am light skinned, I would hear remarks around the towns of Muskogee, Tahlequah, and Warner when I was away from the campus. In the bars, restaurants, shopping centers, and bowling alleys, anti-Indian jokes were the order of the day.

They had to do with the supposed lack of intelligence of the Indian players, their lack of hygiene, their loose sexual habits, and their cowardice.

> "Did you hear about the Indian woman when the garbage man came by? He asked, "Garbage, mam?" She said, "Three bags, please."
>
> "I tried out for the basketball team at Bacone, but they turned me down. I scored too high on the IQ test."

In the county where I was raised in the 1950s, Robeson County, North Carolina, the Indian high schools played each other and the Indian teams in Scotland, Cumberland, and Hoke counties (Brayboy and Barton). The number of teams in the Indian league varied from eight to as few as four. They only played each other. They never played against a white high school or a Black high school.

Segregation was the order of the day. We could not drink from "white" water fountains. We could not eat in "white" restaurants. We could not attend "white" schools.

However, in 1968, the schools of Robeson County were integrated. The Indian basketball league died with integration, and a little of the soul of the people died with it. When I saw games in Robeson, all I heard was cheering. I saw some of the best players in the nation there, including Ned Sampson (the father of famed college coach Kelvin Sampson), Bundy Locklear, my neighbors Bobby and Tim Brayboy, and my classmate Hartman Brewington.

Ned was playing for the college when I first remember him. He later taught and coached basketball for over 30 years in the public schools. He put me in as his pitcher for two years when I played VFW baseball.

Ned was one of the best coaches who ever lived. One of the elders in the tribe told me 25 years ago that Ned could have coached for the New York Yankees. "Why did he never do that?" I asked naively.

"Because they weren't going to have an Indian coach," he said. "The only place Ned could coach was in Robeson County." Ned has pretty brown skin, and is obviously an Indian.

After the girls team from Loneman Day School on the Pine Ridge reservation won their game against Hermosa in 1995, the Hermosa coach, being a bad sport, challenged the gender of the team. He claimed that one or more of them were boys. Before the championship game, he demanded that the girls be checked to see if they really were girls.

When they were, they were allowed to play in the tournament, which was sponsored by the YMCA. The girls and their parents later sued the YMCA for mental anguish and distress. Their parents pointed out that no other team was subjected to inspection of their private parts, but the courts threw the case out, even when they appealed it all the way to the Supreme Court.

In a basketball game between Todd County High School and Stanley County High School in 2001, students from Stanley County called the players from Todd County "prairie niggers" from the stands. Todd County is on the Rosebud Reservation and most students are Indians. Stanley County is in a small border town in Fort Pierre, South Dakota, just outside the state capital of Pierre.

The principal and the superintendent both claimed that they investigated the claim by the Todd County players, but could not find if anyone called them names, or who the guilty parties might have been.

Montana reservation teams have been subjected to the same kind of treatment for years. North Dakota, South Dakota, Nebraska, Oklahoma, and Kansas, and Idaho are just as bad at namecalling to Indian teams when they play white teams from the local area.

Racism in sports in Indian Country adds an extra dimension to what should be wholesome fun. It is often accompanied by name-calling, fights, and violence. Despite the dangers, Indians are confirmed sports nuts.

Probably the favorite sport of Indian Country is baseball and softball, but high school basketball is close behind. It is at these sports events that racism rears its ugly head.

Non-Indian sports fans give Indian teams a bad time, especially when the other team is white and the Indian team is from a reservation and is all Indian. While most contests get played in a team spirit, and without problems, the occasional racist outburst causes everyone grief, often including the hecklers.

They call the Indian team members racist names, from prairie niggers to spear chuckers. They do the tomahawk chop, accompanied by faux Indian music that so many people have gotten used to in watching bad western movies. In their worst incarnations, the fans sometimes call for scalping the Indians, and refer to the Indian team as the tribe.

Coach James Blare's football team from Wyoming Indian School got shellacked by Mountain View from Casper, Wyoming, in February 2007.

"It was one of the funnest games we've ever had. We got smoked 55-0, but they treated our kids great," he said.

However, as his kids were leaving a restaurant later, someone passed in a car, rolled down the window, and yelled, "Go back to the rez!"

The coach said later they get this treatment on nearly every trip off the reservation to play. It may be a war whoop or a racist remark. It is sometimes someone following the players around a store to make sure they don't steal something.

Sometimes, though, the treatment is blatant and discriminatory. Aleta Moss, the coach of the Wyoming Indians girls basketball team, was denied the use of the restroom at the Cenex truck stop in Worland, the coach said. The store clerk pushed a cart in front of the bathroom doors and told the team that the bathroom was closed.

They asked how long they would be closed. "A long time," the clerk said.

Namecalling sometimes accompanies off-reservation games. "I can understand kids saying 'You suck,'" says one parent, Jenni Runs Closer to Lodge. "But I can't understand someone calling a kid a 'prairie nigger.'"

The newspaper article drew 30 pages of comments, with 10% or so saying that Indians were just as racist as non-Indians. Most of the time, the players and coaches reported, opposing teams were not the problem. It was the parents who did the namecalling and the bottle throwing.

Powers-Beck reported how the three leading Indian professional baseball players of the early twentieth century endured racist taunts and namecalling.

- Chief Bender (Chippewa), the pitcher for Athletics and the White Sox, heard "The Chief is on the warpath," and "The Chief has put on his war paint," and "The chief is looking to add another scalp to his belt." These comments, ironically, were from his fans. The comments from fans of opposing teams were downright demeaning. Despite them, Bender proved himself one of the best pitchers of all time.
- John Tortes Meyers (Cahuilla), the catcher, had to let himself be humiliated by a manager who would not let him call any pitches. He resented being treated as a foreigner in his own country.
- Moses Yellow Horse (Pawnee), in contrast, hit Ty Cobb in the leg and watched as he was carried off the field on a stretcher. The racist treatment turned Yellow Horse into an alcoholic, but he recovered and was honored by his tribe on his sixtieth birthday.

The worst case of harassment in recent memory is an incident that happened in the little town of Miller, South Dakota in November 2001. Six Lakota women in a pickup—five teenagers and a 20-year-old woman—were chased by three white boys. The boys fired several shots at the truck, but did not hit anyone.

The incident happened after a basketball game between Crow Creek and Wessington Springs. The game was played in Miller. The Crow Creek players and fans say the crowd at the game shouted racist names at them all during the game. The name-calling continued as the crowd exited the gymnasium after the game.

The three white boys jumped into their cars and chased the pickup through town. Three cars tried to box the girls in their truck. That's when they saw a shotgun sticking out of one of the cars. As they tried to get away, they heard four shots. "I thought they were gonna kill us," said Summer Harrison, a 17-year-old.

As the truck sped back to a lighted area next to the Dairy Queen, the car with the gun pulled up right beside the truck. "He pointed the gun right at my head" and used a racial slur, said one girl. "I heard them straight out. I heard 'fucking Indians.' I heard prairie niggers,'" said Patty Thompson of Stephan.

Three Miller police officers, including the chief, Ernie Sterling, responded to the call for help. They talked to the boys and then let them drive away. They later recovered a semi-automatic shotgun from one of the teenage boys. The police never charged the boys in the shooting incident.

- Police need to intervene to stop violence when Indian teams play non-Indian teams off the reservations. Police who fail to do their job need to be both fired and disciplined.

- Police need to file charges against people who physically attack or harass Indians off the reservation at sports events—something that apparently has never happened.
- Coaches and other sports personnel need to be trained in cross-cultural sociology and anthropology.

NINETEEN

Racism in Stores and Restaurants

Michelle Hoffman, superintendent of the Wyoming Indian School District on the Wind River Indian Reservation, testified before the state legislature in February 2007 that store clerks would offer to serve her, even though Indians had stood in line before her. The clerks in rural Wyoming just assume that Indians have to wait their turn and that white people get waited on first.

She said her students have reported going into stores and being followed as if they were about to shoplift something. She has seen white people refuse to use a restroom if they see an Indian coming out of it.

"I'm embarrassed for my state," she told a group of state lawmakers in 2006.

When I was a kid, we could not eat in the restaurants where I grew up. Lumberton, North Carolina, is the county seat of Robeson County. The population of Lumberton in the 1950s was mostly white, with a handful of Indians and Blacks thrown in. The restaurants were reserved for whites only. Indians and Blacks could go to the back door and put in an order, but we had to take it out to eat it.

It was a regular Saturday thing for us. People would take their orders out to the park to eat it, or take it to their cars if they were lucky enough to have one, or take it to their wagons and eat it sitting behind their old mule's rump.

My cousin Bob Winfree's wife, Mary, went to give her kids some money out of her purse in the Wal-Mart store in Norman, Oklahoma in 1992. Lots of Indian people were shopping there, as usual. She was shopping for Boy Scout supplies. They thought she had shoplifted. She suddenly found herself wedged between two checkout people.

They asked her to empty out her purse and show them everything in it, but she finally refused. They let her go. She was detained for an hour. There was a glitch in their security system. By this time she was in tears at being humiliated. The only reason they searched her and her purse was because she was an Indian, she says.

Bob was in the Navy at the time, stationed at the ROTC program at the University of Oklahoma. When Mary got home and told him about it, he went back to the store and cussed them out, in as loud a voice as he could muster. Bob is a bit larger than the average man, and well-built. He says they apologized to him orally. He wanted to sue them, but he didn't have the money.

When they told the people in their church about it, they said those kinds of things happen all the time to their members. It is an Indian church.

Bob's mother, my cousin Rosa Winfree, went shopping 20 years ago with Mary in Summerville, South Carolina, north of Charleston. Mary says she went about her shopping, and Rosa went on her way to do her shopping. After a while Mary went looking for her mother-in-law and could not find her.

She looked and looked, and finally found her by the door, fuming. One of the store employees had started following and shadowing her as soon as she left Mary. She finally got mad and told the guy to get lost, but he continued to follow her.

"Don't buy anything in this store!" she told Mary. "Let's go. I told that man I knew why he was following me, just because of who I am."

When we lived in Oklahoma in the 1980s, I could tell when my wife, Toni, had been mistreated at a store. She would come home slamming the doors and kicking the dogs, and I knew something had gone wrong.

She is Chicana, but looks like an Indian. In Oklahoma that is not a good thing. She would tell me how she had picked out her blouse or her perfume and had gone to the counter to buy it. However, some blonde lady would come up, and the clerk would wait on the blonde and ignore her. If she spoke up she was doubly wrong. Finally, though, she got tired of the treatment and said we had to move. We went west to New Mexico, and have never looked back. Oklahoma is still treating its Indian citizens this way.

Michael O'Neill (Chippewa) sued Applebee's Neighborhood Bar and Grill of Superior, Wisconsin, in 2001 for refusing to serve him. He showed them his tribal ID card (with his picture on it), but they still refused to serve him, allegedly because of his race and ancestry. His lawsuit was for $9 million, which he announced would be used to help the other 9,300 members of the Red Lake Band who face similar discrimination.

When he visited the restaurant on November 14, 2000, with his wife and his son's fiancée, the restaurant refused to serve him a brandy. He had not been drinking before. The server showed the tribal ID to the manager, Greg Hartnett, who refused to let the waitress serve him a drink. The three left the restaurant mortified over their experience.

"This is humiliating," he said. "Applebee's made me feel awful, the way I felt when I was a child, when the white parents of some of my playmates would not let me into their houses because I was called a 'little savage.'"

The manager explained that since Mr. O'Neill did not have a valid driver's license, he would not serve him alcohol. The tribal ID card, which has much more information than a driver's license, was not enough to satisfy him. Mr. O'Neill explained that he does not have a driver's license, since he does not drive. The Wisconsin law requires proof of age, which the manager interpreted to mean a valid driver's license.

However, the restaurant admitted later that it also accepted state ID cards, U.S. armed forces ID cards, and U.S. passports. O'Neill asserts that the restaurant later served two Caucasians who did not have valid driver's licenses.

There have been times when I was glad to be a swamp nigger. I had a friend named Becky when I was stationed in Waco, Texas. Becky was actually the former girlfriend of one of my friends, who promptly forgot her as soon as he was graduated from Aviation Cadets at James Connelly Air Force Base in Waco, Texas.

Becky was a really sweet pretty girl who lived in Birmingham, Alabama. I met her when she was a senior at Baylor University, which is also located in Waco (we called it "Wacko"). About five of us cadets and Baylor girls spent a pleasant weekend in Dallas a few weeks before they were graduated from Baylor and we were graduated from cadets.

Somehow, Becky invited me to come by Birmingham and visit her when I came through after graduation. I had a thirty-day leave before I had to report to duty in California. I left Waco and went to Virginia to visit my grandparents, then to North Carolina to visit my other relatives, then to Florida to visit my mother and brothers and sisters, and then headed to Birmingham.

I hit there in the early summer of 1964 just as the civil rights movement was starting to take off. I got into town in the middle of the afternoon and decided to have some lunch before I went to meet Becky's mom and dad and take her to dinner.

While I had been in Florida for two weeks I had spent almost every day lying in the sun to build up my tan. When I went into a restaurant on the strip in Birmingham, I was toasted brown. I also had some big lips, which I still have.

I sat in the front near the door, and there were only three other patrons in the restaurant at 3:00 in the afternoon. Two men and a woman were sitting in the rear. They were dressed in work clothes, obviously southern hillbillies. Pretty soon the woman came up to where I was sitting and asked, "Whur yall frum?"

"North Carolina," I answered.

"And what are yall?" she asked.

"I'm an Indian," I answered.

She went back to her companions, and they huddled for a minute or two. They apparently believed me, because they never did anything else. They stayed in their corner and I stayed in mine. I was waiting for them to come up and confront me or harm me, but they never did.

Apparently it was all right to be an Indian in that restaurant, but not a "nigger." I have hated Birmingham ever since, just as I have hated Columbus, Mississippi; Albany, Georgia; Waco, Texas; Jacksonville, Florida; Atlanta, Georgia; Crewe, Virginia; Dallas, Texas; and numerous other southern towns where I have encountered racism.

The worst mistake, though, happened to me in Crewe, Virginia. Grandma and Grandpa used to go to the fair in Crewe every year. They went to the fair in Petersburg, but the fair in Crewe had lots of agricultural and homemaking exhibits, which they loved.

The first time I went was the first year I lived full time in Virginia. Even though I am naturally almost pale, when I spend a lot of time in the sun I tan as brown as a berry. I used to take my hat and shirt off in the summer, especially if I was just plowing, and the sun would turn me a dark brown.

I always got too burned at first, and peeled. However, after that I would turn a dark brown. I had been out in the sun all that summer, so in September when we went to the fair I was dark brown. I had a big time, riding the rides, eating candy apples, and drinking sodas.

I didn't know anyone there, and was all by myself. After a while, the sodas kicked in, and I had to go to the urinal. I was at the urinal, which was one big trough with water running constantly, taking some of the tremendous pressure off my bladder, when two adult white boys walked in. Both were drunk, the first one seriously so.

He looked at me and said, "Git out of hyur, nigger." I couldn't move I was so bloated. If I had been forced to stop, it would have been a disaster.

Luckily for me, his buddy, who was not quite as drunk, looked at me and said, "That ain't no nigger. That's a whatt boy."

I eagerly shook my head in agreement, lying through my teeth. I was white until I finished at the urinal, at least.

In 1959, I had gone to Virginia Beach, Virginia, for the day. My buddy John had gotten an old car that used almost as much oil as it did gas. So we went to Tex Ponder's service station and he gave us a five-gallon can of used motor oil. We took off for the beach. That old Plymouth used so much oil that we had to stop every 50 miles or so and put a quart of oil in it. Thomas Newby, Grandpa's tenant farmer that year, joked about that car, saying that John had to drive and I had to sit on the hood pouring motor oil in the engine to keep it running.

We could not afford to spend the night, so we left early in the morning and got there before 10:00. We hit the beach and had a good time for two hours. Then we got hungry and decided to eat. We probably had five dollars between us. But with hot dogs costing 25 cents and sodas costing a dime, we could afford to eat.

We went into this little hot dog stand with an indoor patio on it. I sat down while John went up to order the hot dogs and sodas. The clerk took one look at me and told John we had to leave.

"You niggers get out of hyur," he said.

"We're not niggers," John said. "We just graduated from Dinwiddie High School." The whole state knew at that time that Dinwiddie High School was all white. The Negros went to Southside High School.

"I don't care," he said. "Git out of my place."

And we did. We went down the beach. John went by himself into another joint and got our hot dogs and sodas. John was obviously not a nigger, but it was bad enough that he was with me, so he was at least a nigger lover.

The first time I went to South Dakota, 1965, there were still signs up in bars and restaurants saying "No dogs or Indians allowed." The next time I was in the state, 1970, the signs were still up. Shortly after that, though, they started to come down. The attitudes stayed up when the signs came down. It is still not a good idea to be an Indian in South Dakota. There is an excellent chance you will be discriminated against.

If you are an Indian and you shop in a store, the employees will probably follow you around to make sure you don't steal anything. They may make you empty out your purse.

If you eat in a restaurant, they may sit you in a special section near the back. Don't expect to get super service. It may take them an hour to take your order.

- Indians need to boycott every store that practices discrimination. The signs will soon come down when sales go down. This worked for the buses of Birmingham, and it can work in Indian Country.
- Indians need to protest to management every time an employee tails them in a store, and demand that it stop.

TWENTY

Racism in Politics and Voting

Indians have had to fight to win the right to vote the way GIs had to fight the Germans in France and Germany—one block at a time. The successful case in a county in Montana has little or no relevance in Oklahoma. The Indians of Oklahoma have to fight their own battles to win the right to register to vote. They have to wage a separate battle to be able to vote for county commissioner. Then they have to wage a third battle to win the right to vote for school board members, and it is the same in every state.

Consequently, the most underrepresented ethnic group in terms of numbers of votes cast is American Indians, and the most underrepresented group in terms of holding elected office in counties, states, and cities is American Indians.

When five of us put together "First Americans for Mondale" in 1983, there was much fertile ground to work on. I was the self-appointed chairman, national coordinator, and newsletter editor. The other members were Roger Jourdain, Chairman of the Red Lake Tribe of Chippewa Indians, Ada Deer, former Menominee Chairman and a professor, Verna Wood from Red Lake, and Wendell Chino, Chairman of the Mescalero Apache Tribe.

We set out to have 25 Indian delegates committed to Mondale, to sign up 25,000 new Indian voters, and to raise $25,000 for his campaign. We succeeded in all three areas, actually going over the goal for new voters, with some 32,000 people signed up. In fact, we had 25 Indian delegates committed to Mondale when we got to the convention in San Francisco.

However, we found that there was not a lot of Indian activity at the local level. Outside of a couple of Navajos in the New Mexico and Arizona state legislatures, and a couple of Alaskan Natives in the state legislature there, Indian Country was bereft of elected officials. There was not an Indian sheriff anywhere that we heard about. There were no Indian county commissioners. There were no Indian school board members to speak of, outside the Indians appointed by the BIA to serve on their boarding and day schools.

Indians typically turn out in low numbers to vote. The NIYC found that only 15% to 20% of Indians were registered to vote in New Mexico and Arizona. In Shannon County, South Dakota, on the Pine Ridge reservation, the turnout was only 38% in 2000, which was the lowest rate in the state, according to an article on July 13, 2001, in the *Argus Leader* newspaper published in Sioux Falls.

The Voting Rights Act was originally passed in 1965 with the intention of removing the barriers that had kept minority people from voting. Ten years later it was amended to include American Indians. It also included provisions for bilingual voting for people who spoke a language other than English.

However, many influential people have worked against it, especially in the states with large Indian populations. Many of these states have a cowboy culture, and many of them have residents who are racist toward Indians. Among the worst states are North Dakota, Oklahoma, South Dakota, Montana, Wyoming, Idaho, Washington, Arizona, New Mexico, and Oregon.

The attitude of the leaders of these states was that Indians living on reservations had no right to vote. In New Mexico, this provision was actually written into the state constitution. It took a lawsuit by Miguel Trujillo, an Isleta Indian and a World War II veteran of the Marines, to force the state of New Mexico to let Indians vote. Miguel is now one of the "Unsung Heroes" of New Mexico. It took a similar lawsuit in Arizona to let Indians vote in that state for the first time.

One of the most infamous Indian haters was William "Wild Bill" Janklow. In 1977 he advised South Dakota's secretary of state, Lorna Herseth, that he intended to pursue both legislation and litigation that would exempt South Dakota from the provisions of the Voting Rights Act. Even though neither remedy was successful, his threat stopped progress toward equal voting rights in its tracks.

When he issued his decision, he was the state attorney general. After two terms in that office, he served two terms as governor. All four times he ran on an anti-Indian platform, threatening to shoot AIM members, and so on. Then he ran for Congress and served several terms, all the while opposing Indian voting and praising the state of South Dakota whenever possible.

Janklow objected to the pre-clearance provisions of the amended Act. This meant that no redistricting in the Pine Ridge and Rosebud Indian reservations could take place without prior clearance from the U.S. attorney general. This sent Janklow into a rage. In addition, in some places bilingual materials had to be provided to Indian voters. In fact, eight counties in the state were required to conduct bilingual elections—Todd, Shannon, Bennett, Charles Mix, Corson, Lyman, Mellette, and Washabaugh.

His threats stopped Herseth and her successors from carrying out the Act for a quarter of a century, according to the ACLU. The ACLU case to resolve the conundrum, *Quiver v. Nelson,* has been called the largest voting rights case in history. The South Dakota secretary of state, Chris Nelson, admitted to more than 800 violations of the Act. In 1985, only 9.9% of Indians in the state were registered to vote.

County registrars only registered people to vote in one place—the county seat. Indians living on reservations thus had to travel to the county seat, and enter a hostile environment, in order to vote. Many Indians found traveling this distance a burden, especially in the days of horses and buggies. State law prohibited the county clerk from appointing registrars on Indian reservations. Registration by mail was illegal in South Dakota before 1973.

When roving registrars were finally allowed on Indian lands, they immediately found themselves accused of voter fraud by local officials, which intimidated people. Dan McCool of the American West Center said the charges of voter fraud were part of an effort to create a racially hostile and polarized atmosphere.

Few Indians were called to serve on juries. They used lists of registered voters to call people to serve on juries, which naturally left almost all Indians out. At the same time, Indians were the leading group in South Dakota that was targeted for arrest, trial, and imprisonment. An Indian in South Dakota could count on having an all-white jury at a trial. (See the chapter on law enforcement.) Juries for a long time in South Dakota were limited to "free white males."

Finally, in 2005 a three-judge federal panel issued an injunction against the state of South Dakota. It said the state officials must comply with the federal Voting Rights Act (VRA). They could not implement a new law that gave the appearance of rushing to circumvent the VRA. Despite the edict of an earlier ruling, the governor and the legislature continued to ignore federal law and issued changes in election laws and district boundary lines without clearing them with the Justice Department in advance.

Marriage between Indians and whites or Blacks and whites was illegal in South Dakota until modern times. It was illegal to provide instruction in any language other than English. In the bad old days, Indians were forbidden to enter any lands off the reservation without a permit. It was illegal for a white person to harbor an Indian within any white settlement.

The state also finally managed, after years of trying, to steal the sacred Black Hills from the Lakota people. The Supreme Court said in a case decades later that a "more ripe and rank case of dishonorable dealing will never, in all probability, be found in our history." The Lakota people have refused to accept the money the United States awarded the tribes as payment for the illegal taking of the Black Hills. They want the lands back.

In South Dakota, Indian reservations were regarded as "unorganized" areas. Counties, which were all off the reservations, were "organized" areas and people living in organized areas could register and vote. People living in unorganized areas could not register and vote. This provision held until 1975.

Even after people in the unorganized areas gained the right to vote, they could still not run for office or hold office until 1980. In the meantime, vital decisions about abortion, education, health care, economic development, redistricting, transportation, legal rights, and a host of other issues were decided with little or no Indian input.

State officials gerrymandered voting districts for school boards, county commissions, the state senate, and the state house, to weaken the Indian vote. Instead of having one state senate district for the Pine Ridge reservation, for instance, it would be cut up into four or five districts, all of which had a majority of Whites.

In one case in Buffalo County, South Dakota, the Indian votes were put into one county commissioner district which had 83% of the total voters in the county. The total population of the county was 2,000 people, including the Crow Creek Sioux Tribe. The other two districts had an all-white population which was just a few hundred voters each. However, the two white commissioners had control of the county over the one who was from the Indian reservation. The Indian residents sued and finally won as recently as 2003. The "packing" scheme had been going on for several decades with no effective opposition to it. They agreed to a consent decree.

In my home, Robeson County, North Carolina, the white voters, who mainly lived in the six towns, voted in the election of school boards for their towns, and also voted for the county-wide school board, which served mainly Indians and Blacks. Janie Maynor Locklear, a courageous and visionary leader, challenged the practice in a lawsuit and won, completely changing the way elections for the school board were held. My great-uncle John L. Godwin was also one of the advocates for the cessation of "double voting."

(The duplicity involved in maintaining racial segregation is evident when busing to achieve racial balance is the topic. Whites objected, and still do, to busing Indian or Black students to achieve racial balance. However, it was all right before that to bus to achieve racial segregation. My bus full of Indian kids used to meet a bus load of white students every morning, and again in the afternoon. They were on their way to attend a private academy in the little village of Philadelphus, which produced most of the doctors, lawyers, bankers, engineers, and other officials of the county. We were on our way to an all-Indian school. We were told not to look at them. One friend told me his daddy told him if he ever got caught looking at the white kids on their bus, he would beat him. We were forbidden to start a racial confrontation even by looking into their faces.)

In the meantime, the United States had been forcing Indians to attend public schools on or near reservations since 1896. By 1938 half of all Indian students were attending public schools instead of BIA schools; today 85% attend public schools and only 8% attend BIA schools. (The others attend contract tribal schools and mission schools.) Indians were being forced for over 60 years to attend public schools where their parents could not vote, where the parents were not welcome, where they were often forbidden to visit, and where they had no official on the school board to represent their interests.

Officials often designate only one or two polling places for an entire school district or a county commission. These polling places were always located in white areas, where Indians were often denigrated, threatened, and humiliated. Several lawsuits in Wyoming, Montana, and South Dakota forced local officials to extend registration deadlines and establish polling places in Indian communities.

Municipalities tried numbered seat provisions to dilute the Indian vote by eliminating single-shot voting. They also had a requirement for a majority vote for nomination in primary elections for the U.S. Senate, the U.S. House of Representatives, and governor.

Election officials also "packed" Indians into house districts to prevent them from having control of the district. In Arizona, Apache County, Navajo County, and Coconino County had discriminated against Indians by packing them, leaving two White senators living only ten miles apart, but representing two geographic areas larger than most states *Klahr v. Williams;* "the Indians were done in" the court said. The counties had also previously used a literacy test to screen out Indian voters, but it had been ruled out by the Voting Rights Act. Yuma County was also tainted by discrimination against Indian voters, the court said.

McCool, Olson, and Robinson documented more than 70 cases of Indians trying to gain the right to vote in their 2007 book. Although Indians were ironically granted citizenship in the United States in 1924 (through the Indian Citizenship Act), local county clerks, state election officials, county commissions, local school boards, and others have fought for 80 years to try to keep Indians from the polls.

Most of the 70 lawsuits have been successful, bringing about change that is much needed. The ACLU has brought many of the lawsuits on behalf of Indian clients. It has been aided by other organizations such as the Native American Rights Fund headed by John Echohawk and the Indian Law Resource Center headed by Tim Coulter. Seven of the ACLU lawsuits were in the state of South Dakota, widely called the "Mississippi of the North" by Indian people.

Indeed, their efforts have largely been successful. In research conducted by the National Indian Youth Council in the 1980s, Indian registration for voting in state and local elections was found to be only 15% to 20%. This is well below the national rates, which run between 40% for poor whites and minority groups to as high as 85% for urban Republicans.

Today, however, 25 years later, there are some fierce battles still going on to let Indians enter the political process. At the same time, there are many barriers to keep Indians from voting and running for office. These include harassment at the county clerk's office, racial harassment and threats, threats to people's employment, threats to the children of adults who become involved in the political process, harassment from anti-Indian organizations, and campaigning on a racial basis.

In the first ACLU Indian voting rights case, *Windy Boy v. County of Big Horn,* the plaintiff successfully won the right to have single-member districts for the county commission. The case was filed in 1983. Previously the elections had been at-large, meaning no Indian had ever won election. With the new election plan, Indians won election to the county commission for the first time. The plaintiff was Dr. Janine Pease Windy Boy, President of Little Big Horn College.

A similar result obtained in Blaine County, Montana in *United States v. Blaine County, Montana.* The United States brought the action against the Blaine County Board of Commissioners and the Superintendent of Elections. The suit was filed on behalf of eight individuals and the Fort Belknap Community Council for the county holding at-large elections which prevented Indians from participating fully in the political process.

Indians constituted 45.2% of the population, but no Indian had ever been elected to the Blaine County Commission. The Ninth Circuit Court of Appeals held that there was a history of racial discrimination against American Indians, racially polarized voting, "voting procedures that enhanced the opportunities for discrimination against American Indians," depressed social conditions for Indians, and a tenuous justification for the at-large voting.

Five Indians from the Wind River Indian Reservation in Wyoming sued Fremont County under the Voting Rights Act, Section 2, and the 14th and 15th Amendments to the U.S. Constitution. The five plaintiffs are Patricia

Bergie, Pete Calhoun, Gary Collins, James E. Large, and Lucille McAdams. The defendants were the five county commissioners, all Republicans—Doug Thompson, Lanny Applegate, Jane Adamson, Gary Jennings, and Pat Hickerson.

The population of the county is 38,504, with 7,113 of the population being American Indians living on the reservation. The Indian population is 16.3% of the voting age adults in the county.

They alleged that their voting rights had been violated; the reservation votes had been diluted by having at-large elections for county commissioners. Wind River had never elected its own county commissioner; their representative has always been a non-Indian who lived off the reservation.

They wanted an election plan that would have single-member districts. The reservation is of such size that it would constitute a single-member district, they said in their complaint filed in October 2005. They won the lawsuit, forcing the county to go to single-member districts. Ironically, the county commissioners used tax money, raised from Indians and others, to try to maintain a racist pattern of elections.

In Montana, the issue was similar in a case filed in 1999 called *Alden v. Board of County Commissioners of Rosebud County, Montana.* The plaintiffs were Charlene Alden, Fred Belly Mule, Holda Roundstone, Danny Sioux, Wilbur Spang, James Walks Along, Philip Whiteman, Jr., Florence Whiteman, all members of the Northern Cheyenne Tribe, and Lynette Two Bulls, who is Sioux.

The Board of Commissioners of Rosebud County, Montana, was accused of racial bias in violation of the Voting Rights Act. Like the Fremont County case, Rosebud County held its elections at large, meaning no Indian could ever win.

"The at-large election process is illegal because it prevents Indians from participating equally in the political process," said the lead attorney, Laughlin McDonald of the ACLU. He filed the case along with the Indian Law Resource Center, representing 11 Indians living in the county, which includes the Northern Cheyenne Reservation.

In the Montana House and Senate, elections are held in single-member districts. This allows an Indian candidate a chance to win. Indians have run frequently in the county, and they have won statehouse seats. With the passing of the single-member plan for the county commission, Indians won seats on the county commission for the first time.

In the other case filed in 1999, the Board of Trustees of Ronan-Pablo School District in Lake County, Montana, was accused of racism in voting patterns by maintaining at-large elections. Even though a majority of the students attending the schools were Indian, no Indians had ever won election to the school board.

The case was *Matt v. Ronan School District 30, Lake County, Montana.* The plaintiffs were Clayton Matt and Jeanine Padilla. Both were tribal members and tribal employees with children attending school in the district, and both had run for the school board and lost. The reservation is the Confederated Salish and Kootenai Tribes.

The majority of the people living in the district are white. Whites own half the land on the reservation, and they maintain that the state should have complete jurisdiction on the reservation. Some of them have called for termination of the tribe's treaty. They have also participated heavily in some of the anti-Indian groups that have sprouted up in Montana in the past 30 years, including Montanans Opposed to Discrimination (MOD) and Citizens Equal Rights Alliance (CERA).

Indians had run 17 times for the school board since the early 1970s and lost every time except one. Ron Bick won a seat on the school board in 1990, at the same time that he became a tribal member. But he lost when he ran for re-election three years later.

Jeanine Padilla, one of the plaintiffs in the case, also ran for the school board. She said, "One white lady said 'we have to get everybody out to vote because there's another Indian running.'" Padilla lost.

"I didn't realize people could be so shallow," she told the ACLU.

Gallup-McKinley County Schools (GMCS), the largest school district in the United States in terms of Indian students, only did away with its at-large election process as the result of a lawsuit. Even though the district is 67% Indian, there had only been one Indian to serve on the county-wide school board in its history. GMCS has 14,000 students, with 9,000 of them being Native. Navajos, Zuni Pueblo, and Hopi students make up the largest group of Indians, with some transplanted South Dakota and Oklahoma Indians as well.

With help from the National Indian Youth Council, the local Navajo people filed a lawsuit calling for single-member districts and won. Finally, in 1998, the district had its first Indian majority on the school board when three Indians won seats on the five-member board. They were Annie Descheney, Young Jeff Tom, and Ernest Bowman, who had already served on the board for several years.

They removed the superintendent, Ramon Vigil, within a short time, and replaced him with Robert Gomez, from California. Bob started the schools on the road to progress, and some were doing much better during his six years at the helm. However, after his retirement, the district slid back into its previous ways.

Vigil had long been known as a fair-haired boy and one of the local favorites. He belonged to the second-largest ethnic group in Gallup, Hispanics. He had been superintendent for over a decade, after starting as a math teacher in the district and advancing to principal. He was only in his early forties when he was released; he went from superintendent to law school.

Even so, Indian students had performed very poorly under his administration. The documented dropout rate for Indians was 65%. Indian students most often did not go to college after graduating from the six GMCS high schools. When they did, they were so poorly prepared that they dropped out at a rate of over 80%. The high schools steered them into bonehead classes, offered them no remedial work to prepare them for college and gave them social promotions to get them through school.

In Thurston County, Nebraska, several Indians filed an injunction in *Stabler v. County of Thurston, Nebraska* asking the court to reapportion their county's voting districts to create a new Native American majority district. They stated that despite the fact that 44% of the population was Indian, no Native American had ever been elected to the county board of education. Furthermore, no Native person had ever been elected to the county Board of Supervisors. They maintained that the at-large voting system violated their voting rights.

The barriers to voting have come down very slowly, and with fighting to maintain the barriers at every step of the way by white local and state officials. In *Bone Shirt v. Hazeltine,* four Native Americans challenged the legislature's redistricting plan in 2001. Alfred Bone Shirt, Belva Black Lance, Bonni High Bull, and Germaine Moves Camp stated that the plan violated Section 5 of the Voting Rights Act because it diluted the minority vote and unlawfully "packed" Native voters into a single district. The court agreed with both contentions.

There have been many other similar cases filed in the state of South Dakota and other states:

- *Little Thunder v. South Dakota,* 1975, struck down a law that prohibited Indians from voting in certain county elections.
- *United States v. South Dakota,* 1980, said a state law that prohibited Indians from holding office in certain counties was unconstitutional.
- *American Horse v. Kundert,* 1984, said that Indians who had been unlawfully denied voter registration must be added to the voting lists.

- *Black Bull v. Dupree School District,* 1986, said the school board had failed to provide polling places to Indian voters in a school board election.
- *Fiddler v. Sieker,* 1986, said the auditor of Dewey County had to furnish Indian plaintiffs with voter registration cards and extend the deadline for voter registration.
- *Emery v. Hunt,* 1998, overturned the state legislature's decision to abolish a predominantly Indian single-member district on the Standing Rock and Cheyenne River Sioux Reservations.
- *Weddell v. Wagner Community School District* challenged the at-large elections of school board members and having only one polling place off the reservation for all voters.
- *Wilcox v. City of Martin* challenged the city's redistricting plan on the grounds that it discriminated against Indian voters. The ACLU brought this lawsuit.
- *Bowannie v. Bernalillo Municipal School District* in 1987 dealt with the rights of Indians to vote. The NIYC filed this suit.
- *Casuse v. City of Gallup,* 1986, also dealt with the right of Indians to vote in school board elections. NIYC brought this lawsuit.
- *Largo v. McKinley Consolidated School District,* 1983, dealt with the right of Indians to vote in at-large elections for the school board. NIYC brought this lawsuit.

All these cases were brought on behalf of Indians by the ACLU and the NIYC.

Much more work needs to be done to allow Indians full access to elected positions and the right to vote.

- States need to pass laws forbidding racial voting practices, allowing roaming registrars, setting penalties for persons violating voting rights, and setting fines for violators of voting rights.
- Indians need to launch voting registration drives all over the United States.
- Indians need to push candidates for offices at all levels, for school boards, county commissions, sheriffs, city councils, state representatives, state senate seats, and other positions.

TWENTY-ONE

Racism in Natural Resources

Indians have been losing land since 1492, slowly at first, and then with a vengeance after the Civil War. When the Civil War started, the United States only went as far west as Kansas. After the war, settlers continued with their wagon trains going to California, Oregon, and Washington. The takeover of Indian land in Oklahoma, South Dakota, Montana, Utah, Colorado, New Mexico, Arizona, and the other western states was rapid. By 1890 it was a *fait accompli.*

The next phase of the Indian land grab occurred when the United States decided that the reservation lands Indians had hung onto were too much. The General Allotment Act (Dawes Act) of 1887 authorized the executive branch to chop up the remaining Indian lands and open the "excess" to sale, lease, and permanent settlement by non-Indians. Out of 150 million acres that Indian tribes owned as of 1885, 90 million were lost within the next four decades.

Within three decades most Indian reservations had lost huge chunks of their land. A piece of land owned by an individual Indian would lie next to a farm or ranch owned by a non-Indian. Next to that might be a piece of land owned by the tribe itself, held in common. The land situation became very confusing, the situation it remains in today.

At Pine Ridge, for instance, the latest report on the economy says that the ranch lands on the reservation generated $33 million a year. However, only a third of the money went to Indians. White ranchers got the other two-thirds. The unemployment rate for Indians living on the reservation is perennially 85%.

The Rosebud Reservation next door to Pine Ridge has over 900,000 acres of land remaining, but half of it is owned by white ranchers. The Indian people there defeated a proposal in 2003 that would have put a huge pig farm on the reservation. The unemployment rate on the Rosebud is close to 85%.

The Indians of Oklahoma lost almost all their lands. Some tribes have managed to hold on to a few hundred acres. One of the largest landowning tribes in the state, the Muskogee Creek Nation, has only 5,000 acres that it owns. There are over 50,000 Muskogee people today. The Indians of Oklahoma ended up losing almost all their lands in the land runs of the 1890s. The biggest loser was the Cherokee Nation, which lost seven million acres.

The result is huge inefficiencies for the BIA and tribes in managing land. The following citation from the case of *Hodel v. Irving* (481 U.S. 704, 713, 1987) illustrates the most extreme example. The U.S. Supreme Court stated in the case in 1984:

> Tract 1305 [of Sisseton-Wahpeton Lake Traverse Reservation] is 40 acres and produces $1,080 in income annually. It is valued at $8,000. It has 439 owners, one third of whom receive less than $.05 in annual rent and two-thirds of whom receive less than $1. … The common denominator used to compute fractional interests in property is 3,394,923,849,000. The smallest heir receives $.01 every 177 years. If the tract were sold (assuming the 439 owners could agree), for its $8,000 value, he would receive $.000418. The administrative costs of handling this tract are estimated by the Bureau of Indian Affairs at $17,560 annually.

Land disputes stir up resentment toward Indians more than anything else. But a close second are fights about natural resources. Minerals, timber, water, petroleum, oil, natural gas, gold, fish, and game animals stir up way more controversy than anything else in Indian Country.

People living on or near reservations put up most of the objections, naturally. They object to Indians not having to get hunting and fishing licenses from the state, even if a treaty guarantees them the right to hunt and fish "in the usual and accustomed places," as many treaties stated. Oil companies and their collaborators in the federal government have stolen billions of dollars from Indians. Non-Indians want to take as much water from Indian reservations as possible, leaving little or none for the Indians living there.

The most famous case in the protection of natural resources of the recovery of money owed to Indians is the current case of *Cobell v. Babbitt.* (The case is now called *Cobell v. Kempthorne,* after being called *Cobell v. Norton.* The name changes as the defendant, a federal appointee as Secretary of the Interior, also changes.)

Elouise Cobell, a Blackfeet woman from Montana, is the lead defendant and the person who brought the case. She has been working on it for the past 30 years without letting up. It is the largest class-action lawsuit against the United States in history.

She actually filed the lawsuit in 1996 against then Interior Secretary Gale Norton. However, she had been working on it for more than two decades by that time. When she was appointed Treasurer of her tribe in 1976, she found that the tribe's interest-bearing accounts were earning a negative interest! The BIA had loaned their money to another tribe, which was not paying it back, and was not paying any interest.

This piqued her interest, and she dug further. She soon learned that oil and gas companies with wells on Indian reservation lands were paying little or no royalties to the people who allegedly owned the land. Occasionally a poor starving Indian would get a check, but it would be very small. She heard story after story about how her Blackfeet people were getting nothing from the oil and gas produced on their rural farms and ranches.

She raised holy hell for almost 20 years. She wrote letters. She attended meetings. Always she asked questions. Finally the late Mike Synar, a congressman from eastern Oklahoma, called a meeting in the White House with the Office of Management and Budget and Interior. Elouise attended the meeting, as did Dennis Gingold, a prominent banking attorney. When the meeting was over, Gingold told the Interior officials, "I'm amazed you guys haven't been sued."

Synar followed up the meeting with the establishment of a Special Trustee to provide a full accounting of the money owed to the tribes with large accounts in the Individual Indian Monies (IIM) and tribal trust accounts. The initial Trustee was Paul Homan, a banking executive with years of experience. He stayed in the position until 1999, quitting in disgust and accusing Bruce Babbitt, who was Interior Secretary under Clinton, of undermining his authority in trying to do his job.

Elouise says "the case has revealed mismanagement, ineptness, dishonesty, and delay of federal officials." The plaintiffs are seeking a complete historical accounting of all Individual Indian Monies (IIM) accounts. The BIA admitted in 1999 that it

- Cannot provide account holders with a quarterly report on funds
- Does not adequately control the income and expenditures of accounts
- Cannot provide reconciliations of the accuracy of accounts
- Does not provide account holders with periodic statements
- Does not have written policies and procedures for trust fund management
- Does not have adequate staffing, and
- Has an inadequate record keeping system.

Babbitt had a huge conflict of interest himself. He is a former governor of Arizona and a former candidate for president. However, he is also the owner of the huge Babbitt Ranch southwest of the Navajo reservation. He is the third generation beneficiary of lots of income from Indian lands. He and his family have made huge fortunes selling cars to Indians, running trading posts, and operating on Indian lands.

Elouise tried for years to see Babbitt about the claims, but finally gave up. Babbitt refused to meet with her, as did the various Assistant Secretaries of Indian Affairs. She finally went to a conference where Attorney General Janet Reno was the main speaker, and went up to her afterward and introduced herself. She asked for a meeting with Reno, and Reno invited her to come to Washington to meet with her. When she got there, however, Reno would not meet with her. Babbitt had obviously warned Reno not to meet with her.

She had to meet with Reno's assistants, who could promise her nothing. She concluded that the only alternative was to bring a lawsuit. She called on Gingold again, asking him to take the case. He agreed, but he said it would be costly. Elouise set out to raise the money, which so far has been over $10 million.

She went to foundation after foundation, finally raising over $8 million to pursue the case. When she won the "Genius" award from the MacArthur Foundation in 1997, she gave that money to the cause, too.

The first judge in the case was Royce C. Lamberth. He was a conservative Texas Republican who had been appointed to the bench by Ronald Reagan. He had many insults thrown at him by the government defendants, but has appeared to bend over backwards to be fair. The problem is that the government itself has acted in bad faith toward Indians. They have acted like thieves in the night. The stealing goes back to the late 1800s. It was institutional racism gone wild.

Interior has always assumed it could do what it wanted to with Indian monies, lands, minerals, and natural resources, and never be accountable to anyone. The situation has been rife for corruption and bribery from the very beginning. Slush funds, hidden accounts, secret exchanges of lands, sweetheart deals, low-balling royalty payments, high appointments to positions as payoffs, and other nefarious deeds have been the order of the day with Interior.

Judge Lamberth eventually cited both Babbitt and the Assistant Secretary, Kevin Gover (Pawnee), for contempt of court for not furnishing the proper records to the court on time. He said Interior "engaged in a shocking pattern of deception of the court. I have never seen more egregious conduct by the federal government." At one point, Judge Lamberth stopped the BIA from shredding and destroying records related to the case. Some records that were destroyed will never be available to be accounted for. The BIA employees destroyed at least 162 cartons of ledgers and checks before the judge could stop them.

Judge Lamberth also accused the Interior of being racist toward Indians. These were strong words coming from a conservative Texan who was a Ronald Reagan appointee. This statement in 2005 caused Interior to ask the court to take him off the case since he was allegedly biased. His removal for the language he used in his decisions was very controversial; it may mean the government can remove any judge it does not want simply by appealing to his superiors (Rutledge).

The U.S. Court of Appeals removed him from the case in July 2006. The court said he had lost his objectivity. He was telling the truth too often, and too loudly. The court said that his actions showed that he believed that the behavior of Interior was "a dinosaur—the morally and culturally oblivious hand-me-down of a disgracefully racist and imperialist government that should have been buried a century ago, the last pathetic outpost of the indifference and anglocentrism we thought we had left behind."

Various experts have estimated the total amount of money still owed Indians at between $27 billion and $100 billion. That's billion with a "b."

The government has carried out economic institutional racism against Indian people for 120 years, since 1887.

- It undervalued the amount railroads would have to pay to cross Indian lands. Indians got paid a fraction of what white landowners got for the same rights-of-way.
- It failed to log thousands of loads of oil hauled off Indian lands by the major oil companies.
- It failed to pay Indians the proper amounts for minerals taken from their lands.
- It undervalued the amounts of royalty payments.
- It has given billions of acre feet of Indian water away to farmers, ranchers, soil conservation districts, game preserves, and mining companies. In some cases, no payment was collected for this water, or made to the Indian owners.
- It failed to tell Indians what they were owed from their IIM accounts and their IMPL (Indian Monies from the Proceeds of Labor) accounts. Moreover, it failed to pay them. In some cases, as in Anadarko, the IIM monies ended in a slush fund that was used to hold year-end parties for BIA employees, pay for BIA travel, and other things. (Newton Lamar, the Chairman of the Wichita Tribe, exposed this sham; the BIA promptly threw him out of office. He sued and was reinstated.)
- It let pipelines cross Indian lands for a fraction of the price that non-Indians right next door were collecting.
- It undervalued the value of coal on Indian lands. Peter MacDonald, the former Chairman of the Navajo Nation, found that the state of Arizona was collecting more from taxes on Navajo coal than the tribe was collecting in royalties on the coal. He renegotiated the coal leases and doubled the amount of royalty payments. They were later quintupled

again. The BIA had initially negotiated the leases with no input from the tribe.

- It fired several people who exposed the shoddy bookkeeping and lack of management of Indian trust accounts, including David Henry and Bobby Maxwell.

The Interior management of trust fund accounts is a largely unfixable mess. Interior has leased Indian lands, issued use permits, given mining permits, sold timber and minerals, and engaged in other activities. In most cases the Indian owners of the property knew nothing about what Interior was doing and were not involved in the decisions. They were legally "incompetent" to manage their own affairs. The BIA had to do it for them.

The Karuk Tribe of northern California has been involved in trying to stop several controversial actions over the past few decades—mining damaging water tables and polluting the rivers, tribal hunting rights being challenged by non-Indians, sacred Indian lands being returned to the Tribe, and other issues. The tribe issued the following statement:

> "Since we have brought attention to instream suction gold mining on both a Federal and State level we have notified our members of our community not to approach miners due to the threat of violence. This notification was prompted by certain statements found on various "chat forums," and of shots being fired at tribal members along the Salmon River at a New 49er claim back in 2004. It is also interesting to note some of the most vocal advocates (Jim Foley, Mike Higbee, Jerry Hobbs) actually are moderators of these forums and allow such nonsense."

The following are some of the comments from their website: http://www.golddregger.com/cgi-bin/dcforum/dcboard.cgi

- My letter to white chiefs asks them to stop anything that "may" or "may not" cause any harm at all. … I want em more fish to gill net!!! I want Big SMOKEHOUSE full. … Me like um smoked fish. Me hope um gill nets full like many moons ago. … Me like to fill back of pinto wagon and sell em fish for $8 pound to pale faces. … Me afford um much firewater. Firewater good.
- "Me like to fill back of pinto wagon." Wrong Chief. Gill netting Indians drive new Dodge 4x4 trucks. Come to West coast and seeum for self.
- "karuks" are not just a name of a band not tribe IMHO [meaning unclear], but are people. http://karuk.us/staff/index.php these people are the ones filing these lawsuits. In reality the karuks were hideout bands that lost many a squaw to early miners.
- No, Russ, we need to do a lot more than that. We need to beat the crap out of liberal commie loving anti-American pansies. We need to start breaking legs. They don't fear lawsuits. They have lawyers to protect

them and insurance companies to cover the losses. But they will stop when they start feeling the pain. You can have all the lawyers in the world and all the most expensive insurances available. It don't matter. Break a leg or two and they'll be fearful of us for a long time. I'd say leg breaking is a great start...hopefully the end is that they are exiled down to Mexico or Belize or some other place where they can do their best to try to screw it up in the name of "protection" ... I kind of get the feeling the locals down there are going to be much less tolerant than we have with this kind of sh*t. See how far legal maneuvers take you South of the border ELF and company...I'm laughing just thinking about it. Drive them out and kick'em in the as* as they cross the Rio Grande and season them with a little rock salt.

- I am having a few pints and throwing a few darts. (Below this is a picture of our Vice Chairman Leaf Hillman)
- I doubt anything short of a civil war will dislodge the parasitic organisms.
- Author unknown. Somewhere a True Believer is training to kill you. He is training with minimum food or water, in austere conditions, day and night. The only thing clean on him is his weapon. He doesn't worry about what workout to do—his rucksack weighs what it weighs, and he runs until the enemy stops chasing him. The True Believer doesn't care "how hard it is"; he knows he either wins or he dies. He doesn't go home at 1700; he is home. He knows only the Cause. Now, who wants to quit?" They may not be the only ones. Time to break legs? Brother, it was time to do that decades ago!
- If you can't appreciate the efforts being made by the groups above and the people that support them, then I suggest that you shut up and go out and get your group of leg breakers and bring them to california (sic) or what ever state that is having these problems and start breaking the appropriate legs. Put your words to work and show us how it is done.
- We need your help.
- Jerry (Jerry Hobbs of People for Public Lands) Time to play cowboys and Indians-John-now quote that Leaf ass wipe!
- Hoser John I agree John but this time lets finish the job. JingleBobs
- It would be more benaficial (sic) for the native fish, If America got rid of the Indians. Billions could be saved and spent on Americans rather than a conquered race of leaches (sic). How's that Bruce? John Adams
- MYSELF If the GD Indians want Government money and Aid they need to give up their Sovereign Nation status or support themselves. I just

wish they'd of finished the Damned indian (sic) wars. Just goes to prove that if you don't finish the job it'll come back to bite you in the a$$. Or as my dad used to say "A job half done is a job done half assed." Jingle-Bobs

- http/www.49ermike.com/ operated by Mike Higbee Medford, Oregon
- If Mike thinks there are "racist remarks" I am sure he will act accordingly. (Jim Foley)
- Those guys going behind our backs was just the only way that those scum of the earth Karuk's (sic) could win this. 150 years ago we the miners would have just killed them all for this
- I haven't played cowboys and Indians since I was a kid. Humm.
- Indians with nets harm fish. It's time to stop the horse$hit we've let the Indians get away with for the last 100 years. They're a citizen, I'm a citizen. NO SPECIAL LAWS OR FAVORS FOR ANY MINORITY!!!! Our forefathers shed their blood to make this country free. Do we need to follow in their footsteps to keep it that way?
- well if past practice is what gives them "the indians" (sic) the right to over fish do dope kill animals with out a hunting licence (sic). Why isn't it the whites right to get the gold and take the indians (sic) land away from them? HAHA Wyatt
- You guys have the mining laws backing you up and i don't see how a few…what are they? what did you call them?...don't matter. crack smoking, bourbon swilling, leftist, so-called indians (sic) who hire a greenpeace (sic) lawyer commie to give the land back to them through frivolous litigation a handful of crack head indians (sic) that nobody even heard of trying to end mining as we know it is just laughable. We sent ours to Oklahoma in the 1830's.
- This anti-American activity must stop if the indian (sic) tribes are to retain any of their honor and respect from other Americans.
- Don't ya just love the Chicken*&<% tribe from San Diego giving testimony on how bad dredging is—they have NO RIVERS—just big bloody casinos and you want to know who is bankrolling the injuns?? they just came outta the teepee. HEAP BIG MINERS PUSHED OFF KLAMATH LAND-UG-NOW OURS-MAKE HEAP BIG'M CASINO AND SCALP PALEFACES!! Hoser John

Indian water rights have stirred up perhaps more controversy in the past three decades than any other issue in Indian Country. Farmers, ranchers, developers, cities, power companies, coal mining companies, and others with big water needs have designs on taking as much Indian water as they can get.

In the water-hungry west, rain is not an option for having water. It is snow and rivers that provide it. Without snow in the Sierra Nevadas, people in Los Angeles and San Francisco would have to leave. Without water from the Colorado River, people in Phoenix and Los Angeles would have to leave. Los Angeles brings water all the way from Parker, Arizona, on the Colorado River Indian reservation. The Colorado never makes it to the Pacific Ocean any more. It dries up in the desert of Mexico because of all the water drained from it upstream.

Without water from the aquifer under the city, people in Albuquerque would have to leave. The water to fill the Albuquerque aquifer comes from the snows of the mountains of Colorado. The water moves down the valley of the Rio Grande River to keep the aquifer full. Even so, the city of Albuquerque is now bringing water from the Chama River up north to meet its needs, and the water level in the aquifer is slowly dropping.

The big call during the Ronald Reagan administration was for "quantification" of Indian water. Tribes resisted this call. They know once their water is quantified, they will be left with a little and the rest will go to other users. The little they are left with will not allow for future growth needs on the reservations. The past hundred years have proven the truth of that statement.

The "Winters Doctrine," settled in court in 1908, states that Indians have prior rights to water over other users. This sets many municipalities, developers, and farmers on edge. They want all the water they can get, regardless of the consequences.

However, most Indian leaders know the history of Los Angeles and how it stole its water from the Owens Valley near Bishop, California. The water that has let Los Angeles grow into a major metropolitan area came at the expense of a small city to the north and Indians to the east. The Owens Valley is now water poor and stagnated. Owens Lake is now a dry dusty lakebed with no water in it at all. Calls for quantification, which James Watt made when he was Reagan's Secretary of the Interior, get resisted with a vengeance.

In 1993, the Navajo Nation sued the BIA and the Interior Department over the handling of the huge coal deposits on the Navajo Nation. The BIA sold the coal, worth trillions of dollars, initially for less in royalties than the state of Arizona was collecting in taxes. The suit alleged the BIA sold the Navajo coal to Peabody Coal Co. in 1964 for $600 million less than it was worth. When John Fritz, the BIA head in 1985, tried to increase the royalty payments, the Secretary of the Interior, Donald Hodel, stopped him. Fritz is an Indian and Hodel is a non-Indian. Hodel had lots of friends in the coal companies and oil companies. Hodel was a good Ronald Reagan Republican.

Despite government rules that forbid contact between government officials and parties in a lawsuit, Peabody hired a good friend of Hodel to lobby him. The friend, Stanley W. Hulett, had worked for Interior at one point and had been a good friend of Hodel's for years. The tribe alleged that Hulett and the Peabody lawyers had actually written the directive that Hodel sent to Fritz ordering him not to act on increasing the Navajo royalties.

Fritz was going to give the Navajos a 20% royalty rate on their coal, the rate the BIA had been forced to agree on. The initial rate they got was an astonishing 2%, not the 20% lower officials at the BIA had agreed they were due! The Bureau in the 1970s had set 12.5% as the minimum rate tribes should get for coal royalties.

The coal, which was and still is furnishing electricity to Los Angeles, Las Vegas, and Phoenix, was costing the tribe $50,000 a day in lost royalties, according to an internal study done by BIA officials. Kelsey Begaye, the Navajo president, said the tribe was not privy to any of the internal meetings between Hodel, Hulett, and Peabody officials and lawyers. The BIA and Interior also cheated the Hopi Tribe, which also has huge coal deposits on its land, out of several hundred million dollars.

The Makah Tribe of northwest Washington won the right in 1998 to hunt a gray whale in their traditional fashion. They had been denied this right for 70 years (Sullivan).

As a result their culture, based largely on whaling and seafood, had changed radically. Their treaty of 1855 allowed them to continue whaling and fishing at their usual places. However, in 1920, because of the decline in the whale population worldwide, they stopped whaling. It had been the center of their culture for centuries.

They went on a whale hunt in 1999, in the midst of protests from numerous animal rights and environmental groups. They used a traditional boat and traditional hunting methods. Greenpeace followed them out into the ocean and tried to ram their boat. The local police wanted to arrest them, but they knew they had no jurisdiction. The hunters finally killed a whale and brought it to shore.

The United States needs to fix its Indian land problem. It needs to change the law to allow the following:

- Reverse the national policy spelled out in the Dawes Act, which aimed at taking as much Indian land as possible and opening it up for homesteading and settling.

- Allow Indian tribes to buy back the land that has been stolen and alienated from them over the years. When leases run out, let the tribes buy back the land and the improvements and make it tribal trust land again.
- Take individual Indian small holdings that are not tribal land and let the tribes buy them back and put them into tribal trust land.
- Affirm the validity of treaties, none of which have been broken by the tribes, to include hunting and fishing rights, landownership, and mineral rights.

TWENTY-TWO

Racism in Oil and Gas Royalties

In the 1960s the nation discovered that the "worthless" land that Indians had ended up with during the Reservation era after the Civil War had some valuable things on and under it. By some estimates, Indians owned about one-quarter of all the energy resources of the United States. These included oil, natural gas, uranium, coal, wind energy, water in rivers and lakes, and geothermal energy such as hot springs and geysers.

Indians owned about a quarter of the coal in the United States. This coal was extremely important to the dozens of companies providing electricity to such places as Phoenix, Los Angeles, San Francisco, Tucson, Las Vegas, and Oklahoma City. New finds in the decade confirmed huge coal deposits on Indian reservations in Arizona, New Mexico, Montana, and South Dakota. When these coal mines were opened, millions of tons of coal were shipped annually to electricity and power producers.

The coal companies, the oil and gas companies, and the utility companies naturally wanted to get Indian resources at the cheapest possible prices. They proceeded to do some high-powered Washington lobbying that netted them billions. They got Indian resources for a song, much less than the value of the resources. On top of that, the federal agency responsible for collecting the royalties let the oil companies operate on the honor system, cheating Indians out of other billions of dollars. Racism in the federal bureaucracy has operated to keep Indians destitute and dependent on the federal government, which can then manipulate Indians any way it wants to.

The Minerals Management Service (MMS) of the Department of the Interior is responsible for collecting royalties from federal lands, including Indian lands. The standard set by the Mineral Lands Leasing Act (MLLA) requires 1/8 of the price to be paid to the owner for onshore leases. Offshore leases require that 1/6 of the price be paid to the owners. These payments have to be made within 30 days. They require strict accounting standards, accurate records, and detailed monthly reports. These records are supposed to count each barrel of oil pumped and shipped away from a well.

In 2000, MMS collected $200 million in royalties from Indian lands. It collected a total of $5 billion on all resources on all federal lands. These royalty payments go to the individual Indian owners of the lands on which the wells are located. In some cases, the Indian wells are sitting very near the wells of white neighbors. They are tapping the same underground pool of oil. In many cases, Indians have gotten a pittance of the money coming from joint ownership, and by law should have gotten many times more.

There are ongoing attempts to rectify the problem. Following the introduction of her legislation on January 19, 2007, that would permit a study of the most accurate methods of collecting royalties on federal and Indian lands, Rep. Carolyn Maloney (Democrat, New York) said, "There may be piles of money owed to taxpayers and Indian Tribes left on the table because we don't accurately collect royalties."

"In August 1996, I released a report that showed that oil companies owed more than $2 billion in unpaid oil royalties nationwide," she added.

Following the Congress's establishment of the State and Tribal Royalty Audit Committee (STRAC) in 2006, MMS announced that it was sharply restricting the activities of the group. Under the directive from MMS Director Mrs. R. M. "Johnnie" Burton, STRAC can only meet once a year. It cannot meet without MMS being present. In fact, MMS will set the agenda for the meeting. This is like asking a deputy sheriff to operate all day with handcuffs on his wrists and no gun. However, Burton and the other MMS people have brass balls. Burton was a Bush appointee and a proud representative of Interior Secretary Gale Norton.

Naturally, Rep. Maloney co-signed a letter to Burton objecting to the restrictions MMS tried to place on STRAC. MMS tried to intervene, even though STRAC is not an Interior body. It was formed by the jurisdictions that were losing serious money on the under-reporting of royalty from oil, gas, and minerals. The initiative to form it came from state and tribal governments.

Associate MMS Director Lucy Denett had stated that STRAC meetings were not worthwhile, according to the letter. The letter from Maloney accused Denett's actions of being in retaliation for STRAC finding loopholes in MMS's monitoring of royalties.

The courts have consistently upheld decisions requiring energy companies to pay adequate royalties to Indian tribes. One such ruling by Judge Terry on August 31, 2000, ordered Alexander Energy Corporation to follow the dual accounting requirements for reporting on royalty payments from Indian lands.

The Supreme Court of Oklahoma ordered the Indian Territory Illuminating Oil Co. to pay an Osage Indian woman her royalties as far back as 1913 (*Leahy v. Indian Territory*).

On January 30, 2008, Interior Secretary Dirk Kempthorne ordered ethics training for all MMS employees who work in regulatory, collections, and enforcement roles. This followed the report of a bipartisan panel he had appointed which was headed by former Senators Bob Kerry (Democrat) and Jake Garn (Republican). Ethics training was just one of 100 recommendations the panel made.

Kempthorne formed the panel after receiving a report from the Inspector General (IG) of his Department that exposed serious management problems at MMS. Within a short time, Mrs. Burton was gone. She resigned in spring of 2007 and departed the agency in May 2007. Kempthorne appointed Attorney Randall Luthi of Wyoming to head MMS. IG Earl Devaney stated in the report that the complaint of oil companies that having to calculate interest on oil payments was a hardship on them was bogus. He wrote:

> This report tells the tale of Mineral Revenue Management (MRM), a program within MMS fraught with difficulties stemming from myriad causes; it presents examples of a systemic dilemma in MMS—that of the bureau's conflicting roles and relationships within the energy industry. It also hints of a profound failure in the development of a critical MRM information technology (IT) system; it reveals a working environment in which poor communication, or no communication, compounded an already existing element of distrust; and it demonstrates a band-aid approach to holding together one of the federal government's largest revenue producing operations. In addition, we discovered a number of other significant issues worthy of separate investigation, including ethics lapses, program mismanagement and process failures.

Despite a new $150 million computer system, MRM, a division within MMS, had reported that its computers could not compute the interest due on Indian oil and gas royalties. The whistleblowers who complained about the inadequacy of the system had 18 attempts at retaliation thrown at them. For his trouble filing against Shell and Kerr-McGee, Bobby Maxwell was fired.

The companies alleged to have shorted the federal government and/or Indian tribes included Kerr-McGee, ENI, Shell, and AGIP Exploration. The amount of money involved is staggering. Mr. Devaney reported that:

> Between 1998 and 2004, the OIG jointly conducted royalty *qui tam* investigations with DOJ that resulted in the recovery of more than $568 million from 25 U.S. companies operating oil, natural gas, coal, and other activities on federal and tribal lands.

Indeed, that amount is just the amount they found, which is only a small part of the total amount involved. The total would probably be well over $50 billion, and could approach $75 billion, based on the annual amount MMS collects, which is between $6 billion and $12 billion a year.

One of the problems with MMS and MRM is that the employees tend to be former employees of the oil and gas companies they supposedly regulate. Many of them will return to their former employees when their federal service is over. There ought to be a law requiring anyone serving in a federal regulatory agency not to have worked for any company which that person would then regulate.

On August 17, 2007, Burlington Resources, Inc., agreed to pay the U.S. $97.5 million on royalties it had underpaid on natural gas wells on federal and Indian lands. A federal whistleblower had filed suit against Burlington. In the same action, Shell Oil had already paid $56 million in underpayments, and Dominion Exploration had paid $2 million (Devaney).

Indian royalties in oil and gas have frequently also been diverted to the benefit of non-Indians. Justice William O. Douglas, dissenting in *United States v. Jim* (409 U.S. 80, November 20, 1972), said the United States (meaning the BIA) had illegally taken money from the Navajo Indians living on the Utah Extension and used it for non-Indians. When oil was discovered on the reservation in the 1930s, the law set aside the royalties for tuition for the Navajo students and for roads. Instead, the Justice said:

> The white man was unconcerned about this domain until oil was discovered; and then he became quite active. By June 30, 1970, the royalties owing the Aneth Extension Indians had increased to $7,039,022.32. Of this, $78,000 was used to pipe water from the Aneth Extension to the adjoining lands of a white man, an "improvement" that only incidentally aided the resident Indians. Another $27,000 of Indian funds was spent for the construction of an airport and connecting road, which substantially benefited a white man's private dude ranch operation. ... When this suit was started, additional expenditures were about to be made: $175,000 to a federal agency to locate isolated water springs on the Aneth Extension and $500,000 to build a hard-surfaced road outside the boundaries of the Extension.

The Council of Energy Resource Tribes (CERT), which represents almost all the tribes in oil and gas resources, says the MMS system of monitoring royalty payments amounts to an honor system. They said the system "unfailingly results in underpayment" to tribes (Andrews, 2007).

Bobby Maxwell worked for MMS for 30 years, eventually heading an office of 120 people who audited royalty payments. When he could not get his superiors, including MMS head Johnnie Burton, to collect adequate royalties from oil companies, Maxwell brought a lawsuit against Kerr-McGee. This lawsuit eventually led to $440 million in underreported royalty payments from 26 oil companies. Kerr-McGee had to pay up. Bobby Maxwell was fired.

The following and other recommendations need to be implemented immediately:

- Congress needs to pass a law forbidding any federal employee being hired who will regulate, monitor, or oversee any actions of his or her former employer.
- Congress needs to stipulate that federal employees leaving federal employment will be barred for five years from working for an employer they have monitored, regulated, or overseen during their federal employment.
- Congress needs to authorize an independent commission of non-federal personnel to review the monitoring and regulation of minerals mining and oil and gas production on federal and Indian lands, and report to the Congress on its findings and recommendations.
- Congress needs to pass a whistle blower protection act that would prohibit such people from being fired unless they have committed a major felony. There are hundreds of potential cases not being filed now because MMS and other federal employees fear retaliation or firing. The law needs to include provisions for whistle blowers that have been fired to be reinstated in their former jobs.

TWENTY-THREE

Racism in the Environment

The poverty on Indian reservations has led solid waste companies, uranium manufacturers, and others to approach tribes with the idea of using reservations as waste dumps. Ruben reports that 42 tribes have been approached with these types of proposals. She says that 30 have rejected the proposals.

Some tribes have become desperate. The Mescalero Apache Nation attempted to place a nuclear waste disposal unit on the reservation a dozen years ago. The proposal generated lots of heat in the nearby New Mexico communities, leading to a suspension of the project. The tribe had accepted a large federal grant to conduct a study of the problem.

The Laguna Pueblo and the Spokane Indian Reservation are the leading two places where the U.S. mined uranium for three decades. Sherman Alexie (Spokane), the writer and moviemaker, is convinced that he will die from cancer. His grandmother died from esophageal cancer in 1980. A quarter of a century ago, his mother and some neighbors started to make red dots on a map where some tribal members had contracted cancer. The roads from the uranium mines were soon full of red dots (Cornwall).

With their high levels of poverty, unemployment, social problems, and lack of political clout, Indian reservations have become easy targets for some of the worst cases of environmental and solid waste abuse. Minerals mining refuse, environmental dumping, and solid waste disposal lead the list of environmental concerns in Indian Country.

Picher, Oklahoma, in the northeast corner of the state, was the site of zinc and lead mining in the first part of the twentieth century. Its newspaper boasted in 1916 that there were 160 mines and mills in or near the small rural community. It was the greatest lead and zinc mining center in the world. But the mines left the community with what the Environmental Protection Agency (EPA) called in 1981 the most polluted community in the United States.

The home of the Quapaw Tribe, Picher could only exist because of negotiations by the federal government on behalf of the town. The BIA took land from the tribe for the mines and the town to be built on. By 1916 the town had grown to 13,000 residents. Today it has only 1,640 residents. The mines played out long ago, leaving only their pollutants for the town to enjoy. It is the infamous home of the Tar Creek Superfund site.

Lead dust blows around the town with the strong Oklahoma winds. Lead and zinc have leached into the surrounding groundwater, lakes, and ponds, many of which still have children swimming in them.

In the PBS movie *The Creek Runs Red,* Picher resident Orval "Hoppy" Ray stated, "Once the mining companies pulled out, the acid water just completely flooded the mines. Eventually the acid water sprung from the ground and flowed into the creek, staining it burnt red."

The waste left by the mines, which have made their profits and are long gone, now cover over 25,000 acres. The biggest moneymakers from the mines were the Federal Mining and Smelting Company and the Eagle-Picher Mining & Smelting Company. Practically all the Quapaw tribal lands have been left polluted. Tar Creek is now literally stained permanently red with the minerals still leaching into it.

Sen. Jim Inhofe and Rep. Brad Carson have both proposed legislation to clean up the Superfund site and to move all the residents out of the town. The legislation is still pending. Inhofe estimates it will take $100 million to clean up the site.

The residents of the Rosebud reservation in South Dakota finally defeated a proposal to place the world's largest hog farm on their reservation. The location north of Cedar Butte would have built 288 huge hog barns in a development that would have cost $100 million. The unemployment rate on the reservation of 60% to 80% leaves the Lakota people there vulnerable for any proposal that promises to provide jobs.

After the previous Rosebud Tribal Council and chairman approved the lease of the land, William Kindle ran for chairman in 1999 on a platform pledged to get rid of the hog farm. U.S. District Court Judge Charles Kornmann ruled in May 2001 that the contract signed by the earlier council was valid, and that the development could go ahead.

Finally in 2005 the courts ruled that the two hog farms already in place could continue to operate. However, the other 11 farms in the original contract would not be allowed. The two farms produce some 96,000 pigs a year. The extended negotiations between the tribe and Bell Farms ended the battle that had raged for almost a decade. U.S. District Court Judge Richard Battey allowed that the agreement was valid and could stand. After 15 years the tribe can buy back the hog farms.

After approving a federal grant to study the feasibility of locating a nuclear storage dump on the Mescalero Apache reservation in 1992, the tribe finally decided that it did not want to store nuclear materials on the reservation. The tribe would have earned about $50 million a year from the facility, according to the late Wendell Chino, who was the leader of the tribe for 45 years.

New Mexico Governor Bruce King fought the proposal. Residents of Albuquerque, where trucks hauling the nuclear waste would have to pass, opposed it. Senator Jeff Bingaman of New Mexico also opposed it. Both King and Bingaman recognized the sovereignty of the tribe, but did not want nuclear waste in the state. The anti-nuclear forces eventually won. In the meantime, a casino, hotel, and other tourist developments have brought many more jobs into Mescalero country southeast of Albuquerque.

The Campo Indian Reservation toyed in the 1980s with the idea of allowing a huge solid waste disposal firm to use the reservation as a waste site. The reservation is 65 miles east of San Diego, in an isolated desert environment. The site would have covered 400 acres and handled 3,000 tons of waste per day (McGovern).

The tribe would have made $50 million over a period of 20 years. For people with 70% to 80% unemployment rates, any jobs looked good. However, Donna Tisdale, a nearby rancher, said the landfill would pollute the groundwater and her drinking water.

Despite opposition from local ranchers and environmentalists, the EPA approved the Campo plan. The 300 Kumeyaay Indians living on the reservation would have benefited from jobs, schools, and housing, according to tribal leaders.

After a decade, and despite the approval of the EPA, the landfill at Campo was dead. In 2004 the tribe announced another proposal to start the dump site again. In the meantime, they had started a small casino, where at least some of their tribal members are now employed.

The Western Shoshone Tribes were not contacted or asked their opinion of the nuclear explosions in the Nevada desert in the 1950s and 1960s. The World Watch Institute reports that the federal government triggered over 1,000 explosions in Nevada. The United States has plans to deposit in Yucca Mountain most of the spent nuclear fuel it has generated in the past half century—this despite the fact that the mountain is in the center of Western Shoshone territory, and is sacred to them.

The government is also proposing a nuclear waste dump site on the Skull Valley Indian reservation in Utah.

Hundreds of Navajos and people from Laguna Pueblo and Acoma Pueblo worked in the huge uranium mine at Mount Taylor just north of Grants, New Mexico, when it was in full swing. Indian children still play on the piles of tailings (Brugge *et al.*). Most of the Indian miners who produced thousands of tons of uranium for Kerr-McGee have died, leaving widows and children with little or no compensation.

Other tribes have rejected proposals for solid waste dumps. The Umatilla Tribe of Oregon, the Kaw Tribe of Oklahoma, the Lakota tribe at Pine Ridge, South Dakota, the Choctaw Tribe of Mississippi, and the Paiute tribe of Arizona have all rejected proposals to build solid waste dump sites on their lands.

- The United States needs to study the effects of uranium mining at Mount Taylor, the Spokane Indian Reservation, and other places where uranium was mined after World War II.
- The United States needs to establish a compensation fund to pay for the early deaths of Indians and other people who worked in the uranium mines and who later suffered from a variety of cancers.

TWENTY-FOUR

Racism in Religion

Racism against Indians started in the first colonies. Roanoke, Jamestown, Plymouth Rock, and the Massachusetts Bay Colony were founded, on paper, not to make fortunes or to settle the New World. Their charters, issued by the king of England, called for them to spread the gospel to the heathen Indians of North America.

Several of the colonies engaged in turning Indians into slaves. It is a little known fact of history that Indians were slaves in several parts of the United States. The infamous Catholic Father Junipero Serra, who is revered by some people, is hated by California Indians because he enslaved so many Indians.

The original English settlers in the United States, at Jamestown and Plymouth Rock, stated in their charters that their main mission in settlement was to save the pagan Indians from their "superstitions" and make good Christians out of them. This rationale was good enough for the King; he gave them their official charters.

Thus, Indian religions had been banned and condemned before any colonists had actually settled in North America. The government finally got around to making Indian religions illegal in 1921. The Religious Crimes Act of that year made it illegal for Indians to practice their religions; guilty Indians could and did go to prison. The government invaded tribal places of worship such as kivas and religious altars, arresting people and sometimes holding them in prison with no charges filed against them.

Some of the earlier Indians who had refused to give up their religions ended up on Alcatraz Island as prisoners in the 1890s. The BIA kept them there for years without any law allowing the government to do this. The BIA officials tore down religious buildings and sites, burned down kivas, and destroyed numerous religious artifacts. Hardly any news of this made the pages of the daily newspapers and magazines in the United States. Indian reservations were so isolated that federal officials could do what they pleased with no one calling them to task.

Indeed, the ban on Indian religions still exists in the minds of some people today. They believe that Christianity is the only true religion, and they try to outlaw or banish any other types of religion. That topic is one of the hot ones even in today's political climate, with politicians trying to out-Christian each other.

In an intercultural exchange some time ago, an Indian elder asked a Christian missionary if he was one of those Baptists who thought only Baptists were going to get into Heaven. The missionary thought for a few seconds, and then replied, "I don't think all the Baptists are going to make it."

From the 1880s until 1978, it was illegal for Indians to practice their Native religions. Indian people were imprisoned for attending religious ceremonies—if they got caught. This period was known as the underground period. Indian people still practiced their religions, but in secret.

Indian people took advantage of living on isolated reservations to practice their religions. Few white men were around on Saturday nights when the Native American Church and other Indian ceremonies took place. While many Indians went to jail for practicing their religion, many more never got caught and never went to jail. Many Indian religions have remained intact to this day.

Many people believe Indian people have no religion. In fact, Indian people are very religious. Traditional Indians pray when they get up in the morning, often facing the east. They use corn pollen or corn meal as a sacred omen; some people also use sage, sweet grass, tobacco, and other plants in their ceremonies. If you have ever been to an Indian religious ceremony, you know that Indians pray about five times longer than white people.

In a Christian church, people get antsy if a prayer goes on longer than a few minutes. In an Indian church, one prayer might last ten or fifteen minutes. In addition, you have to be quiet with your eyes closed the whole time, listening to everything the person praying is saying.

The four areas of conflict over Indian religions have been (1) having access to sacred sites, (2) restrictions on sacred items, (3) attempts to shut down Indian religious ceremonies, and (4) Indian funerary objects. All four have hindered, but not destroyed, Indian religions and the practice of religious ceremonies.

Part of the practice of Indian religions is having access to sacred areas. To Indians, having access to a certain river, forest, lake, or mountain is the same as a Christian having access to a church. In some cases, the relationship is the same as Catholics having access to the Vatican, the most holy of holy places in Christendom.

Non-Indians have long not understood, and have not cared to understand, this relationship. After all, if Indians were going to go away pretty soon anyway, why worry about protecting a site just because they wanted it?

The Forest Service under President Teddy Roosevelt took the sacred area of Blue Lake away from the Pueblo of Taos in 1906, without their permission. The lake, which the Taos people called Ba Whyea, was sacred to them. They refused to take money as payment for the lake.

The U.S. Forest Service promptly "developed" the lake and the 50,000 acres surrounding it. The roads they built let tourists, ranchers, and camps come into the area. They fished in the sacred lake and grazed their cattle on the land. The government allowed clearcutting of timber in the area, which was part of the Carson National Forest.

Paul Bernal, a Taos elder, spent much of his life working to restore the lake to its sacred status. "We are probably the only citizens of the United States who are required to practice our religion under a permit from the government. This is not religious freedom as it is guaranteed by the Constitution," he said.

The Pueblo of Taos enlisted some powerful people in its struggle to regain its sacred lake. They included the famous artist Mabel Dodge Luhan, the writers Oliver LaFarge and Frank Waters, and the Udall brothers Morris and Stuart, both of whom were high government officials. Joining the fight later were Senators Barry Goldwater, Ted Kennedy, and Robert Kennedy.

After 64 years of struggle, and many trips to Washington, they finally got the lake restored to them in 1970. The whole 48,000 acres was restored to its former status as part of tribal trust lands. Nixon signed the bill, HR 471, on December 15, 1970, a year and a month after the Alcatraz occupation brought it to his attention. Only members of the Pueblo of Taos are allowed access to Blue Lake now.

It was one of the victories spurred on by the occupation of Alcatraz. Richard Nixon, facing re-election in 1972, was trying to thwart the effects of Indian protests. His answer was to give Indian people what they wanted. The major action he took was to issue a statement on Indian policy in July 1970. He said Indian programs were under-funded, and that Indian people really wanted self-determination. A few years later the Indian Self-Determination and Education Act made large parts of his policy a national law.

Nixon's policy also ended the hated policy of terminating Indian treaties. To this day, the worst word you can say in Indian Country is "termination." Under this illegal and one-sided policy, 152 tribes were terminated between 1954 and 1968. The clear intent of the government, expressed in House Concurrent Resolution 108 (HCR 108) in 1953, was to terminate all Indian treaties and make "citizens" of all Indians. (The complete list of the terminated tribes is found in my book *Modern American Indian Leaders.*)

Two years after Blue Lake was returned, the federal government returned the sacred Mount Adams to the Yakama Nation. They had also fought long and hard to protect this mountain from logging and mining. They consider it sacred.

The Black Hills of South Dakota is the largest sacred site that has been taken from Indians. As soon as the Lakota, Dakota, and Nakota people were settled on reservations after defeating Custer, the state of South Dakota started scheming to take away as much of their land as possible. The Black Hills were included in their schemes. The Lakota call the Black Hills *Paha Sapa.* The Laramie Treaty of 1868 guaranteed the Black Hills to the Teton Sioux people.

The Black Hills are famous for being the site of Mount Rushmore, where the profiles of four U.S. presidents are carved in granite. When gold was discovered there in 1874, the government soon moved the Indians out and onto other smaller reservations. Ironically, it was George Custer who found gold in the hills in 1874, two years before the Indians killed him and all his men. Like everything dealing with Indians in those days, the Indians were moved from the Black Hills at the point of a gun.

However, they never agreed to give up their sacred Black Hills. When the Supreme Court decided in their favor in 1980 and awarded them a payment of $106 million, they refused to take the money. It has been accumulating interest for over 40 years now, and they still refuse to take it, even though it is now almost $800 million.

Justice Harry Blackmun wrote, quoting the Court in an earlier case, "A more ripe and rank case of dishonorable dealings will never, in all probability, be found in our history, which is not, taken as a whole, the disgrace it now pleases some persons to believe." He blasted the duplicity of President Grant in failing to have federal troops protect the Sioux people on their reservation in the Black Hills.

In the case of the Gasquet and Orleans Ranger Districts in California, a proposed road (the GO Road) to connect the two would have gone through lands that three tribes regarded as sacred. The Yurok, Tolowa, and Karuk regarded the areas that would be affected the same way Catholics regard the Vatican—sacred beyond belief. However, the Supreme Court let the "GO Road" be built, after it had been stopped by federal district court rulings. In an opinion written by Sandra Day O'Connor in 1988, the Court said, "the Constitution simply does not provide a principle that could justify upholding the Indians' legal claims." In other words, you have the right to believe, but not the right to practice.

In a case in Oregon, *Oregon v. Smith,* the Supreme Court decided the state of Oregon could punish two Indians who had used peyote in their practice in the Native American Church. They had been fired for using the peyote, and had appealed. In a 5 to 4 decision, the Court upheld the ruling and allowed the firings to stand.

The most misunderstood concept of Indian people is their relationship to the earth. When an agriculture agent walked with hard shoes on newly plowed ground at the Pueblo of Taos a hundred years ago, a local Taos elder chastised him. "You wouldn't walk on your mother wearing those hard shoes," the Taos man told the white man. So the white man had to take off his shoes to walk in the fields.

The concept of the "Mother Earth" has been improperly and partially grasped by New Agers, Wiccans, and hippies since the 1970s. A non-Indian may understand the concept of the earth as a mother in an intellectual sense, but it takes an Indian growing up with this kind of religion from birth to have the real feeling of closeness to nature, of having the earth as a parent, and respecting all living things. I cannot get people to understand why I won't kill a spider. I think spiders are needed; otherwise we would be overrun by bugs. So I don't kill them, and non-Indians think I am crazy. They want to kill every rat, mouse, spider, snake, tarantula, and other dangerous animal they see.

The Native American Church has 250,000 members, including the late Winnebago Chairman, Reuben Snake. This makes it the largest Native American religious organization. Its most controversial practice is using the cactus plant peyote as part of its ceremonies. Its members compare peyote to the sacramental wine that Christians drink, which to them symbolizes the blood of Christ.

The Sun Dance, where the flesh of the chest is pierced by pulling against ropes tied to a pole, is a controversial practice of the Lakota people. It has spread to the reservations in Montana and a few other places, but it is not for the faint hearted.

The Navajo religion is based partly on "sings," or healing ceremonies conducted by a medicine man. In the 1970s a medical doctor at the University of New Mexico became one of the first non-Indians to believe in the effects of Navajo healing. He soon set up a joint program where Western medicine and Navajo ceremonies were combined to bring about better results for Navajo patients.

People have not understood the relationship between Indian religions and eagles. In the old days, a warrior had to prove his high worth by trapping an eagle and claiming some of its feathers. The most popular way was to dig a pit and sit a live rabbit on top. When the eagle swooped down to grab its prey, the warrior would rise out of the pit and grab the eagle by its legs.

Under the Bald Eagle and Golden Eagle Protection Act, Indians can own eagle feathers, but non-Indians cannot. It has usually been a federal or state policeman who has busted an Indian for having eagle feathers. The Indian usually gets charged with violating a federal law that protects eagles or wildlife. However, the courts have given Indians some strong protections against arrest and harassment in the past quarter of a century.

The Tenth Circuit Court decided, sitting *en banc* (as a full court), that non-Indians cannot own eagle feathers even if they are members of an Indian religion. In a separate case, the Tenth Circuit Court also ruled that eagle feathers seized from an Indian person had to be returned to him since they were essential in his religious practices.

Another controversy has been digging up Indian bones and grave sites. Until the 1970s, if a builder dug up Indian bones which were in a cemetery or burial site, he would often just move them or throw them away. However, then Indians started objecting to having the remains of their relatives dug up, and started protesting. "How would you like it," they asked, "if we started digging up your cemeteries and disturbing the bones of your dead?"

The builders, of course, didn't want to hear it, but eventually the courts and public opinion forced them to take the feelings of Indians into account. In some cases, they and the aggrieved Indians came to some agreement about where to move the bones, and the developers were allowed to continue with their plans to build a strip mall or a parking lot. In other cases there was a lot of controversy; some issues never seemed to get solved.

In California, the American Indian Heritage Commission got involved in some of these cases. Soon it was taking as much time and attention as the other Indian functions of the state government.

The American Indian Religious Freedom Act (AIRFA), Public Law 95–341, changed the U.S. official policy to "protect and preserve for American Indians their inherent right of freedom to believe, express, and exercise the traditional religions of the American Indian …."

The AIRFA became law in 1978. Even so, Rep. Morris Udall, the leading sponsor in the U.S. House, declared that the new law had no teeth in it. It did not guarantee any rights to religion for Indian people. It simply reversed a long-held principle that Indian religions were banned and outlawed, which the BIA had been enforcing since the 1880s. However, it led to the passing of the Native American Graves Protection and Repatriation

Act (NAGPRA) of 1990, under which some objects of religious significance have been returned to Indian people.

Museums tried a variety of tactics to avoid complying with the law. UC Berkeley's Hearst Museum allegedly re-catalogued more than 80% of its extensive collection of Indian artifacts as culturally unidentifiable, according to the December 2007 issue of the *Muscogee Nation News.* The law left the disposition of the cultural artifacts, and their return to the tribes who formerly owned them, up to the museums.

Wikipedia reports that over 110,000 items that cannot be identified by a particular tribe are sitting in museums and archeological sites somewhere. They include shields, war bonnets, beadwork, human skeletons, funerary objects, burial boxes, human tissue, burial cloths, beaded vests, items of clothing, and many other types of things. Most of them were lifted from Indians or traded from Indians in the previous two centuries. The objections of scholars that they need the objects for study have been pretty much overruled by the laws and the courts.

The oldest of these pieces is Kennewick Man, found in the state of Washington. The Umatilla, the Colville, the Yakama, and the Nez Perce tribes all claim that he was one of their people. Their main concern is to reclaim the body and give it a proper burial. They have been fought at every turn by scholars who maintain that the skeletal remains are the oldest one ever found in the United States. The researchers want to keep the skeleton to study it.

Such institutions as the University of California at Berkeley, my alma mater, and the Smithsonian Institution initially fought the mandate of the law to return beaded things, skeletons, and other body parts. Nevertheless, for example, the remains of the famous Yahi Indian Ishi were returned to his tribe for a proper burial. His remains had been in the Smithsonian in Washington, DC, for almost a hundred years before they were returned in the early part of this century and buried in a secret place. My friend Mickey Gemmill, the former Chairman of the Pit River Tribe (Achamowi) of northern California, led the ceremony that gave him a proper burial.

In recent decades, a variety of religious celebrations that had been allowed to lapse have been revived. Among them are the Sun Dance, the Bear Dance, and the Rain Dance.

Indian religions continue to be a sore point in Indian Country. Indian people continue to be persecuted for practicing their religion. Having eagle feathers and peyote buttons in your possession could still get you arrested and thrown in jail by some local ignorant policeman. It could cost you months or years of legal wrangling and take time out of your life.

Moreover, if you go to prison, you will not be allowed to practice your religion e. g., *Randall Trapp et al. v. Commissioner DuBois,* 1995. A group of Indian inmates in a Massachusetts prison had been refused the right to have religious meetings. Prisoners were harassed by the guards. Their ceremonial objects, including pipes, drums, headbands, and feathers, had been confiscated. The prison administration had denied their request to build a sweat lodge within the prison. Finally, in 2003, the prison and the prison administrators settled the issue with a memorandum which the court ordered them to negotiate and file with the court. The prisoners were finally allowed to build a sweat lodge—subject to 11 rules and requirements laid out by the administration.

Unfortunately, this case does not automatically mean that all Indian prisoners in all prisons will be allowed to practice their religion or build a sweat lodge. Prison officials are still not allowing Indians certain religious privileges.

You will not be allowed to wear long hair, and if you come into prison with long hair, they will cut it off over your objections, as in *Griffin v. Brierton,* 1979.

You will not be allowed to have in your possession sage, sacred tobacco, sweet grass, and prayer pipes, and there will be little you can do about it. However, if you want to attend Christian services, no problem; you will be allowed to go.

U.S. v. Dann, 1985, involved the rights to Shoshone Indians in Nevada to graze their cattle on aboriginal lands. The Dann sisters have fought for several decades for the return of their grazing lands that were taken illegally. Their cattle have been seized several times.

- Congress needs to rewrite AIRFA and give it some teeth.
- Congress needs to pass a new law giving NAGPRA some teeth and setting penalties for people and institutions that violate it. If an Indian went into a white cemetery and dug up some bones, he would go to prison for 20 years. In contrast, white people can dig up Indian bones and artifacts and not have any penalties imposed for it.

TWENTY-FIVE

Racism and Suicide

I was driving west on I-40 in 1990, headed for Gallup. Just as I passed Thoreau, with 30 miles to go, a middle-aged Navajo man jumped the fence on the side of the freeway and ran into traffic. A young man and a young woman jumped the fence right behind him and caught him in the middle of the two lanes. They grabbed him and pulled him off the freeway, thereby averting his attempt at suicide. I have wondered for years what drove that man to try suicide that day.

Monica Yellow Bird's cousin hanged himself when she was only 17 years old. The cousin was also 17. He was a good student and had ambitions. However, when he started drinking his life went out of control. The family found him hanging by a sheet. A few years later, in 2004, Monica joined other young people to form a suicide hotline in Minneapolis.

The rate of suicide among Indians is several times the rate for the rest of the population. It is either 300% higher or 200% higher for Indians—or somewhere in between, depending on which estimates you believe. I believe the high figures (see Shaughnessy et al.).

When I spent a week at a school on one reservation three years ago, I got the surprise of my life. The third day I was there the high school got let out for a ceremony at 2:00 in the afternoon. I had to stop my interview, because everyone was going outside.

The principal announced that they were going to let one balloon loose for every student who had attempted suicide within the past five years. A student was holding each balloon. On the signal, all the students released their balloons, and 52 helium-filled balloons took to the air.

The total student population there was 450. I seriously doubt any non-Indian school of that size in the United States had as many suicide attempts in that short a period of time. Six of them had been "successful." The ones who had not been successful were left with scars on their wrists, on their necks, and on their souls for life.

The Suicide Prevention Resource Center says suicide is the second leading cause of death for Indians between the ages of 10 and 34. Among Indian children attending BIA boarding schools, 16% had attempted suicide in 2001—an astonishing rate of one out of six. At the same time, mental health services are "not easily accessible" because of lack of funding, services not culturally appropriate for Indians, and personnel shortages and high turnover rates.

High numbers of Indian young people have been denied their tribal spiritual life for the past 125 years. However, Garroutte cited this as one of the highest guarantees against a suicide attempt. Young people with a tribal spiritual life were only half as likely to try suicide as an answer to their problems as those with no connection to their cultural and spiritual life.

Among the things related to suicide are:

- Drinking alcohol
- Using drugs, including both illegal drugs and prescription drugs
- High rates of poverty
- Poor educational achievement
- Lack of employment
- Assimilation and acculturation
- Loss of Native culture, language, and spirituality
- Social isolation
- Family violence

All these things basically define Indian Country. Indian young people often attempt suicide as an act of desperation. They may be tasked with taking care of younger siblings, starting before they are ten years old. They are often neglected at schools, especially public schools on or near reservations, where 85% of them attend. In most cases, they are in the minority at the public school; whites have taken over the land, the businesses, and the jobs on or near reservations.

This reality leaves Indians in poverty positions, with both parents often having to work hard to eke out a living. Furthermore, in at least a third of the cases, the Indian youngster is living with a single parent who is working against hope just to put food on the table.

When the schools belittle students and put them down, they often become desperate and try suicide. However, only about 5% of suicide attempts are successful. The other 95% are left with physical and psychological scars.

Jail is one of the leading places where Indians commit suicide. In one study (Severson and Duclos), the researchers found that Indians got put in jail mainly for driving without licenses or driving under the influence of alcohol. They also found that suicide is the second leading cause of death among jail inmates. They also found that Indians tended to be unemployed, to have more alcohol-related arrests than non-Indians, to have served more time in jail, and to have been hospitalized more often for alcohol-related problems.

Indians had also suffered more trauma than non-Indians. In addition, they felt that no one at the jail really cared about them. They were often the objects of scorn and ridicule, such as being called "Chief," "Squaw," and "Buck."

Gladwell points out that suicide is not a "stand alone" act. People who attempt suicide, who are much more numerous than those who commit suicide, are often following the example of an outstanding leader of their own community.

The federal government needs to be concerned with suicide in Indian Country. Among other things, it needs to:

- Instigate the development of suicide prevention programs in Indian Country.
- Help provide suicide prevention specialists in areas where suicide rates are high.
- Help train tribal members to become professional psychotherapists, psychologists, and psychiatrists and commit them to serving in Indian Country.

TWENTY-SIX

Racism and Alcohol

Alcohol has been the bane of Indian life for four hundred years. Very soon after the colonies got themselves established in Massachusetts, Virginia, North Carolina, South Carolina, and Georgia, they established rum and whiskey as part of the barter system of white traders with Indians.

President Jefferson believed that Indians should not be allowed to keep their hunting grounds. He thought Indians either had to give up their hunting grounds or be eradicated. To prevent them from keeping the hunting grounds, he encouraged hunters, trappers, and traders to move into Indian Country. They inevitably brought whiskey with them to weaken the Indians and make them subject to manipulation.

Gallup, New Mexico, for decades had drive-up liquor stores, which finally got banned a decade ago. However, it took an act of the legislature, literally, to ban them. The New Mexico State Legislature finally passed an act several years ago that banned them outright. In the meantime, the 30 miles between Gallup and Window Rock, the Navajo Capital, had been labeled "Blood Alley" because of the high numbers of deaths from drunk driving that happened along it. Friday and Saturday nights were the big killers.

Gallup, Gordon, Winner, Chadron, Farmington, Holbrook, Flagstaff, and other border towns have been known for Indians and drinking for decades. Every year several Indians get killed by trains when they fall asleep on the tracks in Gallup. They get killed when they freeze to death after they fall asleep in the open. However, they mostly get killed or maimed when they wreck their cars or get hit by someone who is drunk and driving a car.

I have been working in Gallup or visiting it for some 30 years now. For four years I evaluated the Indian Education Act program for the Gallup schools. One morning in 1989 I was headed to the district office after visiting a school. When I passed the jail, I saw about 75 Indians walking out and heading back downtown. They were obviously hung over.

"What were those 75 drunk Indians I just saw walking down by the jail?" I asked my boss, Boyd Hogner.

"That's just the ten o'clock let-out," he said. "They start about five or six in the morning. As soon as a group is sober enough, they start letting them out. The last one will be about noon."

I calculated that the Gallup police were arresting about 300 to 400 Indians a night—and that was on a week night. On weekends the total is much higher.

The mayor, a Hispanic, was almost recalled a year or two later. He was cooperating with the Navajo Nation to raise money for an alcohol rehabilitation facility. He beat the recall petition by a few percentage points. His sin was admitting that Gallup had a problem with Indian drunks.

White Clay, Nebraska, which is not even large enough to be called a village, is one of the worst places for Indians and alcohol. The total population is 22. It has been the object of lots of Indian protests for decades now. Its claim to shame: it sells more beer to Indians than any other town in the United States. The entire little place consists of less than half a dozen houses—and two beer stores. These two stores, sitting just south of the Pine Ridge reservation, sell beer by the case day and night. Their per capita sales are the highest in the world. The two stores sell over four million cans and bottles of beer each year!

Indeed, the most dangerous piece of road in the world is the road from White Clay back to the reservation. It is not a road to be driving on a Friday or a Saturday night. Almost all of the beer sold goes to people at Pine Ridge, which still has an ordinance forbidding liquor sales or ownership on the reservation.

Just down the road from White Clay is the border town of Rushville, Nebraska. It is in Sheridan County, the same county as White Clay. STAR reports that on July 16, 2005, the jailer found Lino "Jay" Spotted Elk hanging in his cell, a suicide.

He had been arrested in 2003 with some other boys who had held up a service station. He spent a few months in jail, and was released later that year. He had not finished high school. The only work he could get was working as a ranch hand by the day. However, the police would not leave him alone; police harassment was a fact of his daily life. If he was sitting outside his house, they would stop by and say they knew he was guilty of something. Finally the family could not take it any longer, and prepared to move back home to Rosebud in July 2005.

The night before his suicide, the police arrested him for an unpaid speeding ticket. Before midnight, Jay allegedly hanged himself with his belt, which the police had failed to take from him. He had bruises and scratches on several parts of his body.

According to Dr. Jay Shore at the University of Colorado, the abuse of alcohol is associated with five of the top ten causes of death in Indian country. They are accidents, alcoholism, suicides, homicides, and cirrhosis of the liver.

There is an institute in Sacramento that trains Indian people how to fight alcohol. There is another one in Minnesota. The University of Denver has an institute that studies alcoholism and treats it. They are not nearly enough. Gallup and the Navajo Nation may have the only place for Indians to dry out and become rehabilitated.

I was the oldest child of an alcoholic. Researchers now know that such children have to grow up quickly. The oldest children of alcoholics have a huge need for control. If anything is out of place or missing, they "lose it" a little bit until they can find it. I know, because I am that way. An article I read on the subject in *Newsweek* 35 years ago could have been written about me.

The older kids have to take care of younger children, including feeding them, changing their dirty diapers, keeping them safe, putting them to sleep at night, protecting them from harm, fixing their breakfast, and getting them off to school in the mornings when mom and dad may be passed out and incapable of taking care of children.

The health effects of alcohol have been devastating in Indian County. Suicides, accidents, murders, violence, and health problems have all sprung from alcohol abuse. It is widely accepted now that alcohol use and abuse will spread like wildfire among oppressed peoples. The axiom has proved to be true in Asia, North America, Africa, South America, Russia, the United States, Canada, England, the South Pacific, and so on.

BIBLIOGRAPHY

Adams, David W. *Education for Extinction: American Indians and the Boarding School Experience.* Lawrence: University of Kansas Press, 1995.

Albuquerque Public Schools. "School Report Card." Albuquerque: the District, 1999.

Andrews, Edmund L. "Ex-Auditor Says He Was Told to Be Lax on Oil Fees." *The New York Times,* March 29, 2007.

Andrews, Lynn. *Medicine Woman.* New York: Harper and Row, 1980.

Associated Press. "Indian Athletes Experience Racism on the Road." *Billings Gazette,* February 6, 2007.

Banks, Dennis, and Richard Erdoes. *Ojibwa Warrior: Dennis Banks and the Rise of the American Indian Movement.* Norman: University of Oklahoma Press, 2005.

Barker, Rodney. *The Broken Circle: A True Story of Murder and Magic in Indian Country.* New York: Ivy Books, 1993.

Bataille, Gretchen M. *The Pretend Indians: Images of Native Americans in the Movies.* Ames: Iowa State University Press, 1980.

Benedict, Jeff. *Without Reservation: How a Controversial Indian Tribe Rose to Power and Built the World's Largest Casino.* New York: HarperCollins, 2000.

Berkhofer, Robert F. *The White Man's Indian: Images of the American Indian from Columbus to the Present.* New York: Vintage Press, 1979.

Biolsi, Thomas. *Deadliest Enemies: Law and Race Relations on and off Rosebud Reservation.* Minneapolis: University of Minnesota Press, 2007.

Braustein, Richard. *Justice in South Dakota: Does Race Make a Difference?* Vermillion: University of South Dakota, Government Research Bureau, 2002.

Brayboy, Tim, and Bruce Barton. *Playing Before an Overflow Crowd.* Chapel Hill: Chapel Hill Press, Inc., 2003.

Browder, Laura. "'What Does It Tell Us That We Are So Easily Deceived'? Impostor Indians." In *American Indian Studies: An Interdisciplinary Approach to Contemporary Issues,* edited by Dane Morrison. New York: Peter Lang, 1997.

Brown, Dee. *Bury My Heart at Wounded Knee.* New ed. New York: Henry Holt & Co., 2001.

Brugge, Doug, Timothy Benally, and Esther Yazzie-Lewis. *The Navajo People and Uranium Mining.* Albuquerque: University of New Mexico Press, 2006.

Buchanan, Susy. "Sacred Orgasm." *Phoenix New Times*, June 13, 2002.

Byler, William. *The Destruction of Indian Families.* New York: Association on American Indian Affairs, 1974.

Castagna, M., and Dei, G. J. S. "An Historical Overview of the Application of the Race Concept in Social Practice." In *Anti-Racist Feminism: Critical Race and Gender Studies.* Halifax, Nova Scotia: Fernwood, 2000.

Chadwick, Bruce A., Robert D. Day, and Howard M. Bahr, edited by A. Calliste and G. J. S. Dei. *Native Americans Today: Sociological Perspectives.* New York: Harper and Row, 1972.

Chartrand, P. "Aboriginal Peoples, Racism, and Education in Canada." In *Racism and Education: Different Perspectives and Experiences.* Ottawa, Ontario: Canadian Teachers Federation, 1992.

Chavers, Dean. *Exemplary Programs in Indian Education.* Albuquerque: Catching the Dream, 1993, 1996, 1999, 2004.

———. *Indian Students and College Preparation.* Albuquerque: Catching the Dream Publishers, 1999.

———. *Indian Teachers and Indian Control.* Research report. Albuquerque: Catching the Dream, 1998.

———. *Modern American Indian Leaders.* 2 vols. Lewiston, NY: Mellen Press, 2007.

———. "Social Structure and the Diffusion of Innovations." Ph.D. dissertation, Stanford University, 1976.

Cleary, L. M., and Thomas D. Peacock. *Collected Wisdom: American Indian Education.* Boston: Allyn and Bacon, 1998.

Cook-Lynn, Elizabeth. *Anti-Indianism in Modern America: A Voice from Tatekeya's Earth.* Urbana: University of Illinois Press, 2001.

Cornwall, Warren. "Radioactive Remains: The Forgotten Story of the Northwest's Only Uranium Mines." *Seattle Times*, February 24, 2008.

Costo, Rupert, and Jeanette Henry. *Textbooks and the American Indian.* San Francisco: Indian Historian Press, 1968.

Davis, Monica. "Financial Illiteracy and Racism Threaten African American and Native American Borrowers." (accessed January 20, 2008) http://www.lulu.com/davis4000_2000.

DeFine, Michael S. "A History of Governmentally Coerced Sterilization: The Plight of the Native American Woman."

http://geocities.com/CapitolHill/9118/Mike2.html. (accessed March 1, 2008)

DeJong, D. H. *Promises of the Past: A History of Indian Education in the United States.* Golden, CO: North American Press, 1993.

Deloria, Phillip. *Playing Indian.* New Haven: Yale University Press, 1999.

Deloria, Vine. *God Is Red.* Golden, CO: Fulcrum Publishing, 1972.

Devaney, Earl E. *Investigative Report: Mineral Management Service, False Claims Allegations.* Washington, DC: Department of the Interior, September 7, 2007.

Deyhle, Donna. "Navajo Youth and Anglo Racism: Cultural Integrity and Resistance." *Harvard Educational Review*, 65.3 (1995): 403–436.

Di Silvestro, Roger L. *In the Shadow of Wounded Knee.* New York: Walker & Co., 2007.

Dobie, Kathy. "Murder by the Road in Robeson County." *Vibe*, 2.1 (1994, February).

Dorris, Michael. *The Broken Cord.* New York: Harper Perennial, 1990.

Eguiguren, A. R. *Legalized Racism: Federal Indian Policy and the End of Equal Rights for All Americans.* New York: Sun, 1999.

Elliott, Michael A. *Custerology: The Enduring Legacy of the Indian Wars and George Armstrong Custer.* Chicago: University of Chicago Press, 2007.

Fogarty, Mark. "Mortgage Lending Practices Yield New Complaints, Settlement." *Indian Country Today,* June 12, 2007.

Foley, D. "The Silent Indian as a Cultural Production." In *The Cultural Production of the Educated Person,* edited by A. Levinson, D. Foley, and D. Holland. New York: SUNY Press, 1996.

Fromson, Brett. *Hitting the Jackpot: The Inside Story of the Richest Indian Tribe in History.* New York: Atlantic Monthly Press, 2004.

Gallup Independent, April 26, 2000. "'Skin Walker' Found Guilty of Sex Abuse." Staff report.

Garroutte, Eva Marie. *Real Indians: Identity and Survival of Native America.* Berkeley: University of California Press, 2003.

Garroutte, E. M., J. Goldberg, J. Beals, R. Herrell, and S. M. Manson, "Spirituality and Attempted Suicide among American Indians." *Social Science and Medicine,* 56.7 (2003).

Giago, Tim. *The Aboriginal Sin.* San Francisco: The Indian Historian Press, 1977.

———. *Children Left Behind.* Santa Fe: Clear Light Publishers, 2005.

Gladwell, Malcolm. *The Tipping Point.* New York: Little Brown and Co., 2000.

Gordon-McCutchan, R. C. *The Taos Indians and the Battle for Blue Lake.* Santa Fe: Red Crane Books, 1990.

Goulding, Warren. *Just Another Indian: A Serial Killer and Canada's Indifference.* Calgary: Fifth House, Ltd. 2001.

Greenfeld, Lawrence A., and Steven K. Smith. *American Indians and Crime.* Washington, DC: Department of Justice, Bureau of Justice Statistics, 1999.

Gridley, Marion. *Indians of Today.* Chicago: Indian Council Fire, 1960.

Grinde, Donald A., and B. E. Johansen. *Ecocide of Native America: Environmental Destruction of Indian Lands and Peoples.* Santa Fe: Clear Light Publishers, 2001.

Grossman, Zoltan. "Treaty Rights and Responding to Anti-Indian Activity." http://www.dickshovel.com/anti.html, n.d. (accessed February 15, 2008)

———. *When Hate Groups Come to Town: A Handbook of Effective Community Responses.* Atlanta: Center for Democratic Renewal, 1992.

Hamby, Sherry. "Sexual Victimization in Indian Country." Harrisburg, PA: VAWnet, a project of the National Resource Center on Domestic Violence/Pennsylvania Coalition against Domestic Violence. http://www.vawnet.org (accessed March 30, 2008).

Hendricks, Steve. *The Unquiet Grave: The FBI and the Struggle for the Soul of Indian Country.* New York: Da Capo Press, 2006.

Henry, David L. "Stealing from Indians: Inside the Bureau of Indian Affairs." http://dicksovel.com/stealing. (accessed April 2, 2008)

Henzi, Brent. "Student Files Racism Complaint." AOL, May 24, 2006.

Hirschfelder, Arlene, Paulette Fairbanks Molin, and Yvonne Wankin. *American Indian Stereotypes in the World of Children: A Reader and Bibliography.* Lanham, MA: Scarecrow Press, 1999.

Howard, Gary. *We Can't Teach What We Don't Know: White Teachers, Multiracial Schools.* New York: Teachers College Press, 1999.

Huff, Dolores. *To Live Heroically: Institutional Racism and Indian Education.* Albany: SUNY Press, 1997.

Huffman, T. E. "The Experiences, Perceptions, and Consequences of Campus Racism among Northern Plains Indians." *Journal of American Indian Education,* 30.2 (1991): 25–34.

Huhndorf, Shari M. *Going Native: Indians in the American Cultural Imagination.* Ithaca: Cornell University Press, 2001.

Jackson, Helen Hunt. *A Century of Dishonor.* 1881. Norman: University of Oklahoma Press, 1995.

Johansen, Bruce E. *Life and Death in Mohawk Country.* Golden, CO: North American Press, 1993.

Johnson, Natasha Kaye. "Student's Comments Upset Forum Participants." *Navajo Times,* February 28, 2007.

Johnson, Troy. *Contemporary Native American Political Issues.* Walnut Creek, CA: Alta Mira Press, 1999.

Kickingbird, Kirke. *One Hundred Million Acres.* New York: MacMillan, 1973.

Kilpatrick, Jacquelyn. *Celluloid Indians: Native Americans and Film.* Lincoln: University of Nebraska Press, 1999.

King, C. Richard. *Native Americans in Sports.* Armonk, NY: Sharpe Reference, 2003.

King, C. Richard, and Charles F. Springwood, eds. *Team Spirits: The Native American Mascots Controversy.* Lincoln: University of Nebraska Press, 2001.

King, Gail. "Type II Diabetes, The Modern Epidemic of American Indians in the United States." www.as.au.edu/ant/bindon/Ant570/Papers/King/king.htm. (accessed March 15, 2008)

King, Marsha. "Tribes Confront Painful Legacy of Indian Boarding Schools." *Seattle Times,* June 30, 2007.

Landry, Alysa. "Bureau of Indian Education Sued: Wasted Money, Sexual Harassment, Retalition All Alleged in Lawsuits." *Farmington Daily Times,* January 14, 2008.

Lauderdale, Pat. *Racism, Racialization and American Indian Sports.* Armonk, NY: Sharpe Reference, 2004.

Lawrence, Jane. "The Indian Health Service and the Sterilization of Native American Women." *American Indian Quarterly,* 24.3 (2000).

Lomawaima, Tsianina, and Brenda J. Child. *Away from Home: American Indian Boarding School Experiences, 1879–2000.* Phoenix: Heard Museum, 2000.

Lorenzo, J. T. "What Do You Say …" Louisville: *The Racial Ethnic Torch,* 9.2 (1997).

Loza, Moises. *Lending on Native American Lands: A Guide for Rural Development Staff.* Washington, DC: Housing Assistance Council, 1996.

Magnuson, Jon. "Selling Native American Soul." *Christian Century,* November 22, 1989.

Mann, Barbara. *Iroquoian Women: The Gantowisas.* New York: Peter Lang Publishing, 2000.

Mason, W. Dale. "You Can Only Kick So Long. … AIM Leadership in Nebraska 1972–1979." http://www.dickshovel.com/lsa23.html. (accessed January 10, 2008)

Mathiessen, Peter. *In the Spirit of Crazy Horse.* New York: Penguin, 1992.

McCool, Daniel. *Native Waters: Contemporary Indian Water Settlements and the Second Treaty Era.* Tucson: University of Arizona Press, 2002.

McCool, Daniel, Susan M. Olson, and Jennifer L. Robinson. *Native Vote: American Indians, the Voting Rights Act, and the Right to Vote.* New York: Cambridge University Press, 2007.

McDonald, Laughlin. "The Voting Rights Act in Indian Country: South Dakota, A Case Study." *American Indian Law Review,* 29.43 (2005).

McEachern, J. "The Community Context of Domestic Violence: The Association of Pecking Order Violence with Domestic Violence." *The Indian Health Service Primary Care Provider,* 28.6 (2000): 125–129.

McGovern, Dan. *The Campo Indian Landfill War: The Fight for Gold in California's Garbage.* Norman: University of Oklahoma Press, 1995.

Melmer, David. "Boarding School Case Dismissed." *Indian Country Today,* December 6, 2004.

Melmer, David. "American Indians Face Rental Discrimination." *Indian Country Today,* December 19, 2003.

Mihesuah, Devon A. *American Indians: Stereotypes and Realities.* Atlanta: Clarity Press, 1996.

Morrison, Dane, ed. *American Indian Studies: An Interdisciplinary Approach to Contemporary Issues.* New York: Peter Lang, 1997.

Nielsen, Marianne O., and Robert A. Silverman. *Native Americans, Crime and Justice.* Boulder, CO: Westview Press, 1996.

Pace, David. "Casinos Not Benefiting Indians." *Washington Post,* September 21, 2000.

Peacock, Richard. "Tribal Wisdom: A Native American View of Male and Female." http://www.context.org/ICLIB/IC16/Reagan.htm. (accessed January 15, 2008)

Peshkin, Alan. *Places of Memory: Whiteman's Schools and Native American Communities.* New York: Lawrence Erlbaum Associates, 1997.

Phillips, Susan Urmston. *The Invisible Culture: Communication in Classroom and Community on the Warm Springs Indian Reservation.* Long Grove, IL: Waveland Press, 1992.

Powell, Joy. "Author Erdrich Rejects UND Honors over 'Fighting Sioux' Nickname." *Minneapolis Star Tribune,* April 23, 2007.

Powers-Beck, Jeffrey. *The American Indian Integration of Baseball.* Lincoln: University of Nebraska Press, 2004.

Pratt, Richard Henry. *Battlefield and Classroom: Four Decades with the American Indian.* Norman: University of Oklahoma Press, 2004.

Richland, Justin B., and Sarah Deer. *Introduction to Tribal Legal Studies.* Walnut Creek: Altamira Press, 2004.

Rollins, Peter C., and John E. O'Connor. *Hollywood's Indian: The Portrayal of the Native American in Film.* Lexington: University of Kentucky Press, 1998.

Rosenthal, Robert, and Lenore Jacobson. *Pygmalion in the Classroom.* New York: Irvington, 1992.

Ruben, Barbara. "Grave Reservations: Waste Company Proposals Targeting Native American Lands Are Meeting with a Growing Pattern of Resistance." *Environmental Action*, 23.2 (1991): 12–15.

Rutledge, Peter B. "A Judgment Call: Law Professor Says Removal of Judge Lamberth from the Trust Was 'Nothing Short of a Tragedy.'" http://www.indiantrust.com, August 7, 2006.

Ryser, Rudolph C. *Anti-Indian Movement on the Tribal Frontier.* Olympia: Center for World Indigenous Studies, 1992.

St. Denis, Verna, and Eber Hampton. "Literature Review on Racism and the Effects on Aboriginal Education." Prepared for Minister's National Working Group on Education, Indian and Northern Affairs, Canada, Ottawa, Ontario, 2002.

Sarabi, Brigette. "The Ironhouse: Native Americans and Prison." *Justice Matters*, 2001.

Severson, Margaret, and Christine Wilson Duclos. "American Indian Suicides in Jail: Can Risk Screening Be Culturally Sensitive." Washington, DC: US Department of Justice, 2005.

Shaughnessy, Lana, S. R. Doshi, and S. E. Jones. "Attempted Suicide and Associated Health Risk Behaviors among Native American High School Students." *Journal of School Health*, 75.5 (2004).

Sixkiller Clarke, Ardy. "OERI Native American Youth at Risk Study." Bozeman: Montana State University. ERIC Document ED 373–951, 1994.

Smith, Kyle. "Predatory Lending in Native American Communities." Fredericksburg, VA: First Nations Development Institute, 2003.

Specktor, Mordecai. "State Agency Condemns Actions of Minneapolis Cops." http://nativenet.uthscsa.edu/archive/nl/9405/0339.html. (accessed February 15, 2008)

Spicer, Edward. *Cycles of Conquest: The Impact of Spain, Mexico, and the United States on the Indians of the Southwest.* Tucson: University of Arizona Press, 1962.

Spindel, Carol. *Dancing at Halftime: Sports and the Controversy over American Indian Mascots.* New York: New York University Press, 2000.

Stannard, David E. *American Holocaust: The Conquest of the New World.* New York: Oxford University Press, 1992.

Stoll, David. *Rigoberta Menchu and the Story of All Poor Guatemalans.* New York: Westview Press, 2007.

Sullivan, Robert. *A Whale Hunt.* New York: Scribner's, 2000.

Swisher, Karen, and Donna Deyhle. "Styles of Learning and Learning of Styles: Educational Conflicts of American Indian Youth." *Journal of Multicultural and Multilingual Development,* 8.4 (1987).

Terry, James B. "Alexander Energy Corporation, 153 IBLA 238, August 31, 2000."

Thornton, Russell. *American Indian Holocaust and Survival: A Population History Since 1492.* Norman: University of Oklahoma Press, 1990.

Topper, M. D. "Mormon Placement: The Effects of Missionary Foster Families on Navajo Adolescents." *Ethos: The Journal for the Society of Psychological Anthropology,* 7.2 (1979): 160–162.

Trafzer, Clifford. *Exterminate Them: Written Accounts of the Murder, Rape, and Slavery of Native Americans During the California Gold Rush, 1848–1868.* East Lansing: Michigan State University Press, 1999.

Underhill, Ruth. *Red Man's Religion.* Chicago: University of Chicago Press, 1965.

U.S. Department of the Interior, Bureau of Indian Affairs. "Indian Service Population and Labor Force Estimates." Washington, DC: Bureau of Indian Affairs, 1993–2003.

Vacsey, Clifford. *Handbook of American Indian Religious Freedom.* New York: Crossroad Press, 1991.

Walker, Richard. "First Trial for Accused Whale Hunters Jan. 22." *Indian Country Today,* January 8, 2008.

Weatherford, Jack. *Indian Givers: How the Indians of the Americas Transformed the World.* New York: Crown Books, 1988.

Williams, Robert A., Jr. *Like a Loaded Weapon: The Rehnquist Court, Indian Rights, and the Legal History of Racism in America.* Minneapolis: University of Minnesota Press, 2005.

Wolcott, Harry F. *A Kwakiutl Village and School.* New York: Holt, Reinhart and Winston, 1967.

INDEX